Celia Sánchez Manduley

ENVISIONING CUBA

Louis A. Pérez Jr., editor

Envisioning Cuba publishes outstanding, innovative works in
Cuban studies, drawn from diverse subjects and disciplines
in the humanities and social sciences, from the colonial period
through the post–Cold War era. Featuring innovative scholarship
engaged with theoretical approaches and interpretive frameworks
informed by social, cultural, and intellectual perspectives, the series
highlights the exploration of historical and cultural circumstances
and conditions related to the development of Cuban self-definition
and national identity.

Celia Sánchez Manduley

The Life and Legacy of a Cuban Revolutionary

Tiffany A. Sippial

The University of North Carolina Press CHAPEL HILL

This book was published with the assistance of the Greensboro Women's Fund of the University of North Carolina Press.

Founding Contributors: Linda Arnold Carlisle, Sally Schindel Cone, Anne Faircloth, Bonnie McElveen Hunter, Linda Bullard Jennings, Janice J. Kerley (in honor of Margaret Supplee Smith), Nancy Rouzer May, and Betty Hughes Nichols.

Set in Merope Basic by Westchester Publishing Services
Manufactured in the United States of America

The University of North Carolina Press has been a member of the Green Press Initiative since 2003.

Library of Congress Cataloging-in-Publication Data
Names: Sippial, Tiffany A., author.
Title: Celia Sánchez Manduley : the life and legacy of a Cuban revolutionary / Tiffany A. Sippial.
Other titles: Envisioning Cuba.
Description: Chapel Hill : University of North Carolina Press, [2020] | Series: Envisioning Cuba | Includes bibliographical references and index.
Identifiers: LCCN 2019014009 | ISBN 9781469654072 (cloth : alk. paper) | ISBN 9781469654607 (pbk : alk. paper) | ISBN 9781469654089 (ebook)
Subjects: LCSH: Sánchez Manduley, Celia, 1920–1980. | Women revolutionaries—Cuba—Biography. | Revolutionaries—Cuba—Biography. | Castro, Fidel, 1926–2016—Friends and associates. | Cuba—History—20th century.
Classification: LCC F1788.22.S26 S57 2020 | DDC 972.9106092 [B]—dc23
LC record available at https://lccn.loc.gov/2019014009

Cover illustration: Melanie Cervantes, *La Paloma* (2017). Used by permission of the artist.

For my parents, Wade and Gail Thomas,
who always believed I had a story to tell.

For my son, Rhys,
who holds my heart.

For my husband, Trey,
who champions all my dreams.

Contents

Figures

Preface

In April 2018 I received the email that transformed this book. After twenty-two years of filing requests, I was invited to enter an archival world few scholars have ever entered. I am now one of the few U.S. scholars granted access to the highest security archive of the Cuban revolutionary government, the Oficina de Asuntos Históricos del Consejo de Estado (Office of Historical Affairs of the Council of State, OAHCE) in Havana. A hallowed vault of Cuban revolutionary history, the archive houses the papers of Cuba's top revolutionary officials, including Fidel and Raúl Castro and Che Guevara. The archive directorship offered me almost unprecedented access to thousands of pages of personal correspondence, wartime communiqués, diary entries, and official government memos penned by Cuba's most revered female revolutionary heroine—Celia Sánchez Manduley (1920–80).

Sánchez shares within these documents her raw, intimate assessment of life on the front lines of history in the making. Her documents prove the decisive role she played in planning and executing the Cuban Revolution from the mid-1950s until her death in 1980. They also reveal the woman behind the mythology. In her signature block print, Sánchez articulated her hopes and dreams, and even her personal doubts and fears, in ways that reshaped my understanding of her experiences and identity. Exquisite details, like Sánchez's habit of closing her correspondence with the words "Revolutionarily Yours," granted texture and dimension to Cuba's mythologized heroine.

Positioned within twenty-two years of archival and oral history research conducted in the United States and Cuba, the OAHCE documents revealed to me the choices and struggles of a highly private woman who nonetheless stepped willingly onto the precarious stage of international politics, shifting gender roles, and public scrutiny at a time of tremendous national upheaval. While no archive can encapsulate the full complexity of a life, nuances of her personality, beliefs, and experience emerged within her writings. I glimpsed the revolution through Sánchez's own eyes in ways that few ever have. What follows is a critical portrait of a woman who became, over the course of an exceptional life, a revolutionary icon.

Acknowledgments

The list of people who deserve my gratitude for supporting me with this book is long. First on the list of people to thank is Sonia Riquelme, who introduced me to the name Celia Sánchez Manduley in 1995. When she invited me to Cuba to assist her with her research on Afro-Cuban poets, Sonia insisted that I pursue my own research project. I learned so much about the research process from her that summer and only wish she were still alive to read this book. At Southwestern University, I must thank Eric Selbin, who has been a constant supporter of this project for more than twenty years, and of me for even longer. His Latin American politics class changed the course of my life, and his friendship and mentorship continue to mean the world to me.

With support from the Latin American and Iberian Institute at the University of New Mexico, I decided to extend my undergraduate work on Sánchez into an M.A. thesis. My thesis committee—Judy Bieber, Linda Hall, and Elizabeth Hutchison—pushed the work in fruitful new directions. I am also indebted to Jane Slaughter, whose graduate seminar on gender, war, and memory introduced me to a whole new field that shaped in important ways how I thought about Sánchez's legacy. Another of my UNM mentors, Melissa Bokovoy, offered instructive feedback on a section of this work at the American Historical Association meeting in 2016.

At Auburn University, where I have been on the faculty since 2007, I must thank my amazing colleagues for their friendship and support in all things. Special thanks to Dave Lucsko, Donna Bohanan, Ken Noe, Joe Kicklighter, Jim Hansen, Cate Giustino, Kathryn Braund, Charles Israel, Alan Meyer, Jennifer Brooks, David Carter, Matthew Malczycki, Christopher Ferguson, Abby Swingen (now at Texas Tech), and Ralph Kingston. To my amazing Honors College team, I have loved every minute of this new adventure together and look forward to all the great things to come. Many thanks also to Andrew Gillespie and the Office of International Programs at Auburn University, who helped finance my final two trips to Cuba to complete the research for this book through an Internationalization Grant. I feel so privileged to work with such supportive and inspiring colleagues.

I am also grateful for the support extended to me by the staff at a number of U.S. archives. The University of Florida's Center for Latin American Studies awarded me a Library Research Grant in 2016, and my experience with the entire library and special collections staff was stellar from beginning to end. My research in the University of Miami's Cuban Heritage Collection was equally enriching, and the helpful staff there both tracked down the sources I requested and brought others to my attention. I have made countless trips to the University of Texas at Austin's Benson Latin American Library, and each was as helpful as the last. I also appreciate the assistance I received (on both of my books) from library and archival staff at Yale University.

In Cuba, so many wonderful people have supported my research over more than two decades. I am deeply indebted to the staff at the Celia Sánchez Manduley Memorial Stairway (Manzanillo), Federation of Cuban Women (Havana), José Martí National Library (Havana), History Institute (Havana), Celia Sánchez Childhood Home Museum (Media Luna), Celia Sánchez Home Museum (Pilón), Municipal History Museum (Media Luna), Municipal History Museum (Manzanillo), Celia Sánchez Monument in Lenin Park (Havana), and the Colón Cemetery (Havana). To the staff at the Office of Historical Affairs (OAHCE) in Havana, there are no words to express what my time with you all meant to me and to this project. My most heartfelt thanks to Eugenio Suárez Pérez, Jorge Luís Aneiros Alonso, Iliana Salas Lemus, Ileana Guzmán Cruz, Adelaida Béquer Céspedes, and Aida Luisa Moreno Fonseca.

I am also beyond grateful to the many people—some of whom are no longer living—who offered their insights about Sánchez through interviews, conversations, email correspondence, and long-distance phone calls. In particular, I would like to thank Raquel Andino, Adelaida Bécquer Céspedes, Bárbara Cañadilla, Nirma Cartón, Elizabeth Elliottt, Bonnie Fambrono, Alina Fernández, Arnaldo Gómez Satti, Mirtha Hernández, Nexsy Llana, David Martínez, Aida Luisa Moreno Fonseca, Delio Orozco González, Nilda Porot, Margaret Randall, Sergio Rego Pita, Lourdes Sang, and the incomparable Nydia Sarabia. I am profoundly thankful to Efraim Conte for all the many phone, text, dinner, and email chats in which he answered my questions about his family with the most exquisite care and detail. His friendship is one of the greatest gifts this project brought to my life. To other Cuban friends who I consider my family, I send so much gratitude for offering their homes, their friendship, and their insights about Sánchez and about life: Luís René, Mercy, and Luís Carlos in Havana; Pedro, Tamara, and

Tamarita in Media Luna; and Yolanda Díaz Martínez and Bárbara Danzie Martínez at the National Archives. *Los quiero mucho*.

I am grateful as always to the amazing editorial staff at the University of North Carolina Press. Elaine Maisner and Lou Pérez were as wonderfully supportive and encouraging on this second book project as they were on the first, and I am beyond honored to join again the authors of the "Envisioning Cuba" series. Thank you also to the anonymous readers whose key insights and advice improved this book greatly.

Last but not least, I offer my gratitude to my family. They have lived with this project for so many years and supported me at every step. I dedicate this book primarily to my parents, as nobody championed it more loyally and enthusiastically. My siblings, Jared Thomas and Lauren Menn, might be pressed to remember a time when I was not working, in some capacity, on this project. I am so blessed to have siblings who are also my friends. My wonderful husband loves and supports me and my work without hesitation, even when it pulls me away from home for extended periods of time. I am proud to be his wife and to be the mother of our precious son, Rhys, and stepmother to three wonderful young men. Life is beautiful.

Abbreviations in the Text

ANR	Revolutionary National Action
CIA	Central Intelligence Agency
DRE	Revolutionary Student Directorate
FAR	Revolutionary Armed Forces
FBI	Federal Bureau of Investigations
FCMM	Martí Women's Civic Front
FEU	Federation of University Students
FMC	Federation of Cuban Women
FOIA	Freedom of Information Act
INRA	National Institute of Agrarian Reform
M-26-7	26th of July Movement
OAHCE	Office of Historical Affairs of the Council of State
SIR	Military Intelligence Service
SISS	Senate Internal Security Subcommittee

Chronology

9 May 1920	Celia Sánchez Manduley is born to Dr. Manuel Sánchez Silveira and Acacia Manduley Alsina in Media Luna, Cuba.
16 October 1920	Sánchez is baptized and the name Celia Esther de los Desamparados is inscribed in the Registro Civil del Juzgado Municipal de Vicana.
19 December 1926	Sánchez's mother, Acacia Manduley Alsina, dies of malaria in Manzanillo.
15 July 1934	The "Media Luna Massacre" occurs when the Rural Guard attacks protesting members of the Union of Workers and Employees of the Isabel Mill and Its Settlements, resulting in three deaths.
8 May 1935	Antonio Guiteras Holmes, founder of the radical "Joven Cuba" youth protest group, is executed.
7 May 1937	Sánchez enrolls in the Institute of Secondary Education in Manzanillo.
9 June 1937	Sánchez's rumored boyfriend, Salvador Sadurní, hemorrhages to death during surgery to remove a tumor.
20 October 1939	Sánchez's grandmother, Doña Irene, dies, leaving Sánchez as the principal caretaker for her father and younger siblings.
20 May 1948	Sánchez and her father host Eduardo Chibás, founder of the Orthodox Party, in their house in Pilón. Chibás loses in the June 1948 presidential elections.
5 August 1951	Chibás commits suicide while delivering a public address at the radio station CMQ.
10 March 1952	General Fulgencio Batista seizes control of the Cuban government via a military coup.
19 May 1953	Sánchez and her father join an expedition to place a bronze bust of Cuban independence hero José Martí atop the highest peak in the Sierra Maestra mountains, El Turquino.

26 July 1953	Cuban rebels carry out a momentous, albeit disastrous, attack on the Moncada Barracks in Santiago de Cuba. Twenty-seven of the rebels are imprisoned in the Model Prison on the Isle of Pines.
15 May 1955	The imprisoned rebels are freed and regroup under the name M-26-7 in honor of the failed Moncada Barracks attack.
7 July 1955	Castro and other male leaders of the M-26-7 leave for Mexico to begin planning the Cuban Revolution. Sánchez is ordered to stay behind and plan for the rebel landing.
2 December 1956	M-26-7 rebels arrive at Las Coloradas near Belic aboard the overcrowded yacht *Granma*.
23 December 1956	Sánchez makes her first of many trips to the Sierra Maestra to aid the rebel forces.
16 February 1957	Herbert L. Matthews of the *New York Times* arrives in the Sierra Maestra to conduct his famous three-hour interview with Castro. This date also marks the first meeting of Sánchez and Castro.
24 February 1957	Sánchez officially joins the M-26-7.
28 May 1957	At the battle of Uvero, Sánchez becomes the first female member of the M-26-7 to fire a rifle in battle.
24 June 1958	Sánchez's father dies of lung cancer at Havana's Calixto García Hospital.
18 September 1958	Sánchez helps organize the first group of female soldiers, the Mariana Grajales Brigade. The brigade consists of only fourteen women, and Castro designates them as his personal security detail.
1 January 1959	Batista flees the country, granting the rebels a historic victory.
24 March 1962	Sánchez is appointed secretary to the president and Council of Ministers.
4 May 1964	Sánchez officially opens the Office of Historical Affairs in Havana.
1 October 1965	Sánchez is elected as an official member of the Central Committee of the Communist Party, a position to which she is reelected in 1975.
22 April 1972	Lenin Park in Havana, an epic project that Sánchez herself oversaw, is officially inaugurated.

17 December 1975	Sánchez becomes a member of the Organizing Commission and delegate to the First Congress of the Communist Party of Cuba.
2 November 1976	Sánchez becomes a delegate to the National Assembly of Popular Power.
11 January 1980	After years of progressing illness, Sánchez dies of lung cancer in Havana.
12 January 1980	Sánchez's body is interred in the mausoleum dedicated to the Revolutionary Armed Forces (FAR) in Colón Cemetery in Havana. Her grave is marked only with the number "43."
4 October 1980	Sánchez receives a posthumous social sciences degree from La Escuela Superior del PCC "Ñico López." Her diploma hangs in the Media Luna museum.
11 January 1985	A bronze relief of Sánchez by Caridad Ramos is dedicated in Lenin Park. The monument is intended to eventually hold Sánchez's remains.

Celia Sánchez Manduley

CHAPTER ONE

Searching for Celia

Biography and the Politics of Remembrance

> The people know how this symbol was created, but in this
> moment, we are participating in the duty of remembering.
>
> —ARMANDO HART DÁVALOS, "El ejemplo de Celia"

> Memory as a whole . . . is bigger than the sum of its parts.
>
> —ALON CONFINO, "Collective Memory and Cultural History"

Searching for Celia

I first heard the name Celia Sánchez Manduley (1920–80) in August 1995 from a professor who had recently traveled to Cuba. As I had spent much of that summer living in Oaxaca, Mexico, investigating the role of women within the recently formed Zapatista Army of National Liberation, my professor thought that Sánchez's story might interest me. What I discovered upon further investigation into Sánchez's life was baffling. She had played a critical role in the Cuban Revolution, but references to her in scholarly accounts of those events were brief and often confined to footnotes.

I learned that the revolutionary leadership recognizes Sánchez as the first woman to fire a weapon in battle, an achievement that earned her the title of "first female guerrilla of the Sierra Maestra." It also credits her with organizing the first platoon of female combatants, known as the Mariana Grajales Brigade.[1] Following the triumph of the revolution in 1959, Sánchez was appointed secretary to the president and Council of Ministers (1962) and then secretary of the Council of State (1976). In her capacity as a government official, she created several large public institutions and tourist centers, including the Office of Historical Affairs, the Palace of the Revolution, and Havana's 1,900-acre Lenin Park. She also traveled widely—to the United States, Africa, and Vietnam—as an international ambassador for the revolution. Her image appears on two Cuban postage stamps, a commemorative one-peso coin, and in the watermark of the twenty-peso note.

In light of these achievements, I found it remarkable that many published works about the revolution never even mention her. How could this be? How could a woman openly spoken of as "the maximum representative of the

Cuban revolutionary woman" not have at least one biography written about her life?[2] In contrast, the Library of Congress online catalog listed forty-one published biographies of Fidel Castro (1926–2016) and sixty-five biographies of Ernesto "Che" Guevara (1928–67). I was intrigued.

My first research trip to Havana's José Martí National Library, during the summer of 1996, revealed a card catalog with only a handful of references to Sánchez, and several enthusiastic, but honest, librarians who told me that I would be hard-pressed to find much published biographical information about her. Not only was I having difficulty finding materials written about Sánchez, but I was also having difficulty getting people to move beyond the basic biography sketched above. It seemed that wherever I went people offered the same observations about Sánchez's contributions to Cuban history.

I was both frustrated and fascinated by the fact that my interviewees often responded in an almost formulaic way during our interview sessions. One young interviewee responded very honestly to my assessment on this front, stating, "Yes, everyone thinks of her as a hero, but if you ask someone, 'Tell me something about her,' they could probably only tell you about her public works projects after the triumph of the revolution. She is rarely mentioned in school. Mostly the way you learn about her is through government-produced sources . . . you know, '*La flor más autóctona de la Revolución Cubana*' [the most native wildflower of the Cuban Revolution]. The government has preserved and communicates her story that way."[3]

In some ways, the standardization of Sánchez's biography serves a didactic purpose. Centered on a manageable subset of her experiences and accomplishments, it is easy to teach and learn, which promotes its circulation. For some critics of the revolutionary government, however, standardization promotes truncation. The female revolutionary experience is reduced to a handful of talking points, while the male leaders are meticulously eulogized. Ilja Luciak finds that some Cuban feminists even feel that Sánchez's presence in the watermark of the Cuban currency, which "can only be seen if one holds the note against the light," symbolizes the invisibility of women's contributions to the revolution.[4] They argue that despite grandiose plans to transform gender relations and the position of women in Cuban society, the revolutionary government can boast only moderate accomplishments on that front. Pointing to the limited number of female rebels who assumed leadership roles after 1959, they claim that the promised "revolution within the Revolution" never occurred.[5]

Many of my interviewees identified Sánchez herself as the primary architect of the relative silence surrounding her life. Sánchez shunned cameras, interviews, and the press.[6] Her deep sense of personal humility, rooted in a family legacy of service, provides a common explanation for her "allergic" reaction to publicity. Sánchez's long-term colleague, Aida Luisa Moreno Fonseca, a woman who has worked at the Office of Historical Affairs for four decades, refers to Sánchez as a "compañera of ideals."[7] Waldo González López explained in a January 1984 memorial article published in *Muchacha* magazine that Sánchez operated with "the silence characteristic of authentically great people."[8] Several of my interviewees over the years also linked Sánchez's leadership style to the teachings of famed Cuban independence leader José Martí—namely, his belief that "all the glory in the world fits inside one grain of corn."[9] Any silence or mystery surrounding Sánchez's life was, they argued, of her own purposeful design.

I began to question this representation of Sánchez, however, the first time I saw her on film. Before that moment, I had marveled on several occasions that I had never heard Sánchez speak. I assumed that I never would, as in all her years of public service she almost never delivered public speeches or granted interviews. One family member even chuckled when I asked him a question along those lines, noting simply: "She received dignitaries daily, but she was a terrible public speaker."[10] What was so surprising about the first time I saw her on film, therefore, was not only *what* she was saying, but also *how* she was speaking. In the clip, Sánchez recounts her legendary evasion of government troops under the command of U.S.-backed dictator General Fulgencio Batista (1901–73) by dressing as a pregnant woman. I saw nothing in this footage of the camera-shy woman so often described to me. Wearing the bohemian-style dress and large earrings that were typical of her later life, she stood directly in front of the camera. A cigarette dangled from her right hand, and she appeared to be wearing false eyelashes. She spoke eloquently and confidently in the notorious rapid-fire Cuban style, looking directly at the interviewer except in the brief moments when she allowed her gaze to take in the movement of people around her. She was engaged but also aware of her surroundings. Completely at ease and comfortable telling a story about her own participation in the early mobilization efforts of the 26th of July Movement (M-26-7)—the vanguard political party led by Castro that would overthrow Cuba's national government in 1959—Sánchez smiled wryly when amused by a particular memory. She used the pronoun "I" often, but seemed neither boastful nor self-deprecating.

When the film clip ended, I began to wonder about the need to reevaluate Sánchez's legacy. What might imaginings of Sánchez as the self-effacing player behind the scenes obscure in our understanding of her life and of the

Cuban Revolution more broadly? I was reminded of a moment during my interview with scholar and activist Margaret Randall in which she sagely noted that "the official story is often wrong."[11] The narrative of purposeful self-denial and sacrifice that dominates imaginings of Sánchez's career has left little room for alternative readings. The words of my colleague Paula Backscheider also came to my mind as I pondered this issue. Backscheider notes that "Women who understand and are able to maintain a conformist image while striving for their individual successes often do well." She encourages us to consider the "performative self," and the "roles that are available, natural, accepted, attempted, and forced upon a person."[12]

How much of the Sánchez that we can access via photographs, poetry, and commemorative acts is really a reflection of her performative self? To what extent might she have purposefully refashioned herself in order to play the role she wanted to play and have the life she wanted to live? Might a more attention-seeking woman not have risen as high in the ranks of the revolutionary government, as she would appear more competitor than comrade? Furthermore, how much of what we think we know about Sánchez is really just the projection of an image crafted by others?

It became critical for me to find people who had actually had a personal or professional relationship with Sánchez. This quest led me to conduct interviews with women like Nydia Sarabia, Nirma Cartón, and Lourdes Sang. Due to their interactions with Sánchez, all three women were well aware of the difficult task ahead of me. They concurred that Sánchez was one of the most important women in Cuban history, but they also agreed that she was one of the most private. They generously offered their own invaluable insights about Sánchez's life and legacy and encouraged me to seek access to the principal archive of the Cuban Revolution.

The Office of Historical Affairs of the Council of State occupies a former bank at the intersection of Línea and Twelfth Street in Havana and is Cuba's highest-security archive. It houses the memos and communiqués that Sánchez painstakingly recopied during her time in the Sierra Maestra Mountains and stored in a satchel now on display at her childhood home in Media Luna. The archive also contains books, photographs, newspaper clippings, and maps detailing the earliest years of the Cuban Revolution. These records are considered national treasures. A rotating set of uniformed guards stands at the door throughout the day to verify each visitor's credentials. Consequently, only a small handful of U.S. scholars have ever accessed that archive. As Randall noted during our interview: "Cubans are very protective of their heroes and heroines."[13] Attempts to access the Office of Historical Affairs proved disappointing on that and several subsequent trips. I could never have guessed that I would wait twenty-two years to receive authorization to access the archive.

By early 2018, I had almost given up hope of being able to examine Sánchez's papers. One evening, however, I sat down and wrote a final request to the archive director. Much more personal than previous requests, the letter described my research journey and my hopes for the book. I sent the email without any expectation of a response, especially in light of deteriorating U.S.-Cuban relations as a result of rumored "sonic attacks" on U.S. diplomatic staff in Havana. Within forty-eight hours I received an invitation to the archive, and I had purchased a plane ticket within forty-nine.

My unprecedented access to that repository allowed me to complete the first critical biography of one of the most influential female political leaders in twentieth-century Cuban history, if not Latin American history more broadly. Twenty-two years of field, archival, and oral history research pull Sánchez out from the shadow of the bearded male heroes whose life stories continue to dominate our understanding of the Cuban Revolution. While most assessments of Sánchez's life produced within Cuba or off the island—including works by Álvarez Tabío, Stout, and Haney—take at face value the legacy of heroic self-abnegation that frames her state-sanctioned biography, this study offers a more analytical treatment of her life story.[14] Employing a combination of feminist biography and cultural history methodologies, I interrogate the meanings assigned to Sánchez's experiences within official discourse, popular memory, and sites of memorialization. I also examine Sánchez's purposeful and strategic framing of her own public image within Cuba's new brand of revolutionary womanhood. She was more than an object of mythologization; she actively crafted her own legacy. Balancing the careful work of recovery and interpretation, this is a study of the making—and remaking—of Cuba's revolutionary "New Woman" through the life story of one of its most revered national heroes.

Writing Celia

This project has challenged my understanding of biography as a genre of historical writing. As I moved more deeply into the work, the variables with which I would need to grapple seemed to compound upon themselves. How does a U.S. female scholar write the biography of a woman who also happened to be Cuban, who also happened to occupy a high-ranking government office, and who was also notoriously private? As I struggled to account for these aspects of both Sánchez's identity and my own, I discovered a new intellectual cohort whose work offers a critical methodology for considering a project of this nature—feminist biographers.[15] To be clear, placing my work within the field of feminist biography does not mean that I define Sánchez as a feminist. Sánchez placed her faith in the transformational possibilities of the revolution, not feminism. I claim this book as feminist biography not merely because its primary subject is a woman, but because it reveals the historically and culturally contingent process by which Sánchez became the embodiment of Cuba's New Woman.

Feminist biographers reimagine traditional approaches to biography as a coherent, bounded narrative unfolding through linear time. They value cultural forms of evidence (such as memorabilia), recognize the subjectivity of biography as a tool for understanding historical experience, and acknowledge the complexities, contradictions, and tensions in stories told about a person's life. As a feminist biographer, I am disinclined to smooth out the rough edges that appear where public commemorative acts or private, personal reflections from friends and family solder together incongruous pieces of Sánchez's life. That roughness is, in fact, a key area of my interest in this project. My motivation is not only to recover as many facts about Sánchez's life as are accessible, but also to explore how representations of her life developed over time. I acknowledge, however, that the subject of any biography remains, in many ways, a cipher. There are elements of Sánchez's lived reality that we may never fully understand.

Recognizing the potential effect my own presence had on the production of my knowledge about Sánchez is important to this work. Like other feminist biographers, I recognize the subjectivity of biography as a form of historical inquiry. Rather than attempt to disappear within a slick narrative, I acknowledge my own presence within this story and the ways my positionality may have impacted various phases of the project, from accessing sources to interpreting meanings. As Susan Crane states, "Historical research is a lived experience that the self-reflexive historian consciously integrates into collective memory. Historical representation is inadequate to this lived experience only so long as the author remains absent and the textual or site-artifact serves only the function of commemoration."[16]

I also recognize the ways in which Sánchez actively shaped her own story. I balance concerns with fixing in time and space the significant events and accomplishments of her life against frank evaluations of how gender constraints shaped those public achievements. Freed from the limits of traditional biography, I can ask complex questions. What is at stake in Sánchez's own self-fashioning—her performative self—with regard to the (at least per-ceived) strategies she engaged in to enhance her political effectiveness, manage her public and private life, and construct herself as a public figure within a set of available gender roles? These kinds of questions alter and ex-pand the framework within which we understand biographical "truth" and encourage us to read stories about Sánchez's life against a broader discourse of acceptable revolutionary womanhood.

As a scholar of Cuba, I also acknowledge the complex politics that shaped the parameters of the possible with my work. Strained U.S.-Cuban diplo-matic relations became a central character in my research even before I set foot on the island. The Freedom of Information Act (FOIA) requests I filed with the U.S. Federal Bureau of Investigation (FBI) and the Central Intelli-gence Agency (CIA) were both rejected ("we can neither confirm nor deny the existence or nonexistence of records"). The U.S. Treasury Department denied the first travel license request I filed, which almost derailed my plans. When I finally secured permission to travel to Cuba in the summer of 1996, airport security officials detained me for an hour to question me about the purpose of my trip. I found the capital city dotted with freshly painted mu-rals denouncing the Helms–Burton Act, which President Bill Clinton had just used to tighten the U.S. embargo against Cuba.[17] One mural showed a mus-tachioed Adolf Hitler proclaiming "Heil Helms!"

Diplomatic tensions between the United States and Cuba may also have influenced my research in less overt ways. In the summer of 1996, I encoun-tered a climate of simmering distrust in Cuba that colored my personal in-teractions in ways difficult to quantify. A range of historical, political, and personal forces continued to press upon both my formal interview sessions and my informal conversations about Sánchez over the years. Elda Guerra has noted that "written memories are influenced by the weight of past liter-ary models, the conviction of the author, the intended reader, and the am-biance in which the text eventually survives. Oral recollections raise these issues and more, being especially coloured by the relationship between the interviewee and the interviewer, and thus by the communicative past which they establish."[18]

Years into my research, I was surprised to learn that several of the resi-dents of my apartment building in Havana's Vedado neighborhood feared that I was a government agent and questioned my landlady about my activi-ties. I wondered constantly if my interviewees withheld information or avoided subjects that might be sensitive for one or both of us. Might they have felt protective of certain aspects of their personal or national history and decided not to share them with me, a citizen of Cuba's political enemy? I also assumed that international politics played a role in many, if not most, of my declined requests for interviews. Some of the interviewees with whom I have maintained contact over the years have confessed their initial trepidation about speaking with me. In one case, I have chosen to protect the identity of an interviewee due to the sensitive nature of his government work.

Scholars who examine the development of national mythologies know that performances of nation/self contain contradictions and silences. These contradictions and silences may reflect unresolved tensions between official discourses and lived experiences, or they may point to topics considered threatening to broader national goals. When they perceive that discreet acts of remembering may have national or global ramifications, individuals and communities may self-censure. Historian Daniel James notes that the act of sharing stories represents a "profound referential pact between storyteller/ local historian and the community and its needs [that have been] arrived at through negotiation and concession with other alternative narratives within this community."[19] Resulting acts of individual and collective memory monitoring are not unique to oral interviews, to be sure; they can also shape how people present or perform a story in other sites of memory, such as museums, cemeteries, and monuments.[20]

Preserving and promoting a specific set of memories can represent a deeply patriotic act, especially in the presence of an outsider. Sánchez's life story links to a foundational myth—or master narrative—about the revolutionary experience as a struggle for solidarity and survival. This foundational myth is replete with all the nostalgia, aggrandizement, and forgetting typical of any story a nation tells about itself. One of the exercises of good revolutionary citizenship is, however, to promote and maintain coherence in this master narrative. During his speech at her 1980 funeral, Minister of Culture Armando Hart Dávalos (1930–2017) made clear that the revolution intended to bind its citizens to specific forms of remembering Sánchez within this foundational myth when he stated, "The people know how this symbol was created, but in this moment we are participating in the duty of remembering."[21]

Although I sometimes sensed that Cubans I spoke with might not completely agree with the Sánchez master narrative, they seemed to understand that there was, indeed, a story that they should feel duty-bound to promote or at least respect. Criticisms of governmental policies in general—or aspects of Sánchez's story in particular—were typically counterbalanced by reverent acknowledgments of the sacrifices associated with her generation of "authentic" revolutionary leaders. José Quiroga argues that Cubans shape their memories of their revolution through "their at times free, at times coerced, at times implied, and at times suggested right to become one as a people."[22] Sánchez's sister, Griselda, once confessed in an interview that "as Celia's siblings, we watch what we say, how we say things, [and] when we offer critiques . . . whether that be in political or private conversations, in order to never undermine her, and this has been especially true since her death."[23]

It matters that I conducted all of my interviews after Sánchez had been deceased for at least twenty years. Filtered through time, those conversations revealed the vagaries of individual memory and the influence of national mythology as much as (if not more than) verifiable historical truth. The vast majority of the written works I consulted for this book also date after her death and are commemorative in nature. Their purpose is to craft (or contest in the case of some U.S. sources) consensus as it relates not only to Sánchez's story, but also to the goals and aspirations of the revolutionary project writ large. Sánchez is no longer alive to verify, deny, or contradict the resulting narrative. Her death, therefore, structures much of what we know about her life.

Acknowledging that Sánchez's story is *both* a repository of fact and a creation of memory takes nothing away from its significance. Nor does it undermine our ability to glean insights from its contents. In her work on the Spanish Civil War, Shirley Mangini warns that "recounting memories is a slippery task. Questions of truth versus fiction are based on the fickle nature of memory, the passage of time, the need for self-justification, self-compassion, and self-aggrandizement."[24] I have found that it is in engaging the very slipperiness of this task—one not wholly bound by the need to prove or disprove sources—that we come closest to weaving a story worth telling. Quiroga offers that "in a paradoxical manner, memory and not history will allow us a more perceptive vision of the Cuban present and its future."[25] There are aspects of any person's legacy that are born of fact, while others may be born of fiction. Sánchez is no different.

Sánchez's life story sits at the threshold of fact and fiction. My use in this study of a combination methodology, in which I balance both feminist biography and cultural history approaches, positions me at this threshold where history and mythology are often indistinguishable. J. M. Taylor noted in her study of Eva Perón's posthumous legacy that there is no "easily perceptible point at which 'reality' ends and 'myth' begins . . . myths have used reality, and reality has been shaped by these myths."[26] Although Taylor does not identify as a feminist biographer, I see elements of Latin American feminist biography in her work, as I do in Margaret Randall's recent work on Haydée Santamaría and Kathryn Bishop-Sánchez's work on Carmen Miranda.[27]

I invite other scholars of women and gender in Latin America to explore the possibilities of feminist biography as a tool to enrich our understanding of the complexities, contradictions, and tensions in stories told about women's lives. I see ample opportunities for biographical work within my own subfield of Cuban women/gender studies. A growing number of exceptional books produced over the last ten to fifteen years—including those by Bayard de Volo, Chase, Guerra, and Serra, for example—have shed new light on the ways women have engaged the revolutionary project, the government's influence on how that engagement is understood and valued, and the limits of the revolution as a mechanism for female liberation.[28] There is ample room now for more granular studies of specific women's revolutionary experiences to complement these broad works. Retail and library bookshelves are filled with biographies of men, but there is space for biographies of women if we claim it.

Imagining Celia

As a cultural history and feminist biography, this book is attuned to the general chronology of the Cuban Revolution, and the discussion tracks along that time line. Each chapter, however, centers on the *making* of a particular phase of Sánchez's life or afterlife. I draw on a broad range of state-produced (newspapers and speeches), personal (oral testimony and interviews), and cultural (poetry and art) sources to examine *how* and *why* her life story has been imagined and reimagined over time. This approach to biography encourages the reader to distinguish between the "real" Sánchez—who is largely unknowable to us all—and the glorified or villainized symbol of Cuba's New Woman.

Sánchez's early biography begins with her birth in Media Luna, Cuba, in 1920 and stretches through her early politicization in the years leading up to the Cuban Revolution. These are some of the least analyzed years of Sánchez's life. I have always found it odd that historians and biographers of Sánchez—and even family members—often omit from their narratives the years that Sánchez lived in Media Luna. One Miami-based family member even commented, when I mentioned that the book would start in Media Luna, "She didn't really even live there."[29] Biographer Nancy Stout dedicates only a few pages of her book to Sánchez's early years, and those pages focus primarily on her years in Pilón when she was already in her twenties.[30]

Commemorative photomontages produced after Sánchez's death and published in Cuban newspapers like *Bohemia* often visually omitted these years altogether, focusing instead on her thirties and beyond. Truncated in this way, Sánchez's life and resulting legacy centers on the years when she engaged in overtly political work. She is effectively "born" when she becomes a revolutionary leader.

Sánchez herself almost never addressed, even in her personal correspondence, her earliest childhood years in Media Luna. Perhaps she wanted to avoid the memories of personal tragedies she experienced during that time of her life, or perhaps she preferred to live her life looking forward instead of looking back. The reality is that Sánchez lived in Media Luna for her entire childhood, except for a short period when she lived with her aunt in Manzanillo while attending school. Her father accepted a job in 1940 as physician at Pilón's Cape Cruz sugar mill, which was owned by famed sugar tycoon Julio Lobo, when she was already twenty years old.[31] I draw on interviews with family members and neighbors, commemorative writings published in Cuba, photographs, and information provided by the administrative staff working at the house museum in her hometown, Media Luna, to understand this era of her life. These sources reveal not only the critical influences of Sánchez's childhood, such as her father and the harsh economic circumstances faced by her community, but also the ways in which Cubans refract the stories of her childhood through the lens of her later achievements.

Several key events from these earliest years—including widespread sugar worker strikes and her father's failed bid for political office—were critical in shaping Sánchez's own approach to politics. This is also the period when she developed her lifelong devotion to the social and political thought of Cuban national hero José Martí and engaged local and national politics through voter registration drives and community fund-raising and support projects. Understanding Sánchez's own early organizing activities is essential for understanding that she was politically engaged well before her incorporation into the M-26-7. In fact, these early activities put her on the radar of the principal organizers of the M-26-7 in the *llano* (urban plains), who would recruit her into the movement.

Sánchez's efforts to coordinate and support the uprising that would eventually spark a revolution frame much of her thirties. These years figure most prominently within her official biography, overshadowing both her childhood and her postrevolutionary life. History textbooks for primary and secondary school children in Cuba, for example, focus almost exclusively on these years as the foundation of her national significance.[32] Though I do not attempt a full recounting of all of the events of these years, I mobilize previously untapped material to show definitively that Sánchez was a crucial organizer and administrator of the liberated territories, able to draw on her own political skills and relationships in support of the M-26-7.

Sánchez's work to link the rebel army with surrounding villages, towns, and cities—which was critical for stabilizing the revolutionary nucleus—became a key piece in the posthumous story of her status as a "woman of the people." Aside from her role in smuggling arms into the mountains, maintaining rebel communications, bringing international media attention to the movement, and participating in direct combat, I explore the relationships she developed with Cuban supporters in the eastern provinces and with her fellow *compañeros* in the movement. Sánchez's personal correspondence from this period, as well as her only known diary, also offers glimpses into her complex feelings about life as a combatant. She offers clear-eyed reflections on the devastating impacts of war on the lives of rural families, the tremendous sacrifice of young life, and her own heartbreak about living separated from her beloved father and siblings. Sánchez's vulnerabilities, anxieties, and fears are omitted entirely from her official state biography, perhaps to preserve her image as a steadfast and unwavering supporter of the revolution. Yet they appear in these documents as honest and important reflections on the cost of war from a woman standing on the front lines.

With the triumph of the revolution in 1959, Sánchez moved into the ranks of authority, occupying several key positions within the postrevolutionary government. Sánchez's keen eye for design, her resourcefulness, her motivational capacity, and her ability to work autonomously in the Sierra Maestra laid the foundation for the trust Castro placed in her to execute a range of large-scale public works projects after 1959. Although speculation about the nature of their relationship overshadows most accounts of their years working together, friends and family understood them to share deep common roots.

Sánchez's childhood steeped in the works of Martí linked her to Castro—also a devout *martiano*—as did her earlier organizing efforts on behalf of the Orthodox Party. They were also both raised in rural communities at the eastern end of the island and easily comprehended the struggles faced by families living in that zone. As a result of the revolutionary war, they were further bound together by a profound experience of privation, violence, loss, and hope for the future. Sánchez and Castro may have shared a romantic connection—an aspect of their imagined relationship later weaponized by their critics—but the primary foundation of their relationship was as "war buddies" who shared a common set of experiences, values, and roots. The two leaders forged a deep and abiding alliance until her death in 1980, and that relationship continues to figure prominently within framings of Sánchez's historical significance.

Sánchez's conviction that the revolution should reimagine public spaces as expressions of the collective—be they for leisure, business, or educational purposes—defined her postrevolutionary public works portfolio. She initiated and executed with almost complete autonomy a vast array of construction projects, including the revolution's first high-security archive and Havana's famed Coppelia ice cream park. She also traveled widely both nationally and internationally as an ambassador for the revolution. Sánchez's political activities did not, however, concentrate solely in her official capacities as secretary to the president and as a member of the Communist Party. She attended to individual Cubans' daily concerns in ways that shaped how Cubans understood her as an example of the New Woman. Acting as a kind of godmother to the new Cuba, she received thousands of written requests for assistance with housing, medical needs, and family finances. She also took into her home in Havana's Vedado neighborhood a number of children orphaned by the war, personally overseeing their medical care and education well into their adult years.

While rarely appearing in the Cuban media from 1959 to 1980, Sánchez's image served as a prism through which supporters and opponents of the Cuban Revolution understood and judged its significance. As the female revolutionary most closely associated with its famous leader, the U.S press became intrigued with Sánchez. Initially offering an adulatory, even romanticized, portrait of Sánchez's relationship with Castro and her strategic importance for the Cuban Revolution, they quickly refashioned this image when the tenor of U.S.-Cuban relations shifted in the early 1960s. Depictions of both Castro and Sánchez, like the entire revolutionary project, changed dramatically. The U.S. press cast the "woman behind Castro" as a dangerous influence on Cuban state policy in general, and on Castro in particular. Insinuations of inappropriate sexual relations between the two leaders became a key mode through which international observers expressed Cold War reservations about the Cuban Revolution and the island's imperiled relations with the United States.

Sánchez's health declined steadily over the course of the mid- to late 1970s. Her death from lung cancer in 1980 initiated a new phase in a myth-making process that began in the Sierra Maestra. Thousands of Cubans attended her lavish, multiday funeral in Havana, where they bore witness to the crystallization of her official biography at the hands of friends, colleagues, and fellow Communist Party members. The timing of Sánchez's death—when rising attrition rates plagued the revolutionary government—shaped the official narrative of her life and career. The Cuban press published dozens of articles and photos of Sánchez, the majority of which show her standing directly at Castro's side, in order to cement her image as his most loyal supporter. She became mythologized as the epitome of the revolution's New Woman: steadfast, self-abnegating, deferential, and maternal. Circulated both nationally and internationally, this version of Sánchez's story was not without its critics, who seized upon her death as a new opportunity to voice their disdain for the revolutionary administration.

I conclude this study with my reflections on the creation of Sánchez's popular biography since the time of her death, surveying a selection of commemorative sources and sites created by groups and individuals whose identities cross geographic, gender, and racial boundaries. These sources allow us to consider how Sánchez's official biography shapes, and is shaped by, globalized imaginings of her life. The creative spaces generated through these imaginings—whether they take form in paint, poetry, or on the theatrical stage—all engage the idea of Cuba's New Woman. At times reflecting, and at other times refracting, the image of Sánchez cultivated by the revolutionary state, these sites of memory offer unique insights into contemporary projections of her legacy both on and off the island. They also reveal where Sánchez's real and imagined life story intersects with a variety of important themes relating to the Cuban Revolution, such as the politics of memory, gendered constructions of war and revolution, and the contested nature of national mythology.

Finding Celia

Sorting recently through photos from my first research trip to Cuba in 1996, I found one that shows me standing in front of the Celia Sánchez monument in Havana's Lenin Park. I remember being so excited to take the photo, as this was the first monument to Sánchez that I had visited on that trip. Tucked in a lush corner of the park reachable by a wooden footbridge, the 3.25-meter-high bronze relief of Sánchez created by Caridad Ramos stands only yards from a statue of Vladimir Lenin at the top of a nearby hill.[33] At the base of the relief, a bronze plaque states simply: "Celia Sánchez Manduley, 1920–1980" (figure 1).

FIGURE 1 Monument in Lenin Park, Havana, 2018. Author's collection.

Architect Antonio Quintero, who worked with Sánchez to create Lenin Park years earlier, envisioned the site not only as a national monument—a status signaled by the Cuban flag fluttering on a flagpole overhead—but also as an homage to Sánchez's rural roots and her love of nature. Ramos's relief of Sánchez, dedicated on the fifth anniversary of her death (11 January 1985), complements Quintero's vision. Embedded within a large, mossy boulder surrounded by ferns and red ginger flowers, Sánchez stands in her fatigues and holds one of the notebooks that were her constant companions in the Sierra Maestra Mountains. Roger Ricardo Luís's prose poem "Celia entre nosotros" (Celia among Us) evokes the solemn power of the location, stating, "The people say that our Celia is in Lenin Park dressed as a guerrilla fighter. She stands among the jicaros, palms, [and] ferns of her Cuban wilderness, among the rocks as firm as her willpower, among the flowers as simple and perfumed as she was, by the stream of water as clear as her affection and smile."[34]

As a site of memory for individuals who feel connected to Sánchez's story or want to learn more about the Cuban Revolution's highest-ranking female leader, the Lenin Park monument remains a key tourist destination within the larger park complex. I returned to visit the site in April 2018, almost twenty-two years after the date of my photo. To my surprise, the same enthusiastic site manager, "Cuso," who has worked at the site since its dedication, emerged from the small visitor center to greet me. After offering me a *cafecito* (shot of hot Cuban coffee), he ushered me into the receiving area where a pair of glass display cabinets contain a few of Sánchez's medals, a childhood dress, a pen, and her mechanized Bates Listfinder address book. "Cuso" informed me that he lives in a state of perpetual anticipation. Former Cuban President Raúl Castro (b. 1931) indicated on several occasions that he intended to relocate Sánchez's remains from Havana's Colón Cemetery to the base of the Lenin Park monument. The monument staff has no idea if the move will ever take place, but "Cuso" told me that it would be the "greatest honor of [his] life to spend [his] final days watching over her."[35]

The 1996 photo of me standing next to Sánchez's monument reminds me of the excitement I felt to visit Cuba at a time when so few U.S. citizens were traveling to the island. It also reminds me of a time when formal academic training had not yet complicated my simple enthusiasm for the project. I felt no need to deny my position in the story I hoped to tell. The photo is also a reminder that, in many ways, I grew up alongside and through my interest in Sánchez's story. The photo is part of my own "coming to be" story as a scholar, a process that has shaped my vision for the project. Biographer

Kathryn Kish Sklar notes: "I am not the same person who set out to write about [Florence] Kelly ten years ago. Why should she remain the same person?"[36]

The story of Sánchez's life and her contributions to the Cuban Revolution has taken shape through the cross-pollination of voices, memories, and images. Today, official commemorative sites such as the Lenin Park monument or her tomb in the Colón Cemetery have become creative spaces where visitors exchange recollections about her, reminisce about their participation in the revolution, and ascribe their own meanings onto Cuba's national history.[37] In this way the Sánchez we can access is a palimpsest overlaid with generations of memories and projections, judgments and silences.[38] The layering process is perpetual. Through the interjection of new voices and experiences, the mythology surrounding her life is continuously redefined and reinvented. In his speech at Sánchez's funeral, Armando Hart Dávalos acknowledged that "in the history of every true revolution, legend acquires very real characters."[39]

In the 1990s, my quest was to recover the details of Sánchez's life. Now I am guided by Lois Rudnick's admonishment not to "assume that how a woman is defined is who she 'really' is."[40] The work of writing about Sánchez is about both recovery and interpretation; thus, this book tells the story of what Sánchez's life entailed, but also what it means to people living in Cuba and beyond. The great irony is that Sánchez would probably have felt quite uncomfortable with this entire enterprise. Though she grew to understand the power of her influence, she retained a lifelong aversion to the spotlight. I cannot forget how she threatened to change her name as soon as the war was over so as to avoid the detested press. Part of me feels guilty for not respecting her wish for privacy. Sánchez may not have invited, or even wanted, fame, but her place in twentieth-century Cuban history is irrefutable and her story is worth telling.

CHAPTER TWO

Most Native Wildflower

Tales of a Revolutionary Youth

> Nobody could have imagined then that she would become
> one of the most important protagonists of the future changes
> that would revolutionize her country.
>
> —LILIAN CHIRINO, "La niña que fue Celia"

> Readers like tight connections between child and "man."
>
> —PAULA BACKSCHEIDER, *Reflections on Biography*

The Girl from Media Luna

My first visit to Sánchez's hometown, Media Luna, occurred in 1996. Despite the relatively sparse treatment of her earliest years within existing chronicles of Sánchez's life and legacy, residents of Media Luna informed me that it is a tremendous point of pride that Sánchez was born in their small town. They note with irritation that Cuban history textbooks once erroneously identified her as a *manzanillera* (woman born in Manzanillo, Cuba) and the song "Manzanillera combatiente" (Manzanillo's Fighter) is perhaps the most famous of the songs dedicated to their hometown hero.[1] Staking a claim within her legacy, the town is dotted with murals and billboards proudly claiming Sánchez as a *medialunera*.

It matters that Sánchez was born in a remote sugar mill town in Oriente (eastern Cuba), and not in one of the stately mansions that line Havana's Fifth Avenue. Her special knowledge of the people and places along Cuba's southeastern coastline proved useful when orchestrating the rebels' perilous December 1956 return to Cuba from Mexico aboard the overcrowded yacht *Granma*. At a deeper symbolic level, her childhood weaves seamlessly into the story of a revolution birthed in Cuba's eastern countryside. Her birthplace certifies her authenticity as a true rebel at the same time as citizens of Media Luna lay claim to their own intimate link to the revolution through her historical significance. In this way, Sánchez's origin story becomes the origin story of the broader postrevolutionary *patria*. It also offers a geographic explanation for her storied friendship with Castro, who was born in the eastern village of Birán (Holguín Province). Their affinity is imagined to have sprung from common rural roots.

Life in Media Luna flows in a circular motion along a bumpy main road that rings the town. Horse-drawn carts, bicycles, and the occasional lumbering Soviet-era tractor transport people and goods at the unhurried pace that rural life allows. Most people living in the town today work in agriculture or in a circumscribed service industry. The Vicana River snakes lazily through town, a shadow of its former self due to upstream water needs. Everyone in town remembers times when the rain-swollen river washed out the town's principal bridge. The current bridge dates from the 1970s, after one such catastrophic flooding incident.

Like most Cuban towns, Media Luna is a patchwork of colonial and revolutionary-era structures plastered with brightly colored slogans. Strolling the circular route around town, I noted the town's abandoned *central* (sugar mill) where Sánchez's father, Dr. Manuel Sánchez Silveira (1886–1958), worked as a physician during her youth. Local sugar is now refined in nearby Niquero, but Media Luna boasts the largest grain processing plant in Granma Province. The sugar mill's twin chimneys continue to stand sentinel over the town, as they have since 1886. The original owners of the mill— British immigrants Tomás and Ricardo Beattie Brooks—named the mill "Isabel" in honor of their sovereign, Queen Elizabeth.

A partially restored mansion that once served as the Beattie country home sits at the edge of the mill grounds and testifies to the brother's accumulated power and wealth, which included their own shipping company, Empresa Naviera Beattie.[2] In 1968, the Cuban government reconsecrated the sugar mill in honor of revolutionary hero Juan Manuel Márquez and converted the former Beattie mansion into a headquarters for the local chapter of the José Martí Pioneer Organization (Pioneros), Cuba's communist youth association. The mansion and several surrounding buildings are currently undergoing a slow renovation process. Piles of sand and gravel sit on the front veranda under a fading collection of Pionero-inspired cartoons painted on the mansion's façade.

By the end of the 149-day *zafra* (harvest) of 1913, the Isabel sugar mill boasted a production of 138,524 bags of refined sugar and 1,200,000 gallons of molasses.[3] Today, the mill's three massive grinding wheels lie rusting among the weeds near the collapsing laboratory and electrical plant. The broken water tower showers rainwater onto the palm trees below. Sun-bleached graffiti at the electrical plant entrance now reads only, "We Remain in Combat" and "Sugar." Enormous in-ground water reservoirs serve as public swimming pools each summer, and local townspeople have claimed a large patch of ground abutting the old Beattie mansion for a communal garden where they cultivate sweet potato, cabbage, and yucca. Charming wooden chalets that once housed the mill's administrative staff sit beyond the communal garden, though many are in desperate need of restoration. The mill's dedicated rail spur empties into a large machinery shed that houses a Soviet-era engine and passenger car emblazoned with the words Ferrocarriles Granma (Granma Railways). When the train is in service, it offers families a short day trip to a neighboring town. A tank car that once delivered water to local communities also sits in the shed and its faded white lettering proclaims "This is a Brave and Patriotic Community."

The small Catholic church (not the original building) hosts a handful of townspeople for weekly Mass, and a series of fading billboards bear revolutionary slogans or celebrate local heroes. Impossible to ignore is the largest of these billboards, a conspicuous black rectangle placed at eye level that shouts in all capital letters—"BLOCKADE: The Longest Genocide in History"—and an image of the island caught in a hangman's noose. The next billboard honors Media Luna's most famous citizen. It depicts a youthful Sánchez standing in front of her childhood home and the words "Celia, Forever Celia" encircled with mariposa (butterfly) lilies, the national flower (figure 2).

The mariposa lily grows wild in several areas across the island, and is closely associated with Sánchez. Family friend Adelaida Bécquer Céspedes once told me in an interview that "gardenias were actually Celia's favorite flower," but Sánchez "understood the power of the mariposa as a national symbol."[4] She cultivated the heavily fragrant blossoms at her various residences, and planted them around the rebel command station in the Sierra Maestra to inspire the troops. Several photographs of Sánchez taken during the armed phase of the rebellion show her standing in olive-green fatigues with a mariposa in her hair. This imagery connects Sánchez to Cuba's long genealogy of women rebels. National mythology holds that *mambisas* (female independence fighters) transported secret communiques within these flowers during Cuba's wars of independence (1868–98).[5]

Poet Enrique Pineda Barnet reinforces the connection between the mariposa and revolutionary womanhood in his posthumous poem to Sánchez, which begins with the line, "Celia / the orchid in the guerrilla lapel / flourished in the mangroves that awaited the *Granma*."[6] While the flower imagery surrounding Sánchez signifies her rebellious spirit, femininity, and love for nature, her construction as "*la más autóctona flor*" (the most native

FIGURE 2 *"Celia, Siempre Celia* [Celia, Forever Celia]" billboard, Media Luna, 2018. Author's collection.

wildflower) also frames her as a humble woman with deep roots in the Cuban countryside. In Media Luna, a multistory concrete school features a large mural with Sánchez in a cotton dress and a mariposa lily in her hair. The phrase "Celia: The Most Authentic Wild Flower" hovers above her head.

Both of the two parks in town feature monuments to their hometown hero. The smaller of the two parks holds a Plexiglas reproduction of an iconic photograph of Sánchez wearing fatigues and carrying a bundle of documents. Manicured hedges spell out her initials (C. S.). Locals refer to the small and relatively secluded park as "Lovers Park," because young lovers meet there to avoid the vigilant eyes of family and neighbors. Beyond Lovers Park sits the town's central park, which contains an elegant gazebo with a red-and-white-checked roof, a ring of shady trees, and banks of colonial-era benches that once featured the names of the elite families whose wooden chalets surrounded the park. In the years following the revolution, workers chiseled the names of the families from the benches as part of a reimagining of the town's history. They also tore down a nearby statue of a member of the elite.

Now called Parque de los Mártires (Martyrs Park), the park—like every town center across the island—features at its center busts of two national heroes of Cuban independence, José Martí and Carlos Manuel de Céspedes. Sánchez's father, Dr. Manuel Sánchez Silveira, placed them there in the 1930s.[7] Busts of two local heroes stand at the outer edge of the park to commemorate a second generation of martyrs. One man, Vilo Acuña, died in Bolivia with Che Guevara, and the other, Raúl Podio Saborit—for whom the town's main avenue is named—died just days before the triumph of the revolution at the tender age of twenty-one. A billboard in town provides an imagined reunion between Media Luna's three native stars. Acuña and Podio stand flanking Sánchez under the banner, "Loyal and Valiant: They Were, We Are."

The largest and most centrally located monument in Martyrs Park honors Sánchez. A mossy fountain depicts her seated and barefoot at the bottom of a graduated stack of cement slabs arranged like a topographical map. The form of the fountain conjures the nearby Sierra Maestra mountain range, which served as one of the principal fronts during the revolution. A surrounding moat of water evokes the coastline only two kilometers away. Solidly and intimately connected to the land through her bare feet, Sánchez's fatigues and wistful expression evoke her status as a rebel leader and visionary. Participants in the annual 11 January ceremony honoring Sánchez's death process to the park and to this fountain.

Another mural dedicated to Sánchez stands at the edge of the park. Nearly covering one external wall of the local movie theater, the mural differs from the others in town. Less overtly political, the mural features a hazy, almost ghostly, image of Sánchez's face. She seems both present and departed. The mural references local culture and history with images of the mariposa lily, musical notes, a country farmer (*guajiro*), and the five palms meant to represent the nearby Cinco Palmas farm, where Fidel and Raúl Castro reunited following their chaotic landing at Las Coloradas in December 1956.

The town cemetery lies at the edge of town at the end of a road that becomes almost impassible after a heavy rain. A field of simple cement crypts abuts an imposing marble mausoleum dedicated to Cuban veterans who participated in internationalist missions like the one in Angola. Sánchez is not buried in Media Luna, despite maintaining strong ties to the eastern coastal zone her entire life. Both by choice and as required by her status as a combatant, Sánchez was interred in one of the few permanently sealed crypts in the Revolutionary Armed Forces (FAR) mausoleum in Havana's Colón Cemetery. Sánchez's birth in Oriente and burial in Havana marks her personal and professional trajectory from a small-town girl to a revolutionary power broker in the capital. It also grounds her legacy in both ends of the island.

The Green House in Media Luna

The most famous building in Media Luna is the spacious green house where Sánchez was born. Built in 1908 by architect Miguel Rodríguez, the house is a testament to the popularity of the American bungalow aesthetic, introduced to the area via the penetration of U.S. sugar investors between 1875 and 1920.[8] Traditional Spanish-influenced ironwork gave way to American-style façades featuring wooden latticework and thin columns. Dr. Sánchez purchased the home in 1913 shortly after marrying his hometown sweetheart, Acacia Manduley Alsina, and accepting a position as medical director for the Isabel mill's small hospital. It was certainly not typical for a graduate of the prestigious University of Havana to accept employment in a remote, rural town. The new couple wanted, however, to live in close proximity to family in Manzanillo and to Dr. Sánchez's brother, Juan, who was employed as a physician in nearby Niquero.[9]

For citizens of Media Luna with whom I spoke, Dr. Sánchez's decision to eschew a more high-profile position is a key piece of his legacy of humility. They admire his decision to purchase a house in Pueblo Nuevo—the neighborhood for poor workers—and not in the more affluent El Carmen neighborhood where most of the sugar mill administrators resided. His daughter Acacia remembers that her father "wanted us to interact with the children of local farmers and sugar mill workers, with poor children. He was always fighting with the owners of the Isabel mill about the state of misery in which the sugar mill workers and their families were forced to live."[10] Every person I have ever spoken to about Dr. Sánchez claimed that he frequently offered his medical services free of charge.[11] A 1945 desk calendar belonging to Dr. Sánchez contains scribbled notes about historical events and fees his patients owed for medical services rendered. Only a few of the entries are marked "*pagado*" (paid).[12]

One family member reflected that even after she became a high-ranking governmental official, "Celia's attitude and approach to life was pretty Spartan. Like the rest of the Sánchez family, she loved rural life, and rural areas."[13] Fellow rebel leader—and future minister of culture—Armando Hart Dávalos noted in his published account of the war that "she never ceased being the *guerrillera* of the eastern mountains, who liked to sleep in a hammock or follow a mountain path. Her roots among the people, which molded her consciousness as a combatant, were a weighty part of her very nature."[14]

The house became a municipal museum in 1983, the first for Media Luna. In order to secure a coveted national-level designation, the museum staff needed to secure additional — and more valuable — display items. Maritza Acuña Núñez, the museum's first director, related in a 2017 interview with Radio Ángulo that "the little hall devoted to the heroine consisted of just a few photos and an ashtray of the family's. From the very beginning, we felt that the place had much more to offer, that the latent testimony within the house where Sánchez was born and grew for twenty years was the best place to perpetuate her memory."[15] Acuña Núñez and her staff spent the following three years in meetings, conducting interviews, and locating objects, many of which lay in the hands of relatives or the Council of State's Office of Historical Affairs. The national designation could only come via Castro, so it was essential to secure his endorsement for the project.

When Castro announced that he would visit the museum in December 1986 — as part of a tour for the thirtieth anniversary of Cinco Palmas — the staff was both jubilant and anxious. Acuña Núñez remembers Castro's visit as an emotional one for all parties. "Castro was deeply moved, with his hands behind his back, contemplating the original portrait by Carlos Enríquez of Dr. Manuel Sánchez, Celia's father, and then the photos of her. I did not dare interrupt him. I had to respect that instant of so many emotions that I saw in his eyes, and in his silence." She finally worked up the courage to say, "*Comandante*, it's that we want to talk with you. You surely noticed that we only have a few things of Celia's, and we would like to devote a room to her personal possessions.' He immediately called Pedro Álvarez Tabío, at the Office of Historical Affairs in Havana, and said: 'take care of what these *compañeras* are saying.'"[16]

Three additional years of work led to a designation as a national monument and then finally, in 1990, official designation as the Celia Sánchez Manduley Memorial Museum. "Ay, you can't imagine the emotion, hearing that [the] greatest dream that these country girls had struggled for would come true," Acuña Núñez recalls. "Everything was mixed up with laughter, cries, pinches, and hugs. The emotion of the news was only comparable to the moment when we saw the truck arrive and unload the entire collection of 239 museum-quality objects that belonged to her family."[17]

The museum has undergone various revitalization efforts. The most recent round occurred in 2004, and the museum received the National Prize for Restoration and Conservation.[18] It contains the most extensive collection of objects related to Sánchez's life of any historic site on the island, and its beautifully landscaped yard—which was designed in consultation with the Cupaniyu Botanical Garden from Guisa—is perhaps as celebrated as the home itself for the variety of native flowers, ferns, and trees it contains. The museum organizes a monthly education program, called "Celia: Fuego y Canto" (Celia: Fire and Song), which is open to the public.[19] The museum also serves as the primary draw for an estimated 12,000 tourists who pass through town each year, many of them traveling with the commercial bike tours that now crisscross Granma Province. The Havana-based cycling company CanBiCuba even offers a fourteen-day "Celia Sánchez Tribute Ride."

For some Cubans, there is an undeniable spiritual component to visiting her house. Roberto Rodríguez Menéndez—author and producer of a 2005 Celia Sánchez *radionovela* (radio drama) titled *Una muchacha llamada Celia* (A Girl Named Celia)—refers to the Media Luna house as a "holy place . . . for those who love Celia."[20] The museum website notes without irony that "without mythologizing the house and Celia's image, the townspeople feel that this place belongs to them, they identify with and see themselves here. . . . [Her] presence is felt in every space and through her belongings. And this is how the collections housed here become speaking symbols, transmitters of a message of [her] sensibility . . . a piece of our society's history that binds our collective identity."[21] Historian Tiya Miles recognizes museums as "symbolic, referential, and evocative structures" that transport visitors through time and encourage them to reflect upon their own lived experiences even as they consider the lives of its occupants. Visitors to Sánchez's childhood home can unleash their imaginations as they access and engage with revolutionary mythology through the museum displays. Rodríguez Menéndez notes that "the house is an unavoidable character in our memory."[22]

Eschewing the commercial element typical of many museums of its type, the Casa Natal Celia Sánchez does not contain a gift shop offering silk-screened T-shirts, coffee mugs, or tote bags with Sánchez's image. Visitors receive, as part of their entrance fee, a color brochure describing the history of the museum. The museum's website does now offer visitors a virtual tour, which reinforces the site's importance as a national monument and projects Sánchez's story globally in new ways. The virtual tour includes media clips not currently incorporated into the on-site tour. Songs dedicated to Sánchez, clips from documentaries, and even a brief filmed interview with Sánchez animate and enliven the digital tour while reinforcing the museum's core narrative.

The transition from a municipal museum to a national monument gave new significance to the site and to the narrative that the museum communicates. The green clapboard house in Media Luna was no longer just a childhood home; it became a certified classroom for visitors (be they domestic or international) to learn about Sánchez and about Cuban history. The museum's curatorial staff were no longer simply guardians of important objects relating to one historical figure—they became shapers of national memory and identity. Miles reminds us, however, that the creative vision necessary to mount any museum exhibition is "blurred by the passage of time, the distance of place, the biases of the historical record and the blinders of our own culture-bound perspective."[23] The weight of collective memory, individual experiences, nostalgia, and "the faintest reflection of our modern-day senses of self" shape the staff's decisions about how best to tell Sánchez's story.[24]

As editors of a four-dimensional teaching text, the curatorial staff retain considerable power to shape Sánchez's story. Miles urges us to consider "what stories are allowed and disallowed, voiced and suppressed" within any exhibition.[25] Not surprisingly, in light of its purpose, the museum grants no space to any controversy about, or unfavorable depictions of, Sánchez's life and legacy. Largely unexamined also are the allowances afforded by the Sánchez family's comfortable financial status. The eight-room museum is itself a reminder that the Sánchez family enjoyed comforts available to few at the time.

Dr. Sánchez's profession may not have garnered him a large income, especially if he charged as infrequently as reported, yet the family enjoyed for many years the profits received from several properties. Along with his five siblings, Dr. Sánchez was the proprietor of three farms: San Miguel del Chino (60 *caballerías* or 1,998 acres), dedicated primarily to cattle raising and cheese production; Las Lagunas (12 *caballerías* or 399 acres), which was rich with precious woods such as blue majagua; and Los Arroyones (47 *caballerías* or 1,565 acres).[26] Additionally, the Sánchez Silveira brothers were the proprietors of two local pharmacies.[27] According to a bank statement dated 29 August 1941 from Manzanillo's Banco Núñez, Dr. Sánchez had 2,905.16 pesos in that account—he may have had others—which was equivalent to roughly $33,000 in U.S. dollars today (2018). His monthly deposits averaged $270 ($3,095 in 2018).[28] Letters and postcards reveal that Dr. Sánchez vacationed in Europe in 1949, which was a luxury afforded to few Cuban at that time.[29] Sánchez's goddaughter, Eugenia Palomares Ferrales, notes that the Sánchez family owned a piano, an RCA Victor record player, and the first radio in town.[30] The house was also eventually wired for electricity, which Dr. Sánchez needed for his medical practice, and had plumbing in an internal bathroom. I noted that many houses in Media Luna still have outhouses.

One benefit of the family's relative wealth is that it allowed the family to pass some of the household reproductive labor to a hired domestic staff that included (in various pairings over time) housekeepers, gardeners, and chauffeurs. These individuals—many of Afro-Cuban, Jamaican, or Trinidadian descent—stand in family photos as largely anonymous contributors to the precious time and energy that the Sánchez family was able to devote to their intellectual and political pursuits. Brief biographical sketches of five of these important contributors to the Sánchez household—Dionisio Iglesias, Ignacio Brooks, Ofelia Cayayón, Ofelia Cebollín, and Rosalina Morales—appear in Rodríguez Menéndez's *Una muchacha llamada Celia* (A Girl Named Celia).[31] The author moves between historical fiction and testimony, however, and it is often difficult to determine within which of the two genres to place information. Palomares Ferrales also mentions Ignacio Brooks briefly in her work.[32]

The family's ability to hire domestic staff separates Sánchez from the realities of most women of her time, who could not afford such a luxury. The undeniable racial element to this domestic arrangement—which was by no means unique to the Sánchez family—reflects deep cleavages in Cuban history that are difficult to engage even today. The Cuban Revolution promoted, at least at the level of discourse, the creation of a raceless society that has proven elusive.[33]

Sánchez's childhood story filters almost exclusively through Cuba-produced sources, the overwhelming majority of which appeared years after her death. Assembling the story of someone's childhood when the majority of the information about a person was gathered, collected, and published posthumously presents a unique challenge. Addresses, dates of birth, and school records are largely verifiable—although Frida Kahlo famously altered her date of birth to coincide with the beginning of the Mexican Revolution—but what about tales told about Sánchez as an audacious, socially minded leader from childhood? How many of the stories told about Sánchez's childhood are true and how many are projections of an ideal? How can museum visitors separate "the factual from the fabled"?[34] W. Fitzhugh Brundage argues for an understanding of museums as performative spaces and as stages where curatorial staff present history "both as they want to see it and as they imagined the tourists wanted to experience it."[35] The Casa Natal Celia Sánchez is a reflection of these dual imperatives, and each new visitor becomes an actor in the performance.

Tales of a Revolutionary Youth

The green house in Media Luna gives four walls and a roof to Sánchez's childhood story. I first visited the museum during my 1996 trip, and returned in 2018 to find the eight-room structure much larger and better maintained than I had remembered. I was thrilled that former director Maritza Acuña Núñez offered to provide me with a private, guided tour of the museum. She and I walked quickly toward the front of the house, passing through a series of spacious rooms featuring colorful tile floors and glass display cases. As I remembered from my first visit, each room is dedicated to a different era of Sánchez's life, from her early childhood to her formal incorporation into the rebel army and final public appearance in Santiago de Cuba in 1979.

As I walked through the museum, I noted when museum content echoed (or edited) imaginings of Sánchez's childhood as presented in newspapers, biographies, and photo montages. My familiarity with those sources undoubtedly shaped my interaction with the museum's narrative. I also took notes on recurring language that appeared on wall labels around the room and that Acuña Núñez used during the tour: efficiency, courage, authority, sweetness, energy, sensibility, modesty, dedication, austerity, spirit, sacrifice, selflessness, and discipline. The museum encourages visitors to imagine that Sánchez's childhood home was the earliest training ground for the skills and personal characteristics she would need later in life.

Part of the allure of house museums is the belief that they hold secrets about a person's motivations, aspirations, and values. Visitors hope that the collected artifacts will somehow offer glimpses into a person's interior life. As Acuña Núñez noted in her interview for Radio Ángulo, the house holds "latent testimony." Transported through time, visitors want to imagine Sánchez's daily reality and connect to her through shared experiences. Was there something unique in the way Sánchez maneuvered through the mundane elements of life that made the difference? What are the joys and tragedies that shaped her life? Are there hints of later aspirations hidden within the childhood photographs and collectibles encased in glass?

Childhood homes become especially compelling historical sites when the subject is as unwaveringly private as was Sánchez. Visitors must trust in the authenticity of objects on display—perhaps even suspending their disbelief—in order to accept that the spoon in the case was, indeed, her spoon. Connecting the mundane to the extraordinary cultivates a sense of intimacy between the visitor and the subject. The visitor becomes a teleported witness to a time when Sánchez could not possibly imagine what life held in store—both the good and the bad.

The museum offers a curated and crafted story of Sánchez's childhood filtered through her later career and accomplishments. There is a comforting, if sentimentalized, teleology to that kind of curation. Reflecting on a portrait that hangs within the museum featuring a four-year-old Sánchez with a pile of dark hair and a delicate gold pendant at her neck, historian Pedro Álvarez Tabío once remarked, "Her eyes already say it all."[36] It becomes difficult to resist what William Epstein refers to as the "organized trajectory of individual advancement" when Sánchez's military fatigues are clearly visible from the room where her birth certificate rests encased behind glass.[37] Paula Backscheider contends that we "like tight connections between child and 'man.'"[38]

In fact, all but a couple of rooms in the house are filled with objects not from Sánchez's childhood, of which there are relatively few, but from her later life as a guerrilla fighter and then government leader. Three of Sánchez's personal firearms—the most valuable of which is the M-1 rifle that Castro assigned to her in 1957 and that she kept until her death—and a variety of diplomatic gifts from foreign dignitaries link Sánchez's childhood to her accomplishments as an adult. The museum builds a story of a woman who left behind her comfortable life to dedicate herself to the revolution. Her sacrifice is especially noble precisely because of what she gave up. Biographer Adelaida Bécquer Céspedes claims that the "thing that Celia should be most admired for is that she abandoned a comfortable life and a solid economic position, and left everything to face the dangers and vicissitudes of a clandestine combatant."[39]

The room dedicated to Sánchez's early childhood sits to the left of the front entrance. This first room tells a story of a loving and resilient family centered on patriotic values, but marked for early tragedy. The room contains a copy of Sánchez's birth certificate, which gives her full name—Celia Esther de los Desamparados Sánchez Manduley—and her birthdate, 9 May 1920.[40] Catholic supporters of Sánchez consider it almost prophetic, in light of her life path, that she was born near the feast day dedicated to the Virgen de los Desamparados (Virgin of the Forsaken), who is typically depicted holding a lily in one hand and the infant Jesus in the other. Connections drawn between Sánchez and the Virgin Mary run through Cuban imaginings of her life and legacy. During an interview conducted when she was seventy years old, Sánchez's beloved elementary school teacher and family friend, Adolfina

"Cucha" Cossío, described Sánchez as "a very beautiful child. Her face was like a painting of a little Italian Virgin Mary."[41]

The front wall of the first room also displays a copy of the earliest known photo of Sánchez. Taken when she was nine months old, the photo shows Sánchez seated in her mother's lap at the side of the Media Luna house. Adjacent photos of Sánchez's maternal grandmother, Doña Irene Alsina, remind visitors that Sánchez lost her mother to malaria when she was only six years old. In the wake of her daughter's death, Doña Irene moved to Media Luna to help Dr. Sánchez raise his eight children: Silvia, Graciela, Manuel Enrique, Celia, Flavia, Griselda, Orlando, and Acacia. The early absence of Sánchez's mother meant that her father and grandmother shaped and guided her formation as a small child.

As medical director of the sugar mill's hospital, Dr. Sánchez dedicated much of his career to eliminating local epidemics, especially malaria. Media Luna's position as a coastal port town encumbered his efforts. In his 1924 "Informe sanitario" (Sanitation Report), he stated that "malaria and typhoid fever are the dreadful transmissible diseases that have remained endemic to our communities since '95." He modestly added that "thanks to tenacious labors to eliminate them, it has been possible to completely eliminate typhoid, and if such brilliant results have not been possible with malaria, it is because new carriers of the disease arrive here daily."[42]

Described as "dynamic and imaginative," Dr. Sánchez had the ability to find "audacious solutions when the means were not sufficient."[43] When an epidemic of typhus hit Media Luna in 1923, Dr. Sánchez recommended that all extra gasoline from the Isabel mill be dumped into the Vicana River to kill the mosquito larvae. He also taught his daughter, Griselda—then only twelve years old—to administer injections.[44] Working together, they were able to vaccinate a large portion of the town.[45] Despite these monumental efforts, one of the diseases that he so diligently combated took the life of his own wife. On 19 December 1926, only twenty days after giving birth to a daughter, Acacia Sánchez died of malaria in her sister Amanda's house in Manzanillo.[46]

Sánchez never publicly addressed the personal impact of that loss, nor did I find it referenced in any of her personal correspondence, but family members recall that she clung to her ill mother's bedside. When her mother died, Sánchez suffered a deep depression accompanied by high fevers lasting nearly a month, which even her father could not cure. Her uncle Juan, also a doctor, diagnosed her with a nervous disorder and prescribed a home remedy of baths in verbena. Eventually, the fevers passed, but Sánchez remained despondent for a long time.[47] Dr. Sánchez kept his daughter out of school while she recovered from her grief. He taught her himself and hired tutors until she recovered. When she finally returned to school, she entered with her younger sister, Flavia.[48] Her brother Manuel Enrique recalls that in the wake of her mother's death, Sánchez "became more quiet and reserved. It was a terrible time for her."[49]

Aside from the heartache that Acacia Manduley's death caused for her children, her husband was greatly affected by the loss. A family friend described the couple as "very loving [and] Acacia was very much in love with her husband."[50] Manuel Enrique recalled in an interview that his father was so consistently even-tempered that it scared him to see his father so distraught. When he was summoned to his mother's bedside in her final moments and bent to kiss her, his father yelled at him. "I had never heard my father yell with this tone of desperation," Manuel Enrique remembered, "and I wondered if he was scolding me until he told me, 'Kiss her, my son.' That was so difficult."[51] Even in his seventies, Dr. Sánchez is said to have told friends, "*cada día extraño más a Acacia*" (I miss Acacia more every day).[52] He never remarried, and if he formed any romantic attachments, nobody that I spoke with could recall hearing about any particular one. Sánchez's oldest sibling, Silvia, recalls that: "When mother died . . . father decided to dedicate himself fully to us . . . he didn't want us to plunge into mourning, or even to see our grandmother crying. He wanted everything to continue at home as if mother had not died."[53] Griselda recalls that "he wouldn't allow any mourning in the house, [and] he told us to continue listening to music."[54]

The news of Acacia Manduley's death also impacted the community. Her reputation as a generous, friendly, and genteel woman won her the affection of neighbors. It was common for sugar mill workers to pass by the Sánchez home to greet and speak with her. Everyone knew her, and, in turn, she knew the names of all their wives and children. She was interested in their well-being and was always willing to offer aid to those in need.[55] A family friend described Acacia Manduley as "warm and very caring [and] because her husband was the local doctor, she knew when someone was ill [and] would worry as if that person were a member of her own family."[56] Griselda Sánchez offered in an interview that due to her mother's popularity, "for several days they suspended all [local] theater productions and nobody played their radios."[57] Friends and neighbors had, according to Silvia, mobilized during her mother's illness to donate blood.[58] The family buried Acacia Manduley Alsina in her hometown of Manzanillo.

The family's grief over their tragic loss lifted at least partially with the arrival of Doña Irene and her daughter Gloria from Manzanillo. Doña Irene took a firm hold of all aspects of the family's home life, including the finances, and her grandchildren remember her as strict but also loving and generous. Dr. Sánchez and Doña Irene ultimately proved an effective team, despite their religious differences. While Doña Irene was a devout Catholic who prayed the rosary every afternoon and evening, Dr. Sánchez was an avowed atheist. His children recall a letter that he wrote at some point following the deaths of his wife and his brother Juan—both of incurable diseases—in which he declared that the "human mind is the only, and greatest, truth in the world."[59] Dr. Sánchez was briefly a Mason (1927–30), and he engaged with the Theosophy movement, but he "never imposed any kind of religion on his children."[60] According to Griselda, however, her father did discourage her from attending Catholic school in Manzanillo, telling her that "in public school you would be with people from the town where you will become a woman and which you need to know well, suffering with their sorrows and celebrating their happiness."[61]

Despite their religious differences, Dr. Sánchez and his mother-in-law found common ground in their mutual commitment to teach the children their national history. Nights in the Sánchez home were thus filled with stories of the heroes of Cuban history and poetry readings from the works of Cuba's most celebrated poets, like Gertrudís Gómez de Avellaneda (1814–73).[62] Doña Irene remained with her grandchildren until she died on 20 October 1939.[63]

In addition to childhood photos of Sánchez, the first room in the museum contains many of her father's personal items. His lighter, money clip, and pocketknife—all items one would expect a professional man of some means to possess at that time—are all elegant but not ostentatious. The museum tagged several items as gifts. A variety of his medical instruments also are on display. In addition to serving as medical director for the Isabel mill, Dr. Sánchez became the physician for the local insurance company La Sagua and the sole municipal physician charged with attending patients across an expansive zone that extended from Media Luna to Pilón.[64]

Dr. Sánchez also operated a private consultation office from his home. During my tour, Acuña Núñez described Dr. Sánchez as "the classic rural doctor," with his saddled and bridled horse always standing ready in the front yard.[65] He provided a range of medical services, from delivering an estimated 10,000 babies to performing amputations.[66] Unofficial duties included baptizing children and acting as a local marriage counselor.[67] Dr. Sánchez delivered all nine of his own children in the Media Luna house, only eight of whom survived into adulthood. Daughter Graciela María was born

28 January 1916 and died 26 March 1917. Acacia Manduley gave birth to another daughter, who they also named Graciela María, only one week after that terrible loss.[68]

The only original piece of furniture in the museum is an enormous mahogany bookcase that once held Dr. Sánchez's personal library, which is said to have included over 1,000 books. Dr. Sánchez studied voraciously the lives of Cuban independence heroes, which resulted in numerous written works of his own.[69] He also determined the exact location where independence hero Carlos Manuel de Céspedes died in San Lorenzo, Cuba.[70] The busts of Martí and Céspedes that still stand in Martyrs Park in Media Luna were gifted by Dr. Sánchez. He also venerated Antonio Maceo and intended to publish a book titled *Jalones de nuestra historia* (Milestones of Our History), from whose sales he hoped to erect a monument to Maceo in Media Luna, but the project never materialized.[71] Dr. Sánchez's children remember that he organized study sessions for local children and shared his copies of classic works with them, stating that "many [local] children received their first education from him."[72] Manuel Enrique recalls that his father taught him to read by sounding out the names of the heroes of Cuban independence.[73]

Remembered as a multifaceted man with a "curious spirit," Dr. Sánchez maintained lifelong interests in geography, archaeology, and spelunking, which Sánchez inherited.[74] In 1948, he became an official member of the spelunking association Exploradores de Cuba (Cuban Explorers).[75] He was also a founding member of the Asociación de Arqueología del Caribe (Association of Caribbean Archaeology), as well as the archaeological groups Humboldt (Santiago de Cuba) and Guamá (Havana).[76] Dr. Sánchez directed several archaeological digs in the zone where the aboriginal Macaca population lived, and many of the resulting artifacts are displayed in the municipal museum in Media Luna or the Emilio Bacardí Moreau Museum in Santiago de Cuba.[77] Sánchez and her siblings often participated in their father's excavations. "He organized excursions for us to the indigenous cemetery in order to teach us about the life of the aboriginal people. He was always teaching us something," Flavia once noted.[78] It was not uncommon to find small artifacts or shells interspersed with his medical instruments, his children recalled, and his home office resembled a museum as much as a medical clinic.[79]

Dr. Sánchez's love for Cuban history and deep national pride are bedrock for Sánchez's childhood story. In his 1927 self-published essay *Apuntes biográficos de Rafael Morales y González* (Biographical Notes on Rafael Morales y González), Dr. Sánchez identified himself as a patriot committed to "venerating that most important thing a man has—the Motherland."[80] In a personal letter written in 1951, Dr. Sánchez expressed his dream that Cuba would one day become the "Switzerland of the Americas."[81] Biographer Nydia Sarabia claims that "he was not a great thinker nor even a politician, but rather a doctor who was searching during this era for truth, [and] the continuous improvement of ideas [and] human feelings."[82] Rodríguez Menéndez refers to Dr. Sánchez as a "Caribbean Quijote."[83]

Dr. Sánchez maintained an active and varied correspondence with intellectuals of his era—including famed Cuban anthropologist Fernando Ortiz (1881–1969), who coined the term "transculturation"—and with political figures like reformist Orthodox Party presidential candidate Eduardo Chibás (1907–51).[84] He was, however, notoriously suspicious of politicians. In a letter he wrote to Chibás in 1947, Dr. Sánchez noted that he had "the misfortune of always being one of the first to abandon and fight against the party in power because no Cuban government, to the detriment of the Motherland, has ever come close to making good on its platform."[85] In spite of earning a nickname as "the Systematic Oppositionist," the nationalist Cuban Revolutionary Party (Auténtico Party) nominated Dr. Sánchez as delegate to the Constitutional Assembly in 1939.[86] Remarking on his bid for office in a letter to his son, Enrique—who was studying in the United States—Dr. Sánchez wrote, "I feel disappointed with politicians. . . . I am going to help with the restructuring of the [Auténtico Party], but if you were to ask me if this [work] excites me, I would say no, but I can't just stand around with my arms crossed."[87]

Sánchez received her most direct political socialization through her father, but her extended family tree had deep political roots.[88] While I have never seen him mentioned in biographical treatments of Sánchez's life, her maternal great uncle, Rafael María Manduley del Río (1856–1924), was a staunch separatist who was forced into a brief exile before returning to Cuba to fight in the wars of independence. He rose to the position of secretary of war (1896) and later served as delegate (Oriente Province) to the 1901 Constitutional Assembly, where he voted against the Platt Amendment.[89] He served as governor of Oriente Province (1908–13) and became a candidate for the national vice presidency in 1912 under President Alfredo Zayas (1921–25).[90] He also served as president of the Liberal Party in Oriente Province for many years.[91] His image adorns a four-cent stamp produced on the centenary of his birth, and avenues in Holguín and Santiago de Cuba bear his name.

Her paternal grandfather, Juan Sánchez del Barro, a native of Naves (Asturias, Spain), immigrated to Cuba as a young man when—according to family memory—he killed his opponent in a pistol fight to defend his sister's honor.[92] Sánchez del Barro fought with Spain during the Cuban wars of independence (1868–98), and became a highly decorated captain of the Manzanillo volunteer forces. He eventually served as municipal *regidor* (alderman) in Manzanillo in 1873.[93] He married two sisters in succession—Celia and Modesta Silveira Román—but only had children with his second wife, one of whom was Dr. Manuel Sánchez Silveira.[94] Sánchez del Barro was cousins with Cuban President Ramón Grau San Martin (1933–34, 1944–48) and eventually became one of the wealthiest merchants in Manzanillo.[95] The family holds that a street in Spain honors Sánchez del Barro, but I have not been able to confirm an exact location.

The death of the third Silveira Román sister, Isabel—Dr. Sánchez's aunt—remains a sore subject in the family, and one family member thinks that it may have fueled Sánchez's own anti-imperialist sentiment.[96] Isabel Silveira was killed when shells fired from the USS *Resolute* at the end of the Fourth Battle of Manzanillo (12 August 1898) struck the city.[97] Dr. Sánchez's close friend Dr. Augusto Fernández Conde—who would attend him in his final days as well as deliver the eulogy at his funeral—wrote on the first anniversary of Dr. Sánchez's death that "the bombing of the city by the North American fleet, during which he lost his aunt Isabel, was one of the most formative experiences of his youth."[98] Bound by both biology and their shared link to tragedy, the family remained close across generations. Years later, Isabel's great-grandson, Mario Girona, served as the architect for Sánchez's famed Coppelia ice cream park project (1966) in Havana's Vedado neighborhood.

Acuña Núñez and I passed from the room dedicated to Sánchez's earliest childhood into the adjoining bedroom, which holds only two single beds and a dresser, none of which are original to the family. Sánchez shared the small room with her younger (by only one year) sister, Flavia. Of the Sánchez siblings, these two were closest, in terms of both age and amity. In an interview, Flavia Sánchez recounted that "we were really close from the time we were little. When it was time for Celia to go to school, I wanted to go too."[99] The two sisters often dressed in identical outfits, and first attended a private school together in Media Luna's El Carmen neighborhood, where they learned basic language and mathematics skills under Beatriz Pernías.[100] When Pernías moved to Manzanillo, the sisters transferred to the local public school to study with Ismaela Céspedes. Céspedes died of tuberculosis shortly after the sisters joined her class.[101]

While the museum does not display many items from Sánchez's years in elementary school, her siblings all attest that Sánchez's relationship with teacher and family friend Adolfina "Cucha" Cossío was formative. Cossío was the granddaughter of Cuba's independence hero Carlos Manuel de Céspedes, and was committed to teaching the children their national history. She was also committed to teaching the girls domestic skills like sewing, cooking, and managing household finances, which was typical of the era.[102] Sánchez apparently excelled in this subject.

Sánchez also discovered her love for art and design under Cossío's tutelage. She was especially fascinated with silhouettes and won a box of colored pencils in an art contest held by a local radio station.[103] A copy of the winning silhouette—an Asian-inspired landscape featuring a man in a traditional conical hat seated under a tree—hangs in the Media Luna museum. The original is archived in the Office of Historical Affairs in Havana, as is an exquisite mechanical drawing of a table she designed.[104]

Sánchez and Flavia also loved music, and even took piano lessons for a few years before abandoning the instrument.[105] I have never heard that she practiced a sport, but she followed baseball closely, especially the teams from the eastern provinces. She apparently loved to see Havana's Almendares team play when she was in the capital, and followed the National Series closely. Sánchez's childhood friend Berta Llópiz recalls that Sánchez was known—even years after she became a high-ranking government official—for entering a friend's home and asking them to turn on the radio "so that she could hear if her team was winning."[106]

Sánchez's enduring connection to nature also began during her childhood, when she fastidiously cared for the flowers and plants in the yard and enjoyed long visits to the family farms, especial San Miguel del Chino. From references to Sánchez as the "most authentic wildflower of the revolution" to photographs of her wearing military fatigues with a flower in her hair, Sánchez's image is deeply rooted in her love for Cuba's native flora. Many of her postrevolutionary projects also bore the mark of her childhood affinity for nature. Three Cuban presidents have received international leaders in the "Fern Room" within Havana's Palace of the Revolution, which Sánchez filled with dozens of giant ferns shipped from the eastern end of the island.

According to Flavia's testimony, however, Sánchez's principal hobby was cooking, especially *comida criolla* (traditional Cuban food).[107] Friends and family remember her as also having a special talent for baking, especially *"el cake bocabajo"* (upside down cake). Linking Sánchez's domestic skills to her political activities, Llópiz recalls that from a young age Sánchez began selling her baked goods as a way to generate money for charitable causes.[108] Years later that income also helped her purchase supplies and ammunition for the revolution.[109] Bécquer Céspedes—who grew up in Pilón and knew the Sánchez family well—claims that Sánchez later used her cakes as a way to pass clandestine communiqués.[110]

Cossío spoke candidly years later about her surprise that, of all the children she taught over the years, Sánchez became the national hero. In an interview she confessed, "She was so quiet and shy. She didn't participate in class. She never raised her hand to interject. If someone were to have asked me: 'Which of these children will someday become a revolutionary?' I never would have chosen Celia. She seemed so shy, so fragile." On the other hand, Cossío recounted a story that ultimately proved to her that Sánchez was actually "*un poco zorrita*" (a little mischievous).[111]

According to Cossío's testimony, after announcing a quiz one day in class, she began randomly selecting students to answer questions. Nobody knew the answers to the quiz and it became apparent that the students had not studied the material. In frustration, Cossío sarcastically told her students that they should no longer come to school if they did not wish to study. When the final bell rang, all the students returned to their homes. The next day was a Saturday, and, as was customary, Cossío went to Sánchez's house to visit with her grandmother, Doña Irene. Upon her arrival at the Sánchez home, Doña Irene asked Cossío to take a seat to hear about Sánchez's recent escapade. While Sánchez stood silent with lowered eyes, her grandmother explained, "Imagine, Celia went from house to house telling all her classmates that they should not go to school on Monday since you had told them not to." Cossío, frustrated by her students' plot, began to cry. Seeing the emotion of her teacher, Sánchez quickly fled the kitchen and was gone the rest of the afternoon. When Monday arrived, not a single student was missing from class, as Sánchez had returned to the homes of her classmates, "*retirando la consigna*" (withdrawing the order).[112] Recalling this episode from Sánchez's early childhood, Cossío concluded that, "at ten years old, she was already rebellious and audacious."[113]

Stories meant to communicate Sánchez's early rebellious spirit range from playing hooky from school, to turning off the main water valve on a neighbor who was in the middle of a shower, to more complex tricks. One such story involved a traveling photographer who set up a studio in town. On the day of her photo shoot, Sánchez and a friend stole some photos and began anonymously mailing them around town. They sent photos of women to married men and vice versa, causing more than one scandal in town.[114] Another story involved trapping a local policeman's horse and painting a green "for sale" sign on it. There are two versions of the outcome of this particular prank. According to Orlando, the children were never caught.[115] In another version of the story—related by Álvarez Tabío—the terrified horse took off at a mad gallop into the local Europa Hotel, causing a stampede of domino players out the hotel door, and punishment for the young coconspirators.[116] When recalling the "famous horse incident," Orlando recalled, "I repeat to you that it was Celia's idea."[117]

A final story involves an elaborate plan involving the traveling Ramón Espígul theater troupe, which came to Media Luna to perform. Upon his arrival in town, Espígul received an urgent message that a man in town wanted to join the company. Espígul, eager to discover new talent, promptly walked to the home of the indicated person, only to learn that the message was a prank. The initially confused man quickly determined that Sánchez was to blame, as he had been the victim of many of her tricks. Both men decided to laugh off the incident, and Sánchez was never punished.[118] Cossío once noted that "there is something essential that we discuss—her tremendous powers of persuasion. Her interactions with me were always very respectful. I was a lot older than her, but regardless I would say: 'The day that Celia tells me to jump from a roof . . . I will start looking for a low one, because I will surely jump.' It was her art for persuading people that got my brother to infiltrate [General Fulgencio] Batista's army. He was risking his life, but she convinced him [to do it]."[119]

Stories that present Sánchez as a fearless, mischievous, and persuasive child link well with the daring role she would later play in the revolution. Sánchez's sisters claim that she was not afraid of anything—except rats.[120] Historian Magalí Fernández writes that "You can say that Celia wasn't scared of lightening nor thunder . . . nor any of the other animals, ghosts, or phenomena that frighten children . . . with one exception: rats."[121] She apparently retained this fear of rats for her entire life and refused to enter a room where she could smell one.

Otherwise, her siblings remember her as their fearless defender. Sánchez's sister, Griselda Sánchez, recounted in an interview that she saw a man prowling around their house one night and scurried to find Sánchez, as their father was on a house call. According to Griselda, "without much fuss, Celia grabbed father's pistol and went out onto the patio. We still talk about that prowler's rapid retreat when he saw this small, slender— but very determined—young girl with a gun in her hand."[122] Acacia Sánchez recalls the day that a large, shiny oval appeared in the sky over Media Luna. Instinctively, she took her big sister's hand in fear. Sánchez's instinct was to pursue the unknown object. They ran to a home in the El

Carmen neighborhood that had a lookout and from there they glimpsed their first zeppelin.[123]

Strung together in a cohesive narrative that imbues her with personal values—rebelliousness, bravery, persuasiveness, and determination—anecdotes about Sánchez's early childhood provide the first links in the causal chain of her life. They have survived because they are both entertaining and instructional, personal and popular. Sánchez's childhood, like that of several other top-ranking Cuban officials, becomes a parable for a nation creating a new mythology. Stories about brandishing a weapon to protect her family from an intruder become essential pieces of this mythology, whether or not they are true, because they resonate with judgments about the woman and leader Sánchez became. They are the pillars of her "making of" story.

The reach and resonance of these anecdotes extends beyond the boundaries of Sánchez's life story. Historian Daniel James refers to anecdotes as "a concentrated representation of the idealized story that a culture would like to tell about itself."[124] Through the prism of one outstanding life, Cubans can tell a broader story of their nation's political progression through insurrection and revolution toward a dream of sovereignty. Sánchez's political consciousness is imagined to have unfolded seamlessly from her childhood exposure to Martí's teachings, to her early activism and eventual incorporation into the M-26-7, to her total conformity with *fidelismo*—a kind of revolutionary religion centered on faith in Castro's leadership.[125] Stories about her childhood thus help sustain an overarching meta-narrative about Cuban revolutionary consciousness as one birthed in the Cuban countryside, nurtured by workers and civil servants across generations, and brought to full maturity through the dedicated sacrifice of visionary leaders.

Emerging Political Awareness

Teenage photos of Sánchez in the museum show her as active and popular. Her oldest sister, Silvia, remembered Sánchez at that time as "the center of the group who was always organizing the activities."[126] Cousin Olga Sánchez remembers Sánchez as someone who "possessed a talent [*don*] for organizing."[127] Orlando retains a similar memory of those years, but clarifies that "she didn't want to be the boss, she always just really liked taking care of people."[128] One group portrait depicts her with a group of girlfriends, who referred to themselves as "*Los Pavitos*" (The Little Turkeys) to denote, according to Sánchez's cousin Ana Alicia Sánchez Castellanos, "*que eramos muy jóvenes . . . eramos muy felices*" (we were really young and happy).[129]

Considered attractive by her peers, Sánchez was selected by Manzanillo's Club Guacanayabo as their representative in an August 1938 beauty contest organized to coincide with carnival celebrations. According to Griselda Sánchez, Sánchez initially rejected their offer, because "she didn't want anything to do with it and couldn't stand publicity, but she eventually agreed."[130] As with other parts of Sánchez's life, some discrepancy surrounds the contest's outcome. Álvarez Tabío claims that a disagreement between the owners of the club and the contest organizers meant that Sánchez ultimately withdrew from the contest.[131] Stout claims that Sánchez "won hands down," as does her sister Griselda, who also claims that the other candidates simply withdrew from the contest in the face of the "quantity of votes that Sánchez received."[132] Judging from my own interviews, Sánchez's status as a "beauty queen" is well entrenched within memories of her youth, no matter the actual outcome of the contest.

Sánchez's teenage years also provided her deepest, but not her first, engagement with socialist thought prior to the revolution. Media Luna had deep roots in socialism and a history of civic, patriotic, and class-based consciousness. In 1906, Agustín Martín "Martinillo" Veloz organized a section of the Partido Socialista de Manzanillo (Socialist Party of Manzanillo), and, in 1912, agricultural workers in the area went on strike demanding better salaries and working conditions. Dr. Sánchez read Lenin's works and supported worker activism in the zone. One family source also informed me that Sánchez's brother Manuel Enrique was involved with a local communist political group.[133]

A brief move to Manzanillo in the mid-1930s exposed Sánchez to the ideas of new socialist leaders emerging on the national political scene. Upon completing the sixth grade in Media Luna, Sánchez attended the José María Heredia Preparatory School in Manzanillo with her cousin, Olga Sánchez Castellano. Sánchez first met René Vallejo Ortíz—who would serve as Castro's personal doctor and adviser after the revolution—during her time at this school.[134] Sánchez lived during the week with her maternal aunt, Amanda, who was a school principal and maintained a much stricter home than Sánchez was accustomed to. A homesick Sánchez slowly began spending more time at the home of her paternal uncle, Miguel. In her uncle's house, she interacted with a politicized cousin who supported a young former student and activist named Antonio Guiteras Holmes (1906–35), who was a close associate of Cuban Communist Party founder Julio Antonio Mella (1903–29).

Guiteras burst onto the political scene as a staunch critic of right-wing President Gerardo Machado (1925–33), who, despite initial widespread support from Cubans, became increasingly repressive and autocratic by his second term in office. When Machado was forced out of office in August 1933, Guiteras began advocating for a new proletarian political organization inspired by a blend of anti-imperialism, Spanish anarchism, and the nationalism of José Martí. Despite his radical leanings, Guiteras joined forces with more reform-minded individuals such as Ramón Grau San Martín, and when Grau assumed what would prove a short-lived and fraught presidency in September of 1933, Guiteras was appointed his *secretario de gobernación* (minister of the interior).

Dr. Sánchez supported the new Grau government, believing him to represent the only truly revolutionary and anti-imperialist leader on the island. When the Grau government came under attack in late 1933 by the self-appointed chief of the armed forces—and future president—General Fulgencio Batista (1940–44, 1952–59), Dr. Sánchez and his brother Juan helped organize an armed uprising in protest. The uprising drew the support of 300 men and became known as "La Angulema" for the farm in Campechuela from which they intended to launch their fight.[135] According to Manuel Enrique's testimony, the entire Sánchez family contributed to the mobilization effort. He noted in an interview that "the preparation for the operation took place in my house. We children were tasked with carrying shotgun shells . . . and Celia was involved."[136]

The uprising never occurred. Guiteras sent a telegram asking the men to stand down and guaranteed their safety. Dr. Sánchez and his brother were both arrested one year later (January 1934), however, when Grau's "One Hundred Days of Government" ended due to his resignation, forced from him by General Batista. Dr. Sánchez, his brother, and other organizers of the "La Angulema" uprising were imprisoned for one month in the jails connected to the Moncada Barracks in Santiago de Cuba.[137] They were released under a political amnesty when Carlos Mendieta (1934–35)—with General Batista's support—became president.[138] The Moncada Barracks later served in July 1953 as the site of a failed rebel attack under the leadership of Fidel Castro. At some point during this period, Dr. Sánchez made some notes about his involvement in the failed uprising, remarking that "if we needed to repeat the effort in order to defend the nation, I feel certain that we would return to La Angulema."[139]

Following his release from prison, Dr. Sánchez continued to support the ousted Grau, even establishing a Media Luna chapter of Grau's new Auténtico Party in 1934. For his part, Guiteras went on to found Joven Cuba (May 1934), which called for the overthrow of the puppet Mendieta government by armed struggle, assaults on army barracks, and the assassination of policemen and members of the government.[140] Like her cousin in Manzanillo—who officially joined the ranks of Joven Cuba—the young Sánchez supported Guiteras's radical agenda. Any dreams for Guiteras's leadership, however, ended on 8 May 1935. On the day before Sánchez's *quinceañera* (fifteenth birthday) celebration, Guiteras was executed by government agents under the direction of General Batista. A bronze bust marks the spot at the El Morrillo castle (Matanzas, Cuba) where he died, and he is buried in Havana's Colón Cemetery. Sánchez never met Guiteras in person, even though he apparently stayed in her maternal uncle's Hotel Casablanca in Manzanillo at one point. In a letter written to her sister Flavia years later, however, Sánchez recalled that exposure to Guiteras's ideas opened her eyes to the nation's broader social problems.[141] News of his execution is said to have affected her deeply.

Another photo in the museum from Sánchez's teenage years shows her at the family's San Miguel del Chino farm with the dashing Barcelona-born heir to a profitable Manzanillo hardware store, Salvador Sadurní.[142] Sánchez's friends and siblings remember Sadurní as a popular and talented young man who invited Sánchez to the movies and serenaded her in the evenings.[143] Rodríguez Menéndez includes in his book a fragment of a tango, titled "Celia," that Sadurní composed in her honor.[144] Sadurní died tragically on 9 June 1937 when he began hemorrhaging during a surgical procedure to remove a tumor from his leg. He was only twenty-one years old.

Questions remain about whether Sánchez's relationship with Sadurní was actually romantic. Historian Álvarez Tabío claims that Sadurní called for Sánchez during his final moments, but asserts that their relationship was not romantic.[145] Orlando recounts that his sister "liked Sadurní, but . . . they were never a couple."[146] Her cousin Olga claims that "Celia once told me that she was in love with Sadurní."[147] For some family members and scholars, the ultimately ill-fated relationship answers the question of why she never married. Flavia asserts that her sister "really was in love with Sadurní" and that his death caused her to become "inoculated against love."[148] Biographer Nancy Stout devotes several pages of her book to Sánchez's relationship with Sadurní, claiming that the pair bonded over their mutual interest in the Spanish Civil War and that Sánchez became "something of a widow" after his death, "even in light of other romantic interests and her long relationship with Fidel."[149] In my interview with Margaret Randall, she stated, "I don't buy the idea that she never married because she was pining for her teen love that died." Randall posited that Sánchez never married because "she was smart enough to reject traditional male/female relationships. She invented her own story."[150] Bécquer Céspedes once told me that Sánchez told her to "never get married, because you will only become a slave to your husband."[151]

Despite the much larger scope of her career and accomplishments, Sánchez's love life generates considerable speculative energy. Theorizing about Sánchez's teenage relationship with Sadurní mirrors the extensive guesswork surrounding her later relationship with Castro. In the absence of Sánchez's own documented testimony on the matter—which only intensifies the drive for an answer—responses to this question filter as much, if not more, through individual positionality and broader gendered understandings of ideal male and female behavior than fact. Ultimately, only Sánchez knows how she really felt.

Some debate also surrounds Sánchez's educational trajectory during her teenage years. Sánchez began work on her bachelor's degree on 7 May 1937 when she enrolled in the Instituto de Segundo Enseñanza de Manzanillo (Institute of Secondary Education of Manzanillo) along with Flavia and her cousins Olga and Ana Cecilia Sánchez Castellanos. The three oldest Sánchez siblings were studying in Santiago de Cuba (Chela and Silvia) or in the United States (Manuel Enrique). The family rented a house in Manzanillo at León #15—which features a historical marker today—and Doña Irene and their aunt, Gloria Manduley, moved in to care for the children. Dr. Sánchez stayed behind in Media Luna, and Sánchez assumed her position as the eldest of the remaining five siblings.[152] "Celia was always the eldest sister whom we had to obey. . . . At her command, we had to go or do whatever she said," recalled Griselda in an interview.[153]

Sánchez never completed her bachelor's degree, for reasons that may well connect to her father's changing professional and economic position during this period. The Isabel mill's owner, Don Ricardo Beattie, died in 1938, leaving his son-in-law, Dr. Delio Núñez Mesa, in charge of the mill's operations. Dr. Sánchez had a long history of conflict with Núñez Mesa, the primary source of which was Dr. Sánchez's role as a local founder of the Auténtico Party (1934)—whose leader was the former president, Ramón Grau San Martín. Núñez Mesa was an elected representative of the Liberal Party.[154]

Dr. Sánchez had also become an increasingly visible participant in local labor organizing. During the harvest of 1932, sugar workers in Media Luna staged a fifty-day strike to demand the right to receive at least part of their salary in cash rather than store credit. The workers organized themselves as the Sindicato de Obreros y Empleados del Central "Isabel" y sus Colonias (Union of Workers and Employees of the Isabel Mill and Its Settlements) and began bargaining for a sugar agreement. Violations of that agreement promoted additional strikes in 1933 and 1934, the latter of which became known as the "Media Luna Massacre" (15 July 1934) due to the deaths of three protestors at the hands of the Rural Guard.[155] As pushback against the mill's increasingly exploitative treatment of the workers—which included denying salaries to workers injured on the job—Dr. Sánchez began maintaining a list of every injured worker he attended.[156] He also filed a legal claim against the mill's insurance company demanding payment for $9,000 in medical services rendered, which the mill's lawyer attempted to settle out of court for a fraction of the sum owed. Dr. Sánchez ultimately lost his case.[157]

Dr. Sánchez then took his battle against Núñez Mesa into the electoral ring. His children claim that his 1939 decision to run for office was only to undercut Núñez Mesa's own campaign to become delegate to the Constitutional Assembly. On the day of the election, Núñez Mesa attempted to buy supporters by providing a free meal to anyone who would vote for him.[158] The Sánchez children, who helped with their father's campaign, were elated to learn that Dr. Sánchez still secured the popular vote despite Núñez Mesa's ploy. They were equally devastated when—for reasons that are not entirely clear, but are typically linked to systematic corruption and the power of the Beattie family—he did not win the election.[159] Manuel Enrique recalled that "the people ate the food and still voted for father. [Núñez Mesa] never forgave him for that and made his life so miserable that our father decided to move us to Pilón" that same year (1940).[160] Sánchez was especially devastated by the outcome. Álvarez Tabío claims that the incident "left a bitter taste in her mouth regarding the business of politics."[161]

For his part, Dr. Sánchez's distrust of politicians only deepened. In a drafted article typed on the letterhead of the Pilón mill where he began working in 1940, Dr. Sánchez sarcastically encouraged his fellow citizens to "vote for [Delio Núñez Mesa] so that your children can continue living a miserable life and so that you can keep seeing your children sick and starving to death. . . . Vote for Delio so he can make sugar from your bones."[162] Dr. Sánchez eventually broke with the Auténtico Party and threw his support behind Orthodox Party leader Eduardo Chibás, whom he saw as more ethical and civic-minded.[163]

Sánchez appears to have truncated her formal education at some point during these events, as she did not return to the Institute of Secondary Education of Manzanillo for the 1938–39 academic year.[164] Sánchez's extended family was apparently furious with her decision. Two Sánchez biographers link her withdrawal from school to an incident in which a professor chastised her for her handwriting and declared her exam illegible. Álvarez Tabío claims that due to Sánchez's "extraordinarily firm character," she resolved to never return to school, and he quotes a letter Sánchez wrote to her sister Silvia asserting her position on the matter, "One of us is wrong here: either the professor does not know how to read or I should not be pursuing my bachelor's degree."[165] Her cousin, Ana Alicia Sánchez, claimed in an interview that it always bothered Sánchez when, years later, newspapers referred to her as "Dr. Celia Sánchez." Ana Alicia recalls that Sánchez always protested that she had "already told them that [she didn't] have any titles."[166]

Álvarez Tabío claims that another repercussion of the incident with the professor was that Sánchez largely abandoned cursive writing in favor of printing, often in all capital letters.[167] I can attest from my own work with Sánchez's papers that her slanted and looping cursive is exceptionally challenging to read, and several of her archived documents are simply tagged as "ILLEGIBLE." Proving she was aware of the issue—and as part of her document preservation project within the Office of Historical Affairs—Sánchez generated transcriptions of some of her early documents. Thankfully, the majority of her later communications were written in print or composed on a typewriter. Whether or not her penmanship shifted as a response to teenage insecurity, Sánchez's writing style had the benefit of becoming much more legible, which was an asset for a woman managing rebel communiqués and, later, presidential memos.

Biographer Nancy Stout wonders if the handwriting incident provided a way for Sánchez to avoid going to university, as she had been a fairly uneven student, except in history, where she excelled. Her cousin Olga Sánchez notes that "she was an average student . . . she never really like to study."[168] Stout sees her decision not to return to school as "her first step toward nonconformity," as a "fall from grace," and as "her first big confrontation with both authority and the fact she wasn't perfect."[169]

Perhaps Sánchez really just wanted to return home and care for her father, which is what she ultimately did. When Dr. Sánchez left his job at the Isabel mill, the family's economic situation rapidly deteriorated. Cattle sales were down at the time, but Dr. Sánchez negotiated a barter situation with a local store owner who agreed to accept cows from the family's San Miguel farm in return for store credit to purchase necessities.[170] While it is unclear if these changed economic circumstances shaped her decision to leave school, Sánchez soon became her father's constant helpmate and confidant until she joined the revolution. Friends and family offer stories of her packing his suitcases for trips, planning meals, preparing his clothing, and assisting him with patients. Offered as proof of her sacrificial character and devotion to family, stories that center on Sánchez's caretaking role with her father also foreshadow her almost maternal dealings with the rebel troops, with Castro, and with the many Cubans who sought her aid and assistance over the years. Bécquer Céspedes told me in an interview that "Celia was the way she was *before* the revolution. The revolution didn't make her personality, she brought her strengths to bear on the revolution."[171]

The director of the Municipal Museum of Media Luna, Elizabeth Elliott, shared with me her amazement that Sánchez achieved such significant success despite never attending college. She noted that "staying with her father meant that rural, coastal life became her university, and the relationships she forged during this time would come in handy later when she was helping to arrange the logistics of the rebels' coastal landing." Elliott argued that the years that Sánchez spent with her father were the years that forged her reputation as a "woman of the people."[172] Sánchez eventually resumed her studies at the end of her life and was only two courses short of graduating when she died. She received a posthumous degree in social sciences on 4 October 1980 from La Escuela Superior del PCC "Ñico López." Her diploma hangs in the Media Luna museum.

As the flagship memorial to Sánchez, the Casa Natal museum presents as comprehensive a view of her life as its collection permits. Acuña Núñez walked me through the remaining rooms, which flow chronologically through the end of her life. Like bookends, the photo of Sánchez perched contentedly on her mother's lap sits directly across the hall from a photo taken at her final public appearance in November 1979 at the twentieth anniversary celebration of the rebel uprising in Santiago de Cuba. When Acuña Núñez and I parted ways after the tour, I immediately made plans to travel to Pilón, where Sánchez moved with her father and younger siblings when he left his job at the Isabel mill in 1940. Like the Casa Natal Celia Sánchez in Media Luna, the Pilón home is currently a public museum. As the only museum in town, however, it also displays objects and memorabilia relating to the broader history of the community. If the Media Luna museum told a story of an exceptional child born in a rural sugar mill town who was marked for greatness, the Pilón museum would tell the story of a young adult whose experiences prepared her to accept that call.

Moving to Pilón

Scholarly, press, and popular treatments of Sánchez's biography often minimize or eliminate altogether her earliest years in Media Luna and Pilón. Launching her life story from the moment of her incorporation into the M-26-7 serves a political purpose. Instead of recognizing Sánchez as a fully politicized woman in her own right, she becomes a woman made political by the revolution. This understanding of Sánchez's earliest biography grants ultimate credit (or blame) for her achievements to the revolution, and, by extension, to its leader, Castro. Interviews with friends and family reveal some pushback to this deferential, gendered narrative. They remember the years in Pilón (1940–57) as the most politically formative of her life, when Sánchez honed her leadership skills and developed the personal networks that facilitated her underground organizing efforts in support of the M-26-7. For her most intimate circle, Sánchez's childhood experiences and her own innate character traits primed her for rebellion. This alternative narrative of her youth frames her as a rebel who *found* her movement, more than a rebel *made* by a movement.

Removing the patina of nostalgia, politics, and fate that has formed on the surface of Sánchez's biography, we can consider yet another reading of her early life. Sánchez clearly possessed a set of personal skills, values, and life experiences that prepared her well for a revolution that she could not have known was coming but chose to join. She was charismatic, organized, and well-connected to local communities through her father's medical work and her family's early political and philanthropic activities in the eastern provinces. She was also raised as a *martiana*, steeped in the rich history of Cuba's long struggle for sovereignty and the writings of José Martí. There is no room within Sánchez's official biography to consider an (admittedly ahistorical) scenario in which she chooses not to join the M-26-7 when local organizers came to Pilón to recruit her. Doing so reminds us, however, that Sánchez's eventual power and influence within the movement—and later within the new revolutionary government—were a result of timing, the particular needs of the movement, and Sánchez's own choices. Nothing in Sánchez's story was inevitable.

CHAPTER THREE

Compañera of Ideals

Forging a Revolutionary Identity

> I never thought about writing a diary. My uninteresting life has
> consisted of silly things not worthy of writing down. This war
> and these circumstances obligate me to note some interesting
> happenings so that Cuba's true history might be known.
>
> —CELIA SÁNCHEZ, personal diary, 1 March 1958

> What we most would like to know is forever out of our reach;
> we would like to have the diary of the most obscure of these
> popular leaders; we would then be able to grasp, in the act
> so to speak, how one of these great revolutionary days began.
>
> —GEORGE LEFEBVRE, *La Révolution Française*

The Road to Pilón

I took a day trip to Sánchez's childhood home in Pilón, a small fishing town
nestled between the Sierra Maestra and the coast about forty-five minutes
from Media Luna. The Mareón highway that leads you into Pilón was so
named for the heavy excavator—affectionately referred to as "Marion" by
her operators—that spent seven years (1925–32) carving the original highway into the hillside. The hard rain from the previous night had left all of
the highway's potholes full of water and mud, so my driver spent much of
his time weaving to avoid them. We stopped at a string of historical markers indicating the path taken by revolutionary units under the command
of Raúl Castro and Juan Almeida Bosque (1927–2009). The units had been
scattered following an encounter with Batista's troops at Alegría de Pío
shortly after the disembarkation at Las Coloradas. A series of turquoise
and white concrete monuments that each feature a painted portrait of a
local revolutionary hero—Sánchez's is the first in line—guided us along
the final stretch into Pilón. A large billboard at the entrance to town features Sánchez alongside revolutionary heroine Vilma Espín (1930–2007)
with the national flag behind them, a bouquet of mariposas between them,
and the words "Heroines of the Homeland and of the Revolution" flying
above their heads.

Pilón was an isolated town for much of its history—merchandise and supplies from Santiago de Cuba arrived by boat for decades—and it retains a somewhat remote quality today. Pilón's inhabitants live primarily by fishing, agriculture, or by working in the small service sector connected to a few local beach hotels. When we finally parked in front of Sánchez's former home, after stopping to ask for directions several times, we were joined by a group of students in starched uniforms from the elementary school across the street. My tour guide was a young ex-teacher who had started working at the museum only two years earlier. The museum job provides her the opportunity to share her local history with visitors while balancing her caregiving duties as a single mother of two toddlers. Energetic and enthusiastic, her only misstep occurred when she mistakenly attributed Sánchez's death to a brain tumor rather than lung cancer.

The formal tour began on the breezy front porch of the spacious home. Prior to its occupation by the Sánchez family, the house was the residence of the principal administrator of sugar baron Julio Lobo's Cape Cruz sugar mill, which was renamed the Carlos Enrique Carracedo mill following the revolution. My guide described the extensive renovations to the house undertaken in the 1980s by a local construction brigade directed by Eduardo Fergusson. Truckloads of wood transported from Pinar del Río (at the far western end of the island), a coat of vibrant orange paint corresponding to the home's original color, and new landscaping brought the house back to life. She also directed our attention to the national historical marker in front of the house, which declares that Sánchez lived there from 1940 to 1956, and to the original porch swing. The house—like all of the houses in town dating from the period—sits on stilts to protect it from flooding as well as to facilitate its relocation.

Passing through the front door, visitors are greeted by a wall sign that positions Sánchez's years in Pilón within her broader legacy. The sign states: "Celia came to Pilón when she had just turned twenty years old. In addition to her youth, she brought her nobility and profound humanity, which she shared with this town from the moment of her arrival. Her infancy in Media Luna and adolescence in Manzanillo also shaped her. She matured between the sea and the mountains [where] her devotion to the humblest [countrymen] and her leap into the mountains carried her toward immortality and legend." The first room presents an overview of the town's history by way of a few precontact artifacts, including a small fertility idol that Dr. Sánchez discovered during his archaeological excursions. The room also features objects from the sugar mill and photos from the construction of the Mareón highway. Local residents donated memorabilia from their participation in the revolution's national literacy campaign and international missions, as well as 26th of July bonds and uniforms, and an issue of the rebels' *Sierra Maestra* newspaper.

The museum also displays artifacts from Sánchez's life, which were donated by members of her family or by local residents who, according to journalist Augusto Benítez, "guarded [the objects] like precious relics."[1] The museum displays articles of clothing and a pair of heels, an enamel peacock pin, a large piece of coral that Sánchez recovered from the ocean, a lighter, a coffee pot, a china set, and Acacia Manduley's (Sánchez's mother) purse. The museum possesses an original signed passport that Sánchez obtained in April 1960 for her first postrevolutionary diplomatic tour to the United States, Canada, and Argentina. The only bathtub and sink in the house feature labels claiming them as original to the Sánchez family. My driver noted quietly that even the metallic soap dish featured the label: "Soap dish used by the Sánchez family." The museum also displays Sánchez's fishing net, a hook, and photos of Sánchez fishing in the nearby bay. Bécquer Céspedes claims that Sánchez spent hours out on the bay in a tiny boat that her father gifted her and which she nicknamed "La Piraña" (Piranha).[2] Her intimate knowledge of the area's coastline later became a considerable asset when it was time to plan the male rebels' arrival from Mexico aboard the yacht *Granma* in December 1956.

Sánchez adapted quickly to life in Pilón and established a place for herself in the community. Bécquer Céspedes remembers that Sánchez sewed the robes for the Virgin of Charity statue that sat on the local Catholic church's altar.[3] She also apparently began offering her organizational and artistic skills as a wedding planner. "She would handle everything from organizing the buffet, baking the cake, arranging the bouquet, designing the dress, decorating the tables, and even crafting the toast," remembers Lilian Chirino.[4] Sánchez quickly made friends in Pilón. Bécquer Céspedes claims that "Celia was always the center of our group. She had something special about her! I don't know if it was her resolute and firm character or her way of organizing activities and accounting for the most minute details."[5]

Chirino also recalls Sánchez's reputation for being especially generous and concerned with the well-being of others in town. She notes that "Celia's humanity had no limits [and] she gave everything she had without asking anything in return. . . . She had a keen ability to find the heart of a problem quickly and resolve it . . . she never thought in terms of obstacles."[6] As the daughter of a doctor, she was especially preoccupied with health concerns.

Sánchez is said to have assisted at the births of her siblings' children (totaling fourteen), cared for her fraternal uncle Miguel when he became ill, and even paid for trips to Havana for people who needed specialized medical attention. She also taught herself to drive her father's small Ford truck, which she used to assist her father on his medical rounds.

Sánchez was impacted by the poverty of the people living in Pilón. She knew that many workers in the area only had employment for one-third of the year, during the sugar harvest (January–April), and she resented the fact that certain local vendors took advantage of this seasonal influx of money into the community to hold fairs where they sold liquor and beer to local workers. Angry that the hard-earned money of these rural workers fell into the hands of a handful of merchants, Sánchez decided to organize a festival of her own. She gathered donations of money and supplies from local friends and sympathetic business owners, some of whom donated livestock for a raffle. Sánchez used the proceeds from the festival to help offset expenses for families who needed medical treatment in Manzanillo. Her community organizing efforts provided the genesis for a sustained local relief project named the Comité Pro-Pilón (Pro-Pilón Committee). Years later, the revolutionary government inaugurated the Celia Sánchez Hospital in Manzanillo to honor her work to secure health care for Cubans living in that municipality.[7]

Chirino and others have also cast Sánchez as especially generous with the children in town, especially those who were less fortunate than herself. Bécquer Céspedes remembers seeing Sánchez driving around Pilón in a small red convertible car that was "filled with ragged, barefooted children . . . who all called her godmother."[8] Chirino notes that "Celia's open personality and warmth left no room for prejudices."[9] She also claims that Sánchez conducted a detailed survey of Pilón—identifying the names, addresses, and ages of all the children in town—and gathered donations in order to make sure that each child received a toy at least once a year.[10]

Berta Llópiz notes that Sánchez "organized raffles and dances to obtain money and also asked local farmers to make donations," and then traveled to Santiago de Cuba to purchase the toys.[11] She had the toys sent back to Pilón in private vehicles. Berta Llópiz recalls that "nobody who worked year-round received the toys, Celia wouldn't permit it, only the children of poor, rural workers could get them. When the money ran out, she often bought toys with her own money."[12] A small photo hanging in the Media Luna museum, taken on Día de los Reyes (Three Kings Day) in 1955, shows Sánchez standing with a cluster of small children each holding toys that she had collected for them. Sánchez maintained the tradition even after the revolution, which fortified her legacy as a godmother figure to rural families.

Exiting the home into the large back yard, my guide directed me toward a large mango tree whose heavy limbs reached down to the ground in such a way as to create a kind of interior room around the trunk. The Sánchez family decorated the space with chairs, a table, and colored lights, and christened it the Mango Bar. The privacy provided within the resulting lounge area was ideal for social gatherings and, later, political organizing. According to my tour guide, Sánchez first met Frank País, the rebel M-26-7 coordinator of the *llano* (urban plains), under that tree in early January 1956 when he arrived in Pilón to recruit her to the revolution.[13] There is, as will be discussed below, some debate about the details of that story. The yard also features a small tree house, which now sits on stilts, that Sánchez designed and hired a local carpenter to construct. While Sánchez intended the treehouse as a gift for her nieces and nephews, she later used it to meet secretly with supporters of the revolution.

When Sánchez's Aunt Gloria—who had lived with them in Media Luna— left Pilón to care for her widowed sister Amanda in Manzanillo, Sánchez assumed primary responsibility for the household duties. She was assisted by two hired domestic workers, Juana and Ernestina González. Sánchez continued to nurture her talent for decorating, cooking, and gardening. She also devoted herself to her father's care in ways that echo descriptions of her caretaking role in Castro's life years later: bringing his morning coffee, organizing his clothing, cooking his meals, and preparing his books and medical instruments for work. Sánchez's elementary school teacher and family friend, Cossío, offers that Sánchez was "an incredible housekeeper. She cooked wonderfully, was a skilled baker, and could sew and embroider; all of these facets [of her life] were hidden because of her modesty and because of the political life she lived." Cossío also remarked on the devoted care she gave her father, noting, "She was always planning trips for her father. She wanted to keep him active and happy. She planned where he would stay and what he would do, to the point that she would pack a schedule in his suitcase."[14]

Bécquer Céspedes recalls that Pilón had only "one small, miserable hospital with various beds with mattresses that were infested with bugs."[15] As he had done in Media Luna, Dr. Sánchez received patients at his home office and laboratory—often free of charge—and he also treated sugar workers from his clinic at the mill. He apparently lived entirely off his salary from the mill. The museum displays some of Dr. Sánchez's medical instruments, a few patient receipts, a hairbrush, a personal seal, a pocket-sized chess game, and a Romeo y Julieta cigar box and pipe case. My guide noted that Sánchez chose not to attend university in order to care for her widowed father. She accompanied him on his medical rounds, helped maintain his records, and even learned to administer injections.

Sánchez and her father also engaged in several public works projects, such as building a school and memorial park in town that required fund-raising efforts by way of dances, fairs, and raffles.[16] Their largest public works project occurred in 1953 when Sánchez and her father participated in a collective effort to honor José Martí's life and legacy on the centennial of his birth. Historian Nydia Sarabia recounts that members of the Cuban Institute of Archaeology and the Alumni Association of the Martí Seminar (Havana) grew impatient with the government's tedious debates about how to memorialize the independence hero, and decided to take the matter into their own hands. The group chose Jilma Madera—who also sculpted the Christ figure that stands over Havana Bay—to sculpt a bronze bust of Martí and a set of bronze medallions they could sell to finance the project. On the morning of 19 May 1953, a fifty-member expedition set out from Santiago de Cuba's Santa Ifigenia cemetery to place the finished 163-pound bust atop *El Turquino*, the highest summit in the Sierra Maestra (975 meters above sea level).[17]

Sánchez and her father—who was almost sixty-seven years old at the time—joined the expedition as filmographer and guide, respectively, though Sánchez's footage has never been located.[18] The strenuous two-day climb took an unexpected turn when the group discovered it had been infiltrated by four agents of the Batista government. According to testimony gathered from the group, the infiltrators were discovered when one of them accidentally stabbed himself in the foot while trying to kill a snake. As an act of gratitude for the expeditioners' medical assistance, the agent informed them of rumors that the group intended to collect a helicopter delivery of foreign weapons in the mountains and launch an insurrection. Despite the harrowing encounter with the government agents, the expedition proceeded as planned. A photo taken after the mountaintop celebration that followed the installation of the bust shows Sánchez standing proudly alongside her father, Jilma Madera, and their friend Anibel Díaz. A bronze plaque mounted to the bust's stone pedestal features a quote from Martí stating, "Few are the men who know how to look out from the mountains and truly feel a sense of patriotism, or of humanity, in their entrails." The bust still stands today. Cubans and tourists alike clamber their way up the steep peak as either a personal pilgrimage or photo opportunity.

Photos published in Cuban newspapers in the years following Sánchez's death show her enduring connection to the Martí bust over the course of her life. She orchestrated an elaborate graduation ceremony at the site—to which she famously coordinated the delivery of large containers of ice cream—to honor the first cohort of medical students to complete their training in the mountains.[19] Photos from the celebration show the young graduates in their scrubs posing proudly in front of the bust. Another photo shows Sánchez and Raúl Castro standing in front of the bust alongside a group of similarly whip-thin rebels in fatigues, all brandishing their rifles under a waving Cuban flag.

The installation of the Martí bust remains a hallowed anecdote within Sánchez's official biography. It certifies the authenticity and durability of Sánchez's patriotic values and cements her status as a "permanent revolutionary," as Haydée Santamaría's daughter once characterized her.[20] Told with the end of the story already known, this anecdote also functions as a kind of foundational myth infused with an element of destiny. Typically displayed as a sequence, photos of Sánchez with the Martí bust present her as a bridge between the frustrated dreams of the postindependence generation and the fresh aspirations of the revolution. In his posthumous poem dedicated to Sánchez, titled "I Ask Permission from Death," famed Cuban poet "El Indio Naborí" (Jesús Orta Ruiz) wrote:

> One day, with your father, you climbed the mountain range
> Carrying a bust of Martí
> That you installed in the heights.
> But a Martí of stone couldn't
> Illuminate the Motherland's night,
> And you stayed in Pilón
> Looking toward the mountains.
> You climbed again.
> This time you did not carry a monument.
> You came with a Martí of flesh, blood, and bone.[21]

Sánchez connects the rebels—and Castro more specifically—to Martí through the bust. Nydia Sarabia once offered a similar observation in a brief article titled "Martí en Celia Sánchez" (Martí in Celia Sánchez), noting that "Celia helped finance and place [the bust] in the Sierra so that it could serve as a beacon and guide to her own generation and to future generations of Cubans and Latin Americans."[22]

Anecdotes about the various civic projects—including the bust installation—that Sánchez initiated or participated in during her years living in Pilón are as essential to her legacy as are stories of childhood mischief in Media Luna. They pull the threads of her essential character—brave, unselfish, determined—into her twenties and thus provide additional links in the causal chain of her life. They also frame her as an inherently social and politically engaged being, whose love and care for the poor predated her joining the revolution. Sánchez's elementary school teacher, Cossío, is firm on this point. She asserts that Sánchez's father was her main influence on that aspect of her personality, "with his patriotism and commitment to emulate Martí's social conscience."[23] Núñez Acuña similarly notes that "her father's strong personality left deep prints on her spirit [and] she acquired from him her fortitude, her tenacity, her pure intentions, her patriotic sensibility and many other traits that characterized her for her entire life."[24] The key point underscored in these testimonies is that Sánchez's character was well defined before the revolution and remained consistent throughout her life.

Sánchez's love for the people of her community, and her willingness to share her belongings with *los más humildes* (the humblest people) later formed the core of her legend. Sánchez's special ability to move people to action aided her throughout life, and she relied upon it often. Even at this young age, however, Sánchez came to understand that while her civic efforts temporarily assuaged the suffering of her neighbors, they did not solve the social problems lying at the roots. Just as her father had accepted warfare as a path to change when he joined the La Angulema uprising, Sánchez understood that Cuba's national dilemmas might require militarized action to resolve. In a letter written to her friend Elsa Castro Mestre in December 1957, Sánchez affirmed that "every sacrifice that we make for this revolution is worth it. Time will show this to be true."[25]

Becoming Politicized

The years that Sánchez lived in Pilón are cast in popular memory as the most politically and personally formative of her life. Her father maintained his involvement in local and national politics as a director for the Auténtico Party for Media Luna, Niquero, and Pilón. He became, however, increasingly frustrated with the state of national politics. The Auténtico Party remained in power between 1944 and 1952, first under the leadership of Ramón Grau San Martín (1944–48) and then later of Carlos Prío Socarrás (1948–52). Despite the high hopes of Auténtico supporters, both presidencies were marked by accusations of political corruption, anticommunism, high unemployment rates, and concessions to U.S. interests. Dr. Sánchez, along with many other supporters of the party, began to lose faith in their leadership. In his essay "Authentic Frustration," Dr. Sánchez wrote that "we now know one incontestable truth: that this government cannot continue [and they] must evacuate the Palace and the Capital."[26]

A fiery reformist named Eduardo Chibás entered the Cuban political scene during this period of low faith in the Auténtico Party. In 1947 Chibás founded a new party—the Orthodox Party—to promote the orthodoxy of José Martí's teachings and advance an anticorruption and pro-reform platform. Headquartered in Havana, the party slogan was *Vergüenza contra dinero*" (Shame against Money). In a letter to Chibás dated 19 May 1947, Dr. Sánchez officially broke with the Autétentico Party and pledged his support to the Orthodox Party. Embracing his new affiliation, he proclaimed, "on this symbolic day of our Patriotic Calendar [the day José Martí was killed at Dos Ríos in 1895], I have decided to abandon the Auténtico ranks to become one more in the Orthodox group over which you preside with your public spirit and customary valor."[27] He went on to lament the state of the nation, however, noting that "way before you lost your faith in the Presidential Myth, I had already lost it myself and felt pain in my soul because of our people's disillusionment."[28]

Dr. Sánchez articulated his perspective on the party's slogan in an undated article in which he states that "shame against money means that the people cannot commit suicide [by] giving their vote to a Fernández Casa or a Delio Núñez Mesa—owners of sugar mills—who have spent the last thirty years fighting tooth and nail against the workers' unions and Cuban farmers and throwing them off their land."[29] Dr. Sánchez became a founder of the Orthodox Party in Pilón and supported Chibás when he announced his intention to run in the 1948 presidential elections. In his essay "Authentic Frustrations," Dr. Sánchez articulates passionately his hope that the election would bring real change at the highest level of Cuban government, stating, "the opposition will sweep away Cuba's pre-1948 false apostle-exploiters . . . they will not continue, they will not continue because the Cuban people are the embodiment of real Cuban spirit, they know Martí, and they recognize the false prophets."[30]

In order for the Orthodox Party to become an official national party, Chibás and his supporters needed to submit a petition signed by at least 2 percent of the national electorate. Sánchez joined many other young people across the island in a door-to-door campaign to secure signatures. A photo hanging in the Pilón museum shows Sánchez with a group of young Orthodox militants in Niquero in 1947. Locals remember seeing her working the area between Pilón and Manzanillo, the precise area that she would five years later mobilize in support of the revolution. While only 50,000 signatures were necessary for the effort, Chibás supporters secured more than 140,000 signatures.

With his candidacy thus ratified, Chibás launched his election campaign and began traveling the island. When he visited Pilón, he stayed in the Sánchez house, as there was no hotel in the small town. The Sánchez home quickly became an unofficial way station for affiliates of Chibás's Orthodox Party, of which Dr. Sánchez was a municipal officer. Sánchez engaged enthusiastically with the conversations and debates that filled her home. At least one member of the family also believes that Sánchez "was a little bit in love with Chibás" at the time. In two photos from the tour taken in Pilón, Sánchez appears directly at Chibás's side. The first shows Chibás riding through town on horseback with Sánchez standing in the crowd near him, and a second is a group photo with Sánchez standing directly at his side during a rally. Auténtico candidate Prío Socarrás won the presidency in 1948, but Sánchez and her father continued their work in support of the Orthodox Party, primarily by registering voters and fund-raising.

While she was deeply entrenched in local community organizing efforts, Sánchez traveled regularly during these years. She often visited her sister Flavia, who was attending the national university in Havana. In 1948 Sánchez also traveled to the United States to visit her brother Orlando, who had lived in New York since 1946, and to receive treatment for a severe case of allergy-induced hives. Her treatment was successful, but she decided to extend her trip and spent six months exploring the city, visiting the sights, and witnessing her first snow.[31] A postcard to a friend describing her trip to Niagara Falls stated *"todo es belleza"* (everything is beautiful)."[32] I also discovered an anonymous love poem tucked within her personal documents from this period that suggests Sánchez formed a romantic connection during her time in New York. The poem, written in November 1948, shortly before her return to Cuba, refers to her as a "white dove with soft wings" who needed to "always keep flying, leaving the unnamed miracle of your sweet presence wherever you go."[33]

A family member recalled in an interview that Sánchez also reflected deeply on her future during those months in the United States. In the days before she returned to Cuba, she apparently purchased for her brother a copy of a book about José Martí. On the inside cover of the book she wrote: "When I meet a man like this, I will dedicate myself completely to him." The family member I interviewed considers this gift an indication of a kind of personal and political awakening in Sánchez. She was, he insinuated, primed for the kinds of experiences that awaited her upon her return home (figure 3).[34]

Álvarez Tabío claims that the period after Sánchez returned from New York represents a time in which she "channeled in a concrete way her commitment, concerns, eagerness, and hopes for a solution to the nation's political and economic problems." Despite suffering a loss in the 1948 election, the outpouring of support from Cubans encouraged members of the Orthodox Party to consider the real possibility of a Chibás victory in the presidential election of 1952. Chibás never made it to the 1952 elections, however, as on the afternoon of 5 August 1951, while delivering a public address at the radio station CMQ, he pulled a .38-caliber pistol from his belt and shot himself in the abdomen.[35] Chibás insiders link the incident to his inability to substantiate his public accusation that the minister of education, Aureliano Sánchez Arango, had embezzled education funds to purchase a mansion. They claim that as a man of integrity, Chibás could not stand the humiliation of having his credibility called into question. Some scholars argue that he was merely trying to regain the allegiance of an electorate that could guarantee him the presidency, and had no intention of actually killing himself.

Sánchez was in Havana with her father when she learned that Chibás had shot himself on live radio. Chibás remained in critical condition for eleven days and then died on 16 August from a massive infection. Sánchez remained in Havana throughout the tragedy and attended his funeral. By all accounts, his death was a devastating blow.[36] She both admired him as a man and believed in his potential to have been a contender for the presidency. Though Sánchez would not meet him in person for another five years, Fidel Castro—former president of the University of Havana's law student association and an active supporter of the Orthodox Party—also attended Chibás's funeral.

Later that same year, Sánchez wrote a letter to her sister Griselda in which she states that "Everything has gone badly for me this year." In addition to Chibas's death, she endured two breakups with boyfriends—one of whom, an engineer in Manzanillo, she discovered was married—and her beloved uncle Miguel was diagnosed with lung cancer and died the following year (11 May 1952). Her year would not improve. In the wake of Chibas's suicide, some of his most ardent supporters stepped up in new ways to fill the vacuum he left. Castro ran for the House of Deputies in the 1952 election as an Orthodox Party candidate on the anticorruption platform espoused by his mentor, Chibás. He garnered strong support from Orthodox members in both rural

FIGURE 3
Portrait, 1948.
Cuban Photograph
Collection, Cuban
Heritage Collection,
University of Miami
Libraries, Coral
Gables, Florida.

and urban areas across the island and was considered the front-runner in that race, but the election never happened.

The U.S. embassy in Havana observed the emergence of Cuba's new political players with a mixture of suspicion and fear. The U.S. government saw the possibility of members of the Orthodox Party's leadership—young men and women with a clearly articulated anti-imperialist stance—obtaining seats in the Cuban Congress as the first step in what might become a parliamentary group openly hostile to U.S. interests in Cuba. Not coincidentally, on 10 March 1952, the U.S.-backed general and former president, Fulgencio Batista, seized control of the Cuban government via a *golpe militar* (coup) and President Prío Socarrás fled the country.

In reaction to the illegality of Batista's actions, and the corruption, censorship, terror, and torture that characterized his dictatorship, dissenters began meeting clandestinely to discuss strategies for addressing the mounting crisis. Crossing the boundaries of age, class, and profession, they debated both the errors of the past and the shape of the future. Opposition groups characterized by geographic dispersion and methodological heterogeneity quickly sprang up across the island, though they concentrated in the most densely populated urban areas, like Havana and Santiago de Cuba, which also boasted the island's two largest universities. Many of the participants of these opposition groups, including Sánchez, had been swept up into national politics during the 1948 elections through voter registration and canvassing efforts in support of Chibás and the Orthodox Party. This was not the institutionalized movement that Castro would galvanize within a matter of years, but an atomized, effervescent demonstration of mass discontent. University students, women, and the working class became politicized in new ways, and their activities shook the entire island.

Within the new landscape of mass politicization that took shape in the wake of the May 1952 Batista coup, four groups merit special attention for both their impact on the revolutionary process and for what their mobilization efforts reveal about this period of mass upheaval: the Federation of University Students (FEU) at the University of Havana; Revolutionary National Action (ANR) under Frank País in Santiago de Cuba; the Martí Women's Civic Front (FCMM) in Havana; and the nucleus of what would become the M-26-7. While Sánchez never officially joined any of the first three organizations, she collaborated with several of their members who were later formally incorporated into the M-26-7. Her own efforts in support of the M-26-7 were more localized in the area around Pilón until she was recruited into the movement.

José Antonio Echeverría (1932–57) was on vacation in his hometown of Cárdenas, Cuba, when he learned of Batista's coup d'état.[37] A fiery and popular architecture student—known as "El Gordo" to friends—Echeverría served four consecutive terms as FEU president between 1954 and 1957. When he learned of the coup, Echeverría raced back to Havana and began galvanizing opposition to the regime. He forged a largely anticommunist, middle-class, and Catholic contingent of supporters who used public rallies, protests, and processions to articulate their demands for a democratic government in Cuba. Echeverría and his closest allies suffered arrest and imprisonment in Havana's Castillo del Príncipe for their actions. Increasingly convinced of the need for more direct, offensive action against the dictatorship, Echeverría eventually forged an armed wing of the FEU on 23 February 1954 called the Revolutionary Student Directorate (DRE), many of whose members were graduates of the University of Havana and former FEU affiliates. The DRE embraced the power of public spectacle, even staging a protest in front of the presidential box at the March 1954 carnival celebrations, but would eventually turn to more violent means to secure change.

At the eastern end of the island, in Santiago de Cuba, Frank País helmed another significant opposition group, the ANR. Like the FEU, the ANR drew heavily on student support, as País was elected president of the student association of the Normal School for Teachers in Santiago de Cuba in 1952. The stepson of a Baptist minister of modest means, País was both deeply religious and humble, according to his biographer, José Alvarez.[38] He was also especially sensitive to the plight of local agricultural workers in the area—a mutual concern that bonded País and Sánchez from their first meeting. Like Echeverría, País suffered arrest and police beatings for his protest activities, but successfully constructed an expansive network of collaborators—including future revolutionary leader Vilma Espín—upon which he founded the ANR in 1954. The ANR not only engaged in public protest, but also staged strategic strikes on police stations and elite hunters' clubs to gather firearms. As Guerra notes, "by the time Castro's emissaries arrived in Oriente to request the incorporation of País's vast network of revolutionary cells of activists, they were not only disciplined and loyal to Frank País, but armed and ready to go."[39]

Several women's organizations also formed and found their place within this new landscape of activism and resistance. Smaller women's groups, like Mujeres Oposicionistas Unidas (United Opposition Women) had as few as forty members, while the FCMM eventually boasted hundreds of members in thirty registered chapters.[40] A clandestine group aligned with José Martí's political and social philosophy, the FCMM embraced revolutionary struggle as the clearest path to overthrowing the Batista dictatorship. Aida Pelayo, Olga Sánchez, and Carmen Castro Porta became the principal organizers of the group, which was made up primarily of middle-class women, while others were laborers, housewives, or employees of local businesses. As an organization, the primary activities of the FCMM consisted of distributing anti-Batista propaganda, housing fugitive insurgents, aiding political prisoners, going to the morgue to identify bodies, transporting arms and explosives, and even publishing their own daily newspaper titled *News and Commentaries*.

In Havana, Castro also began formulating a plan to topple the Batista regime. With the support of a group of 160 young collaborators, many of whom were Orthodox Party affiliates, Castro orchestrated an attack on the Moncada military barracks at the eastern end of the island in Santiago de Cuba.[41] The barracks represented a symbolic target for the group due to its affiliation with the national military, but Castro also hoped to seize weapons and establish a headquarters of resistance far from the seat of Batista's political and military power in the national capital. Castro also intended to begin transmitting radio messages from the captured barracks that would telegraph to the entire island (and beyond) his vision for establishing true representative democracy on the island. In an interview with Carlos Franqui, Sánchez noted that "Moncada was the birth of the Revolution."[42]

Several FCMM women expressed a desire to participate in the attack, but to no avail. This restriction infuriated Melba Hernández (1921–2014). "I protested to Castro that we were just as revolutionary and that it was unjust to discriminate against us for being women. Castro hesitated; we had made a sensible point. . . . We couldn't believe that we would be left behind after we had considered ourselves an essential part of the group."[43] Haydée Santamaría (1922–80) and Hernández were finally allowed to join their male *compañeros* in Santiago de Cuba, but only as nurses.[44] Guevara later wrote in his book *Guerrilla Warfare*, "the part that the women can play in the development of a revolutionary process is of extraordinary importance, but in the case of the Cuban Revolution, their primary role was to perform a relief task." In Guevara's opinion, jobs in communication, transporting ammunitions, teaching literacy, and nursing the wounded were perfect for women, as women possess a "gentleness infinitely superior to that of [their] rude companions in arms."[45]

The 26 July 1953 assault on the Moncada Barracks was an unequivocal military disaster. The element of surprise that Castro's group had banked on due to local carnival celebrations backfired when they crossed paths with troops returning to the barracks. The ensuing gunfire killed dozens of the young rebels, while many more were captured and brutally tortured to death. Twenty-seven of the captured male rebels—including the Castro brothers—were placed on trial, charged with treason, and imprisoned in the Model Prison on the Isle of Pines (now Isla de la Juventud) off Cuba's southwestern coast.[46] Despite the limitations to their participation, Santamaría and Hernández were also caught by Batista's forces and imprisoned for seven months.[47] Santamaría's later recollection of this event illustrates the precarious situation that women revolutionaries, many of them from middle-class backgrounds, faced upon challenging societal norms of proper female behavior: "the Supreme Court wanted to free us. It was not the custom for women of so-called decent families to go to jail. I belonged to a rural family of position and culture, not of the street. But . . . we were part of [the rebellion], and what would I have done when I got out? I couldn't get a job. I would have had to go home."[48]

The brutal methods employed by the Batista regime to punish the coconspirators granted the young rebels a moral victory, despite their failed mission to take the barracks. Inspired by the sacrifice of the *"muchachos del Moncada"* (kids of Moncada), new and existing resistance groups across the island mobilized to support the cause during the twenty-month incarceration of the young rebels. Two of the most important leaders of the coming revolution—Frank País and Celia Sánchez—had not yet met, but mounted impressive support campaigns in their respective spheres of influence. In Oriente Province, Frank País worked diligently to organize new cells of the ANR, requesting that his collaborators prepare a list of potential recruits who could be trusted to join the opposition. Members of these cells then began gathering weapons, medicine, and money in anticipation of a future uprising.

In Granma Province, Sánchez also reacted quickly when news of the rebels' failed attack on the Moncada Barracks reached her and her sisters in Pilón. They mounted a fund-raising campaign, selling bonds in support of the imprisoned rebels and their families. Drawing their inspiration from Cuban patriot Bartolomé de Jesús Masó Márquez (1830–1907)—who was elected president of the "Republic in Arms" in 1897 and later opposed the Platt Amendment—the small group of collaborators named themselves the Masó Revolutionary Movement.

In Havana, FCMM women like Aida Pelayo, Carmen Castro Porta, and Gloria Cuadras recognized that consistent communication between the incarcerated leadership and the urban underground was imperative. Despite the restrictive measures of the prison, which limited the goods that could be brought to the prisoners during visiting hours, the women began to establish new channels of communication. One highly successful strategy developed by the women involved concealing notes in cigar boxes. This task was accomplished by removing the tobacco from a cigar with tweezers, planting small notes within the casing, and then replacing the tobacco at either end of the cigar. The boxes were then repacked and carried into the prison on visitation days. The guards rarely searched the women, which seems an odd oversight considering that Santamaría and Hernández were considered highly dangerous by Batista's police force. Additionally, on 28 January 1956, the *Diario de Cuba*—published in Santiago de Cuba—ran an article titled "Six Women Arrested by the SIR [Military Intelligence Service] Delivered to

Police." The six women arrested—Enma Surí, Aida Pelayo Pelayo, María Castro de Rodriguez, Delia Socarrás Olazábal, Estrella González Boudet, and Isabel Benavides—were members of the FCMM. No mention was made of the specific charges against the women.

A second, and perhaps more precarious, communication method utilized during these early years was the ordinary mail system. Lidia Castro, the sister of the revolution's captive leader, was the center of an elaborate process of composing and receiving letters, which at first glance described only the most mundane of life's occurrences (the weather, neighborhood gossip, family news). Lidia Castro, Hernández, and Santamaría gathered these simple notes and, by passing a hot iron over their contents, revealed a second message written between the lines of the letter's inked text. The incarcerated rebels used lemon juice taken from their own lunch trays to continue managing mobilization efforts and communicating with their far-flung collaborators.[49]

These various letters sent by Castro to his sister, his mistress Natalia Revuelta, and other members of the FCMM were then collected and discreetly typewritten at Melba Hernández's home at Jovellar 107 in Havana.[50] In June 1954, the first fifty-three words of Castro's famed self-defense, *History Will Absolve Me*, appeared beneath the hot iron.[51] Nearly one hundred pages in length, the document provided the initial propaganda for the revolution. The mobilization of popular support was critical in these beginning stages, and Castro himself affirmed this fact in a letter written to Hernández and Santamaría on 19 July 1954: "Our immediate project is to mobilize public opinion in our favor; divulge our ideas and garner for ourselves the endorsement of the masses. Our revolutionary program is the most complete, our line the clearest, our history the most sacrificed: we have the right to earn the faith of the people, without which, I repeat a thousand times, no revolution is possible."[52] The innovative methods of communication utilized by the FCMM illustrate the ways in which women were able to manipulate dominant assumptions concerning women's roles in society to the advantage of the revolution. Due to the gendered presupposition that they were at home cooking, sewing, and caring for children, these women were able to type copies of a revolutionary manifesto without suspicion.

In addition to distributing nearly ten thousand copies of the revolutionary manifesto *History Will Absolve Me*, members of the FCMM, as well as the mothers of the incarcerated rebels, played a critical role in attaining the freedom of the male insurgents. Women such as Lidia Castro, and Delia and Morelia Darías Pérez—members of an amnesty committee dedicated to freeing the male rebels—helped gather 20,000 signatures, which were then presented to the Cuban Senate. Additionally, in May 1954, family members of the rebels produced a document titled "Cuba, Liberty for Your Children" directed to the "Mothers of Cuba."[53] Appealing to the Cuban people in the name of the "crucified mothers of the heroic young men of the Day of Santa Ana [26 July 1954]," the document pleads for the release of the condemned heroes.[54] Their labors proved effective. Under pressure from the protests and feeling unduly confident about the stability of his regime, Batista freed Castro and the other prisoners on Mother's Day, 1955.[55]

Hope Deferred

Castro and his supporters relocated to Mexico to gather the necessary money and weapons to relaunch the movement under the banner M-26-7, in honor of the failed 26 July attack on the Moncada Barracks. Among their financial supporters, the M-26-7 counted the ousted Cuban president, Prío Socarrás. Also during this time, Castro met a brilliant young Argentine physician who would become one of the most iconic figures of the coming revolution, Ernesto "Che" Guevara. Guevara was no stranger to national resistance movements. He was exiled to Mexico with his wife, Hilda Gadea, in the wake of his actions to support Guatemalan President Jacobo Árbenz who was ousted by a U.S.-backed coup in 1952. Guevara brought his experiences in Guatemala and deeply held Marxist beliefs to bear on his collaborations with Castro as they worked to define the next moves in Cuba.

During his months in Mexico, Castro also worked to consolidate the various resistance organizations that had formed over the preceding months. He invited DRE founder Echeverría to Mexico to discuss the possibility of uniting the two organizations. Following a set of intense deliberations, the two young leaders established a unity pact, known as the Carta de México [Pact of Mexico], which they both signed on 30 August 1956. Frank País was also in attendance during the deliberations. Despite the signed agreement, the two leaders never completely synchronized their strategy. Echeverría advocated for swift offensive action to assassinate Batista, while Castro wanted to pursue a slow guerrilla war. Due to their differing opinions, Echeverría never agreed to subordinate the DRE under Castro's leadership, but instead continued to operate autonomously in pursuit of his dream to decapitate the Batista regime through a presidential assassination.

Castro also sent a letter to Carmen Castro Porta requesting that the FCMM merge with his embryonic M-26-7 movement. Hailing the "decisive" nature of the FCMM's previous collaborative efforts, Castro asserted that his forces lacked an "important component: a feminine arm," and that this special status had been reserved for the FCMM.[56] Though some FCMM members joined the M-26-7, the two groups never formally merged.[57] According to Aida Pelayo's testimony, the FCMM officially disbanded on 28 January 1959, though some members continued to meet socially for years.[58] Most members of the group were lost in the reshuffling of the revolutionary deck, leaving only a few women to remain as prominent female figures within the revolution.

Castro also requested that Frank País formally align his ANR group with the M-26-7. Castro needed access to País's extensive networks in eastern Cuba, where he planned to reenter the country and relaunch the revolution. País agreed to the merger in the summer of 1955 and thereafter became the movement's principal organizer of the *llano*, the island's eastern urban plains. He was responsible for coordinating under the black and red banner of the M-26-7 all mobilization activities in Oriente province, collaborating with the Sierra wing that Castro would establish in the wake of the landing. País became one of Castro's most important partners, as reentry in the east offered the nascent M-26-7 not only geographic distance from the political and military center of Batista's power in Havana, but also the security offered by the mountains. By tapping into the vast network of organized cells of resistance that País had established in the wake of the Moncada attack, Castro expanded his movement's reach exponentially. Castro never intended that the Sierra wing of the movement would operate independently from the *llano*, as he understood the critical importance of securing support from the civil resistance organized in the urban lowlands. It was not until April 1958—years after País was executed by government troops in the streets of Santiago— that the Sierra was reframed as *the* principal revolutionary front. Prior to that shift, the two wings of the movement worked in tandem, although often with tension between them, especially regarding supply issues.

Castro and País considered several specific landing sites for the returning rebels, but determined that a landing near Pilón held special promise. Both men knew of Sánchez's earlier work in support of the Orthodoxos, her fund-raising efforts on the rebels' behalf through her Masó Revolutionary Movement, and her family's sterling reputation within the working-class populations of the zone. Sánchez is also rumored to have gone to the Orthodox Party headquarters in Havana when the rebels were released from prison, hoping to meet Castro and offer her support to the cause.[59] She did not meet Castro until February 1957, but the trip did connect her to other key members of the movement.

It is unclear whether or not País personally recruited Sánchez into the movement. According to local sources, including guides at her museum in Pilón, País identified Sánchez as a key local ally to help coordinate the landing and traveled to Pilón in July 1955 to recruit her into the M-26-7. Museum guides share with visitors that País and Sánchez met for the first time under the large mango tree in the home's backyard, which the family had playfully nicknamed the Mango Bar. Álvarez Tabío claims that the lead M-26-7 organizer in Manzanillo, Manuel Echevarría, made the original contact with Sánchez in Pilón and—having secured her agreement to join the movement—directed Sánchez to Santiago de Cuba to meet with País.[60] In her testimony to Carlos Franqui, Sánchez notes that she first met País when he came to Pilón to check on the progress that she and Pedro Miret were making with their study of potential landing sites, which suggests that someone else (perhaps Echevarría) had already recruited her for the task.[61]

In an undated interview held in the Office of Historical Affairs, Sánchez does, however, offer her reflections on that first recruiting meeting, stating, "the southern coast of Oriente offered all the possibilities for the landing Castro was planning. The mountains penetrate the sea, creating openings where [boat] landings are possible. It is a zone linked by sugarcane fields that connect three sugar factories and three well-equipped guard stations. The various guard stations disseminated [throughout the zone] watch over the big sugar and cattle operations."[62] From the moment of her incorporation into the M-26-7, Sánchez began working closely with the rebel leaders to prepare the material and human support necessary to effect the planned landing.[63]

The official plan was that Castro and his supporters would depart from Tuxpán, Mexico, on 29 November 1956 in a small yacht called *Granma*. They would arrive on the beaches of Pilón, at either El Macho or La Magdalena, on 2 December. With the help of a local guide, Castro and the others would then advance across the coast, obtain sufficient arms to initiate the insurrection, and board the transports awaiting them. Although she had originally hoped to accompany the passengers of the *Granma* to Mexico, Sánchez and others realized the value their many connections in Cuba would have in securing the eastern provinces. País later praised Sánchez, stating that she "was decisive" during the months of planning the landing.[64] He quickly grew to respect her opinions and entrusted her with increasingly high levels of responsibility for organizing and managing key sectors of the mobilization effort.

Riding in a small motorboat, Sánchez inspected the beaches between Pilón and Marea del Portillo, carefully noting water depth and the topography of surrounding areas. She befriended the captain of a boat in Pilón and obtained navigational charts for all ports along the coast, which she sent to Mexico via Pedro Miret along with detailed maps of the area.[65] Those charts were all found on board the *Granma* yacht when the rebels landed, and the ones stamped "Cabo Cruz" (the name of the mill in Pilón) led authorities to the Sánchez family. According to Sánchez, "[the authorities] found the maps and took them to father's house wrapped in a brassiere in order to convince father that I had arrived with the disembarkation."[66]

An adept organizer with an intimate knowledge of the Oriente provinces and their people, Sánchez was well suited to the task of organizing support and troops for the M-26-7. Utilizing her family's progressive legacy and her own connections with sugar mill workers, students, and farmers in the towns of Manzanillo, Sofía, Estrada Palma, Calicito, Campechuela, Cuba Hueca, San Ramón, Media Luna, Niquero, and Pilón, within a few short months Sánchez had assembled a considerable clandestine force. Sánchez built this base of support from the ground up. According to her own testimony, the "zone featured ten sugar factories and a strong fishing base. . . . We based each sector around a sugar factory, and [each sector] had an officer who coordinated the industrial workers, the agricultural workers, the farmers, the fishermen, and the students."[67] Acacia Sánchez later noted in an interview that the organizers "did not have a single supporter from the upper classes, the whole [movement] was built on *campesino* [farmer] supporters."[68] Hart Dávalos notes that "not only did she grow close to the Movement. The Movement drew close to her. Sánchez exerted a remarkable and growing political influence in those days among the poorest sectors of the population."[69]

Sánchez's recruits monitored the guard stations and tracked the daily movements of naval frigates and the Coast Guard with the help of one of Sánchez's most important recruits. Sánchez recruited to the surveillance force Randol Cossío—the brother of her beloved elementary school teacher—who was the personal pilot of Coronel Alberto del Río Chaviano, commanding officer of Batista's forces near Santiago de Cuba. Cossío kept a detailed log of shipping activities in the area between Santiago de Cuba and Niquero that allowed the M-26-7 to pinpoint the ideal timing for the landing.[70] Collaborators also stationed trucks and gasoline tanks along the coastline to help the returning rebels make their way to the reunion site at the Cinco Palmas farm. They threw sugarcane into the beds of the trucks to disguise the supplies hidden inside. They also prepared a group to cut all telephone lines running between Pilón and Niquero, denying Batista's army its main means of communication. According to receipts archived in the Office of Historical Affairs,

Sánchez's sister, Acacia, helped gather radios and other supplies for the landing.[71] País organized an uprising in Santiago de Cuba to coincide with the landing and distract government troops in the area.[72]

A central problem for the nascent armed forces was locating and smuggling automatic weapons. In her testimony about the variety of challenges encountered during preparations for the landing, Acacia Sánchez lamented that "nobody had any guns."[73] For this reason, roughly 95 percent of the arms used were the personal property of the young combatants, and many collaborators were unarmed. In the words of one combatant, it was *"puro heroísmo"* (pure heroism). With the help of Cuban sympathizers like Ricardo Reitor — the leader of the M-26-7 in Niquero — Sánchez and her collaborators were eventually able to stockpile enough arms to facilitate the arrival of the revolutionaries. They stationed themselves around the zone and waited for the landing.[74]

Despite careful planning, the operation met with immediate complications. The first was that upon leaving Manzanillo for the coast, Sánchez was recognized by an agent of the Military Intelligence Service (SIR) and was arrested. She was taken to Campechuela, where she was detained for questioning in a café. Sánchez described the scene in an interview conducted years later with French journalist Deena Stryker, noting, "I couldn't stand it anymore. I asked if I could buy some cigarettes, got up and went to the counter. Then I sat down again, and a few minutes later, I took out a coin and showing it, asked the girl if she also had chewing gum. She said yes, and I came up again, without asking permission, casually, with the coin in my hand. She bent over to look for the Chiclets, and I started to run."[75]

Soldiers, under orders to kill her, pursued Sánchez for miles. In a document filed in the Office of Historical Affairs, Sánchez gives her testimony about the resulting events. She recalls that she "just started running. I mean running! . . . They fired shots into the air and I was running through the streets of Campechuela with no idea of where to go. I was turning and looking behind myself. I ran and ran."[76] She decided to hide in a thicket, assuming the police would not follow her there, and quickly became disoriented. Guided by the sound of cars passing on the nearby highway, she hid on the ground waiting for a vehicle to pass that was not a military jeep from a nearby barracks. When a civilian vehicle passed, she waved down the driver and was relieved to discover a friend behind the wheel who agreed to take her to Manzanillo.

Though suffering from a fever caused by the thorns that gouged her as she crawled through the thicket, Sánchez arrived safely at the home of Ciro

Redondo in Manzanillo, where she quickly fabricated a disguise and cut her hair so as not to be as easily recognized by government troops.[77] Years later, on the twenty-fifth anniversary of the FAR, Sánchez described her escape, stating, "The thorns you have seen in the crown of Christ, I had them all over my body."[78] Her language vividly portrays the persecution she felt at the hands of Batista's forces, and reinforces the "divine" nature of the rebel struggle against tyranny. Additionally, this statement illustrates Sánchez's own capacity for perpetuating and performing representations of herself as a self-sacrificing saint in ways that complicate her legacy of humble self-effacement.

The second dilemma involved the uprising in Santiago de Cuba, which Frank País orchestrated to begin on 30 November. Intended as a diversionary tactic to draw the attention of Batista's troops away from the arriving rebels, País and his nearly three hundred collaborators planned synchronized attacks on the Maritime Police, the National Police, and the Moncada garrison for that date.[79] The operation failed. Nonfunctioning weapons, police standoffs, the arrest of numerous collaborators (including País himself), and even widespread executions of activists in the streets of Santiago rendered the uprising almost completely ineffectual. Collaborator César Vallejo noted in an interview that another unforeseen issue occurred when the parents of activists—unaware of their children's clandestine political activities—informed authorities that their children had been missing for several days. In so doing, the parents unintentionally tipped police off about the actions afoot and forced their children into hiding.[80]

Furthermore, when País launched the uprising on 30 November, support cells scattered throughout the region moved into action, understanding it as the sign that Castro and the rebels had landed. Sánchez remarked on the resultant confusion, noting, "We were very confused because Frank had told us that the uprising in Santiago would occur simultaneously with the landing; when Castro arrived they would rise up. We thought they had received news of Fidel in some other way. . . . Well, that is what caused our confusion and we headed out to give orders to our fellow collaborators."[81] They had no way of knowing that the landing had not yet taken place. Acacia Sánchez also remembered the confusion that accompanied the news that the Santiago uprising had occurred, stating, "we had no news, we didn't have anything . . . the whole thing failed [and] we were totally disoriented and with so much responsibility for all of the people that we had mobilized."[82]

The third dilemma was that the band of eighty-two combatants did not arrive at the planned location or on the prescribed day. In addition to the confusion this error caused for waiting support cells, the arriving rebels lost the opportunity to access the vast network of supplies stationed by Sánchez and others throughout the target landing zone. Sánchez later lamented in an interview that "if the [arriving rebels] had debarked right on the beach instead of at the swamp, they would have found trucks, jeeps, gasoline. It would have been a walkway."[83] It is actually fairly miraculous that the rebels landed at all. Anyone who has seen the yacht that the rebels purchased to carry them from Mexico to Cuba is astonished. I had the opportunity to board a replica of the *Granma*—the original is on display at the Museum of the Revolution in Havana—and was in disbelief that the original once carried more than eighty grown men and their supplies from Mexico.

Though they had set their course to land at the Cape Cruz lighthouse, the arriving rebels ran aground at a marshy beach known as Las Coloradas near Belic, which was not an ideal location for a military disembarkation. Visitors to the national park at Las Coloradas can walk a 1.3-kilometer pier suspended above thick red-mangrove vegetation and mud to see the disembarkation site where the stranded rebels were forced to swim the seventy meters to shore. Guevara once described it as less a landing than a shipwreck.

When I visited the park at Las Coloradas, my enthusiastic park guide described the perilous landing as "impossible," "incredible," and "destiny" and marveled at the trials endured by the rebels as they struggled with their heavy packs in the dark. He paused at a sharp bend in the sidewalk meant to indicate where the disoriented and seasick rebels shifted course when they saw signs of a home in the distance. The *bohío* (small thatch hut) that they encountered that night has been reconstructed for tourists, and the campesino who received the rebels with a humble offering of food and water is honored as a national hero. With tremendous effort, the rebels eventually reached Alegría de Pío, only to be surrounded by Batista's soldiers. The Cuban media, parroting the Cuban government, declared that Castro was killed in the resulting gunfire.

The news struck the nascent combatants like a bomb. Believing that Castro was indeed dead, their initial enthusiasm foundered, and questions about the movement's feasibility began to take root. According to her official state biography, Sánchez played a critical role in securing the revolutionary nucleus in this moment of uncertainty. Not knowing if Castro was alive or not, Sánchez is said to have realized the disastrous effect that a loss of morale could have on the revolution's outcome. It became her personal mission to maintain everyone's spirits and their faith in victory. Arming herself with courage, she began shouting that Castro was alive and already climbing the hills. Sánchez repeated the refrain with such conviction that she eventually succeeded in rebuilding confidence and reminding her *compañeros* of the value of their goals.

Despite a strong government offensive at Alegría de Pío, a small subgroup of the original combatants had indeed escaped. Later consecrated as the mythical "Los Doce" (The Twelve) in state-produced revolutionary mythology—a number meant to reflect the twelve apostles—the number of survivors actually totaled eighteen and included Fidel and Raúl Castro, Camilo Cienfuegos, and Che Guevara. Over a period of a few weeks, Castro was able to gather his scattered troops and make the long trek into the Sierra Maestra. Cadres of the M-26-7 spread the word of the rebels' arrival to one another via a coded message: "María, come eat your meringue."

Hart Dávalos recalls the emotion he experienced when he first heard the news for himself. He recalls that "We had agreed with Cayita Araújo that as soon as she learned Castro was alive, she should notify us urgently in code and by phone. . . . One day we heard the sweet and clear voice of Cayita who had become our guardian: 'Yeyé, meringue! Little meringue! Big meringue!' All of us were ecstatic; confidence grew."[84] The news energized the movement, and Sánchez was finally able to begin preparations for the first contact between members of the M-26-7 and the nascent insurgents. She relocated to Manzanillo, where she had strong personal connections that could help her acquire supplies to support the rebels in the mountains.

Guerrillas in the News

The first days of February 1957 brought new moments of great preoccupation, as Cuban radio stations once again declared that Castro had been killed. Sánchez and the others refused to believe it. Days later, they discovered that the rebel leadership had been bombed when Eutimio Guerra, a member of the M-26-7, had betrayed their location. Castro and the others were informed of the impending attack in time to change locations, and Guerra was executed. Some sources indicate that Guevara executed Guerra himself, having acquired a reputation as having a "cold-blooded willingness to take direct action against transgressors of the revolutionary norms."[85]

Eager to provide visual proof that he was alive—and realizing that government censorship would prevent Cuban journalists from publishing the truth about the rebel forces—Castro allowed foreign news correspondents to visit the rebel base. Perhaps one of Sánchez's most important contributions to the Cuban Revolution during this time was that she helped facilitate their travel. On 16 February, Herbert L. Matthews of the *New York Times* arrived in the Sierra Maestra to conduct his famous three-hour interview with Castro. A member of the M-26-7, Javier Pazos, acted as interpreter. Matthews's report proved to fellow Cubans that Castro was indeed alive, despite Batista's false allegations, and launched news of "Comandante J" (Castro) and the other Cuban revolutionaries into the world at large. It was an official, world-wide cry for recognition on the part of the revolutionary forces.

It bears mentioning that U.S. journalists focused almost exclusively on operations in the mountains, and not in urban areas like Santiago de Cuba or Havana, where men and women also mobilized in support of the revolutionary cause. Viewing rebel activities through such a focused geographic lens was largely the product of rebel design, especially after the spring of 1958. As Chase has discussed, following a failed urban strike in April 1958, the male revolutionary leadership maneuvered to recenter the imagery of the revolution in the Sierra Maestra as a means to deemphasize the perception of failure on the urban front.[86] Journalists Herbert Matthews and Robert Taber, who both visited the Sierra in 1957, became key (if unknowing) collaborators in this purposeful reimagining of the revolution as primarily a rural crusade carried out by a group of exceptionally dedicated and unified young visionaries. In order to combat any doubts about the revolution's success, it was essential that the leadership communicate and telegraph imagery of rebel fortitude in the mountains to not only a domestic, but also a global audience. The male leadership, and especially Castro, thus directed the way journalists viewed the mountain operations.

While U.S.-Cuban relations remained friendly, depictions of the rebels were generally sympathetic and positive, if notably sentimentalized and chauvinistic. Most U.S journalists who traveled to the Sierra Maestra, including Matthews, were initially sympathetic to the revolutionary cause. They viewed the rebels as largely moderate, white, and middle-class patriots guided by a vision shared by their American neighbors—the pursuit of representative democracy. The rebel leadership understood the importance of perpetuating this moderate vision of the revolutionary project and went to great lengths to present the camp as an environment that upheld traditional values.[87]

The integrity of the rebels' political commitment became linked to their moral purity. Two purposefully crafted archetypes—the *barbudo* (bearded male rebel) and his quasi-maternal *compañera*-in-arms counterpart—helped communicate an image of the revolution in fundamentally moderate terms.

The *barbudo* was presented as a pillar of sexual restraint and the female combatants as quasi-maternal figures in the camp.[88] Making sure that the foreign media captured views of separate living quarters for men and women and of the rebels participating in gender-appropriate tasks—with men marching in formation and women catering to domestic needs—transmitted a view of rebel life palatable to dubious viewers. Historian Michelle Chase notes that the perception was that the "gendered division of insurrectionary labor between men and women seemed to obey 'natural' laws" about the relationship between the rebels.[89] By extension, the revolution was cast as one that did not aim to subvert wholly the social order.

Beginning with the earliest U.S. press coverage of rebel camp life, descriptions of women's contributions fell in line with broader contemporary imaginings of women's proper place in society. Journalists tended to emphasize their domestic support role and femininity and deemphasize aspects of their participation (such as armed combat) that disrupted that narrative. One U.S. journalist noted that these "gun-toting girls" "rarely fired rifles," and only "participated in a couple of easy ambushes [but] protected by strike forces of guerrillas [they] suffered only a few flesh wounds."[90] Journalists instead emphasized the women's "petticoat efficiency" in terms of provisioning, nursing the injured, and maintaining domestic order within "Castro's disorganized camp."[91] U.S. journalists were especially impressed that Cuba's new female rebels operating in the "primitive setting of the Sierra" still tried to "cling to femininity" by continuing to dress and look attractive, despite a scarcity of cosmetics.[92] Observations that, despite meager resources, women rebels operating in the Sierra Maestra provided regular meals to combatants, cultivated a pleasing domestic aesthetic in the camp, and refused to neglect their feminine appearance portended a return to normality once the fighting ended.

The Matthews interview placed Castro and the rebel army on the international stage. Some scholars of the Cuban Revolution cite Castro's new fame as the primary motivation for a set of dramatic actions that took place in Havana in March 1957, the month that the article appeared in print.[93] On 13 March 1957, Echeverría moved on his own strategy to bring democracy to Cuba with an attempted seizure of the Presidential Palace in Havana. The plan was that fifty DRE collaborators would seize the presidential palace and kill Batista while Echeverría and a smaller cell would take over Radio Reloj to announce the assassination. The palace seizure ultimately failed, as Batista was not in his office when members of the DRE burst into the building. Most of the attackers were killed within the palace.

For his part, Echeverría successfully seized the radio station and delivered his prepared three-minute announcement—not knowing that the assassination attempt had failed—and departed for the University of Havana, where the DRE planned to headquarter a new provisional government. His car was intercepted by police, however, and he was quickly killed in the resulting machine gun fire. Despite the ultimate failure of his plan, some scholars have noted that had Echeverría's plan to assassinate Batista succeeded, Castro and the M-26-7 would have become a "suddenly irrelevant factor in the revolutionary equation."[94]

The failed presidential assassination pushed repressive action on the part of the Batista government to dramatic new heights. The new leader of the Orthodox Party, Pelayo Cuervo Navarro, was killed—though he played no part in the attack on the palace—because the Batista government assumed that he was the intended new provisional president of the republic. The DRE never fully recovered, though several surviving members regrouped and, embracing Castro's guerrilla warfare strategy, moved into the Escambray Mountains to open a front in that major coffee-producing area of central Cuba. Despite some limited initial successes in consolidating local support for the revolution, leadership struggles ultimately undercut their efforts.[95] Weakened and largely ineffectual, the group was tagged by Castro for absorption into the M-26-7. When Che Guevara arrived in Las Villas in October 1958, he asked that the Escambray contingent sign a unity pact and merge with the M-26-7, marking the official end of the DRE as its own organization. The FEU remains today an important and respected student organization at the University of Havana.

A Historic Meeting

The day Sánchez escorted Herbert Matthews into the rebel command station in the Sierra Maestra marked another historic meeting. After months of preparation, Sánchez finally met the leader of the revolution she had been working so hard to realize. Commenting on the emotion of that first meeting with Castro on 16 February 1957, Sánchez stated that "to know of the well-being of Fidel and the other *compañeros* enlivened us tremendously in order that we might continue to fight."[96]

Though Castro had never met Sánchez, he was well aware of her efforts, and they did not go unnoticed. He later commented on her importance to the revolution, stating that she was "responsible for logistics, contacts, information . . . everything. She acted clandestinely and ran enormous risks in the fight, she demonstrated tremendous valor; she was crucial to the reorganization of our forces." He went on to explain that "Sánchez helped [the rebels] a lot . . . she sent the first provisions, the first clothing, the first money."[97] For her part, Sánchez's writings in the Sierra reveal her deepening faith in Castro in the wake of their first meeting, not only as a military commander, but as the future leader of the nation. If she disagreed with any part of his vision, I found no evidence of such differences in the documents I was permitted to access. In a postwar interview with Carlos Franqui, Sánchez praised Castro as a visionary, noting that "Fidel spoke of those things up in the mountains and now you see them all being realized. . . . He foresaw everything."[98]

Despite harboring secret hopes that she would be allowed to remain in the Sierra following her first meeting with Castro, Sánchez understood that she needed to continue channeling supplies, troops, and information from the *llano* into the Sierra. She would not join the mountain forces permanently for another eight months, but instead moved regularly between the rebel command station and her own base of operations in Manzanillo, at increasing risk to her own personal safety. The intervening months were physically and emotionally intense. Sánchez became the first woman to fire a weapon in battle and she suffered the loss of two significant people in her life.

Communiqués sent between Sánchez and other members of the M-26-7 following her final move into the Sierra in October 1957 document her growing understanding of her place within the movement as she transitioned from organizer to quartermaster to strategist. They also reveal the lead role she played in the design and execution of projects that would transform life in the Sierra Maestra, such as hospitals, schools, labs, and factories. These facilities offered critical support to the revolutionary troops and birthed a new generation of rural teachers and doctors who became a key vanguard of the postrevolutionary state.

CHAPTER FOUR

First Female Guerrilla

Life on the Front Lines of Revolution

Celia Sánchez! Celia Sánchez!
They look for her! They chase her!

But a unanimous heart defends her.
It's the heart of a heroic people.

—ADELINA VÁZQUEZ, "Celia: Sentimiento y raiz del pueblo"

The state . . . provides its own vision for the future and motivates
citizens again and again to emulate heroic figures in every action.

—JOSÉ QUIROGA, *Cuban Palimpsests*

Journey to Manzanillo

My driver picked me up and we made our way to Manzanillo to visit the hospital and park dedicated to Sánchez in that city and to photograph at least a few of the homes that Sánchez utilized as safe houses during the days of her clandestine organizing efforts. We battled a downpour the entire trip that converted long stretches of the road into a flowing, muddy river. I noted that many of the sugar fields we passed were now standing in water, which was sure to delay the harvest. I sympathized with a man walking down the street holding an enormous patio umbrella over his head. My driver was quieter than usual, but I registered his fear when the car threatened to bog down in the rain. When we finally reached Manzanillo, we stopped at the Celia Sánchez Hospital.

At my request, we pulled into the hospital and parked. I noticed a green-tiled mural dedicated to Sánchez beside a nearby gas station and crossed the street to get a closer look. The mural features Sánchez's portrait bordered in mariposa orchids and a quote from Hart Dávalos's funeral speech: "She is and always will be the Revolution's most authentic wildflower." Several passersby watched curiously as I snapped pictures. Reentering the hospital grounds, I noted an enormous billboard featuring the same image of Sánchez that appeared on the tiled mural across the street. The billboard also draws on familiar symbols—a cluster of mariposa orchids and the gazebo in Media Luna's Martyrs Park. A quote from Castro, in which he referenced both Sánchez and Manzanillo, sits atop the imagery: "If this woman is who you say she is, then there is no place better for her to be than in Manzanillo, where she will be most useful." Castro refused to allow Sánchez to join the rebels in Mexico in 1956 because he needed her to stay and prepare for their return. The quote—which appears on several billboards around Manzanillo—celebrates Sánchez as a well-connected local, but also as a faithful civil servant willing to set aside her own desires in order to serve the revolution in the way its leader deemed most advantageous. It is both commemorative and instructional.

As I approached the front entrance to the hospital, I glanced into a large open window and saw a portrait of Sánchez hanging on a far wall of the room. A uniformed woman seated in the window disappeared for a few minutes when I asked if I could view the portrait. She returned with another uniformed woman who sternly informed me that the hospital did not have any portraits of Sánchez. Walking back to the car, my driver explained that my cool reception was likely the result of a recent incident at the hospital that had prompted tighter security measures. Rather than press the issue, I decided to move to the next destination.

The reception at the Celia Sánchez Plaza was considerably warmer. An imposing concrete monument dominates the expansive plaza that serves as the staging ground for local rallies and celebrations. A large star formed from a series of metal poles sits between iron reliefs of the *Granma*, an image of Sánchez in fatigues, and the faces of a number of male heroes. The same quote from Castro that adorns the entrance to the local hospital—in which he denies Sánchez's request to travel to Mexico and asserts her usefulness on the home front—is spelled out in large metal letters at the base of the monument. As I scribbled some notes, my driver slipped off to locate any guards or workers on the site. He returned within a few minutes and informed me of a small office under the monument. I rounded the monument to find two women seated in a small, abandoned office space. They welcomed me with smiles and allowed me to step through an open window. We spoke at some length about my research and they apologetically pointed to the few well-used books that were all that remained of a small museum dedicated to Sánchez. They graciously offered to write a short letter of introduction for me to present to the staff at the local municipal archive and even made a quick call to alert the staff of my plans to visit.

We traveled the short distance to the municipal archive through a slackening rain to find two archive staff members. After a brief conversation, they grabbed umbrellas and began helping me locate the safe houses that Sánchez utilized during her clandestine organizing efforts, most of which are marked with commemorative plaques. The family currently living in one of the homes allowed me to enter and photograph the main living room area, where they operate a small daycare center. My new friends from the municipal archive also showed me the last safe house that Sánchez used in Manzanillo before making her final ascent into the Sierra Maestra to join the rebels. The Hernández family no longer lives there, but Mirtha Hernández received us eagerly at her walk-up apartment in the center of town.

Hernández settled into a rocking chair beneath a fanciful wooden mobile of tropical fish and began telling the story of the first time she met Sánchez. In 1957, Hernández was living in the large and centrally located home of the aunt and uncle who had raised her since the age of five. She recalls that one evening she was seated in the entrance to the home with her family and noted three individuals approaching. She thought nothing of them until she noted that one of the individuals was injured and the other was her family's own security guard. She did not recognize the other figure, who was later introduced to her as Celia Sánchez. The security guard explained that the young man was from Santiago de Cuba, and because he had just undergone an operation he needed a safe place to recuperate before he would be strong enough to make the trip up into the Sierra Maestra. Apparently without hesitation, the Hernández family agreed to take the young man and Sánchez into their home. Sánchez explained to them that her aunt's house in town was being closely watched and that she was no longer safe there. Hernández remembered that the young man, Ramón, was later killed.

Over the course of the following thirty-seven days, Sánchez established an elaborate covert operation to gather money and supplies from local supporters of the revolution and to collect and distribute messages from the mountain rebels. Hernández recalled that Sánchez only accepted visitors from 8 o'clock to 11 o'clock every morning and kept records of every donation received. A glass case at the Media Luna museum displays a copy of one of Sánchez's handwritten donation inventories. It includes the name of the donor, the date, and the amount of money or other goods collected. Most of the entries list financial donations or cases of bullets.

At 11 o'clock each day, Sánchez would announce "Ya terminé" (I am done), and no other visitors were allowed into the house for the day. She then spent a few hours writing coded messages to Castro — Hernández knew only that they utilized a numerical code — that detailed the day's inventory of supplies. As Hernández had access to a vehicle, Sánchez would then put on a pair of dark sunglasses and a scarf to disguise herself and the two women spent most afternoons hiding the clandestine fighters en route to the mountains. Hand-written notations in documents now housed in the Office of Historical Affairs (such as "Ricardo Ramírez's house, 19 hidden, $20") reveal the volume of recruits Sánchez was responsible for receiving, preparing, and protecting. They also reveal the vast network of collaborators she developed throughout the city to assist her in the endeavor.[1] Hernández's eyebrows shot up repeatedly as she recounted the tension and risk surrounding this operation. Her family had to dismiss one of the three house servants whose boyfriend was a police officer, as they feared that she might leak information regarding Sánchez's presence in the home.

Those who lived with Sánchez during her time in Manzanillo describe her as being in a constant state of activity at all hours of the day and night. If she was not attending to some task related to the movement, receiving a *compañero* bringing information from the Sierra, writing a message, or talking on the phone with a contact, she was helping with the daily domestic chores of the home in which she was taking refuge. The clandestine life was difficult for someone with Sánchez's energy, as was the solitude and lack of contact with friends and family.

In order to combat anxiety and restlessness, Sánchez frequently emerged from hiding and went in search of aid for the guerrillas. Receipts dating from December to April 1957 reveal the vast quantity and variety of goods that Sánchez gathered from local shops in Manzanillo to send to the troops: lanterns, cigarettes, boots, toothbrushes, medicine, towels, candy, hammocks, scissors, stamps, crackers, bullets, and revolvers.[2] Another member of the movement always accompanied her on her outings, and she often traveled in disguise, donning glasses and a wig in order to move through the city undetected.

Dressed in this way, Sánchez met with powerful Cubans like the sugar baron Julio Lobo—owner of the Cape Cruz sugar mill in Pilón where her father had worked—the wealthy rice farmer Pedrito Álvarez, and other influential businessman in Manzanillo, asking each to donate money to the M-26-7. Hart Dávalos noted that "it's true that Celia had great influence in Manzanillo among various popular sectors, which was extraordinarily useful for the work she did. But the value of her efforts lies in the fact that, although known by wide sectors of the population, she always managed to work clandestinely in the zone preparing audacious operations without being discovered."[3]

Recalling the activities of those early years of the revolution, Sánchez's friend Micaela Riera stated, "We went out every day to cafés, to banks, to stores, and businesses to gather funds for the movement. Celia always got straight to the point. She spoke clearly. She would say: 'Look, we are from the 26, and we are looking for money to buy guns to overthrow Batista.' And that was that! Celia was fascinating. Some people helped us; others didn't because they were afraid." Rafael Sierra, a shop owner in Manzanillo during those years, also remembers Sánchez's activities. "One day the *compañeras* Celia Sánchez and Micaela Riera asked me for some money. Immediately, Celia began to speak to me of the need for people to cooperate with the movement in one form or another. And so, under Celia's influence, I became active in the '26.' Celia possessed unique qualities she was energetic, persuasive, and analytical." One family member, in an interview with me, shared his own observations on this front, stating that "it is a strange business to persuade people to do your bidding. She had charisma. She projected self-confidence."[4]

First Reinforcements, First Battle

Shortly after the first meeting of Castro and Sánchez in February 1957, Castro assembled the directors of the M-26-7, which included Vilma Espín, Haydée Santamaría, Armando Hart, Frank País, and Celia Sánchez. He gave orders that day (17 February) to organize reinforcements in Santiago de Cuba and send them to the Sierra. País sent Sánchez back to the Oriente province, and placed her in charge of organizing, lodging, and sending to the Sierra a contingent of more than sixty men.[5] This was one of the most important missions Sánchez executed. It reinforced the rebel army, which, at that time, had only a handful of men. During his February 1957 interview with Matthews, Castro had apparently ordered his small band of combatants to march repeatedly around the rebel camp to create the illusion that they were a sizable military force. Castro later joked with Matthews about the ruse at an April 1959 Overseas Press Club luncheon in New York. Sánchez confessed that they "prepared everything so that Matthews would get a good impression."[6]

Sánchez's work to boost the size of the rebel army thus represented a milestone moment for the movement. In an interview with Carlos Franqui, Sánchez noted that they established a camp to "recruit troops at Manzanillo and to send men and arms from there to Fidel. It was on a small rice farm, not far from the prison. There in a coffee plantation, we set up camp. No one would suppose there was a camp in that treeless area. We had some people there, and more came from Santiago. That was the first Manzanillo group."[7] Hart Dávalos notes in his published account of the war that "the operation, carried out in the early months of 1957, consisted of moving an armed contingent of some sixty men from Santiago and other parts of Oriente to Manzanillo, sheltering them for over two weeks in the marabú thickets a few kilometers from the entrance into town and just steps from the Bayamo–Manzanillo highway, and then moving them to the Sierra. These were tasks that demanded courage, organizational ability, handiness, talent, and audacity. Without a doubt, that first enlistment of men and weapons from different zones of Oriente to the Sierra was of extraordinary value in sustaining the guerrilla nucleus and allowing it to develop later on."[8]

The process of awaiting the arrival of and outfitting the new troops lasted around twenty-two days. When a new member arrived, Sánchez gave them a uniform, inoculated them, recorded their belongings and noted their name, their address, and the names of their family members. One soldier recalled, "Celia helped a lot. For me, those earliest days were really exciting. While there in the camp I was so enthusiastic about the cause, and I learned to have faith in something that I really had little knowledge of. Furthermore, [Celia] was always concerned for us. She never abandoned us. She was always busy and often had to leave the camp, but we always felt her presence and her influence there with us during all our activities." It was this personal attention to the group that helped Sánchez promote a sense of cohesion, comprehension, and unity among these newest members of the M-26-7.

On 15 March, only one month after Castro first gave his orders, the band of reinforcements began the arduous trek into the Sierra Maestra. Originally, Sánchez had hoped to join the troops on their ascent into the mountains, but instead she decided to stay and facilitate the arrival of journalist Bob Taber and photojournalist Wendell Hoffman from the Columbia Broadcasting System, who wished to interview Castro. In the interim, her sister Acacia brought their father to where Sánchez was hiding in Manzanillo.[9] Government agents had come to the house in Pilón—led by the navigational charts stamped with "Cabo Cruz" found aboard the *Granma*—and interrogated the Sánchez family. Griselda even received a telegram from General Batista offering total amnesty if she would "present Celia to him."[10] Dr. Sánchez pleaded with Sánchez to take every precaution regarding her personal safety, not knowing that he would actually be the one arrested shortly thereafter.

Robert Taber and Wendell Hoffman arrived in Havana on 18 April, and Haydée Santamaría guided them to Manzanillo to meet Sánchez where she was hiding in the home of her friend René Vallejo. She had just been through an ordeal with local authorities that had rattled everyone's nerves. Despite precautionary measures to conceal her location, government soldiers under the command of Lieutenant Pino arrived at Vallejo's house while Sánchez was sleeping. The soldiers searched the house, even tearing open pillows in search of rebel documents. Without any possibility of escape, Sánchez was forced to hide under her bed. Luckily, she was not discovered, and the soldiers moved on to search elsewhere, but tensions were running especially high.

When Taber and Hoffman finally arrived in Manzanillo, Sánchez accompanied the two reporters, as well as her *compañero* Celianito Fernández, his brother Marcos or "Nicaragua," Marcelo Fernández, and Haydée Santamaría into the Sierra. They arrived at the rebel headquarters on 23 April.[11] The two reporters and their five guides remained in the Sierra until 29 April. Sánchez was allowed to remain at the base after their departure, a welcome—if temporary—reprieve from the stress of life in Manzanillo. During her stay in the Sierra, Sánchez was invited to become the first official female member of the guerrilla force in the Sierra. She soon also became the first woman to fire a rifle in battle.

At the Battle of Uvero on 28 May 1957, Sánchez, with M-1 in hand, fought alongside her male *compañeros*. The battle was made possible in large part by the reinforcements she sent into the Sierra. Without the infusion of rebel combatants that she provided, Castro would never have been able to carry out the operation. Castro's goal was to destroy the military base at Uvero, located sixteen kilometers from the rebel base in the Sierra. On the night of 28 May, a band of eighty troops, including Fidel and Raúl Castro, Camilo Cienfuegos, Che Guevara, and others marched in darkness to the barracks at Uvero. Castro gave the signal to initiate the attack by firing his rifle in the air, and thus began an onslaught of random gunfire. Having been told by their superiors that the rebels assassinated all prisoners, Batista's soldiers battled fiercely for their lives. The battle was a quick victory for the rebels, lasting only two hours and forty-five minutes. The leader of the government troops at Uvero threw a white handkerchief to the ground at the end of the battle, shouting: "*¡El cuartel de Uvero se ha rendido!*" [The Uvero base has been taken].

Casualties were low on both sides. The rebels had six dead and nine wounded—including Juan Almeida Bosque—while Batista's troops suffered the loss of nineteen men and fourteen wounded. The fourteen wounded were taken as prisoners of war, treated by Guevara, and later released to a hospital in Santiago de Cuba.[12] The battle of Uvero was the first victory of the Cuban Revolution. It served to advise the world that Castro and the rebel army were a force to be reckoned with. Within the revolutionary army itself, the victory caused a resurgence of confidence and commitment to the cause that sustained the rebels during the remaining twenty months of their occupation of the Sierra. At Uvero, Sánchez not only fought in combat, but she also attended to the wounded and noted the exact location where each fallen soldier was buried, thus facilitating their later identification. Sánchez's participation at the Battle of Uvero helped her gain legitimacy as a combatant. It proved that women were capable soldiers, and could be a tremendous asset to the revolution.

Less than one week after the Battle of Uvero, the commanders of Batista's army decided to send an infantry battalion consisting of 800 U.S.-trained and outfitted soldiers to the Sierra Maestra. At the same time, Batista began a massive effort to denounce all campesinos suspected of giving aid to the rebels. Hundreds of men and women in Santiago de Cuba, Bayamo, and many other cities were linked to the revolution and suffered eviction, heavy fines, or incarceration. The government also announced, with great fanfare, that it was fighting the revolutionary troops near El Turquino and that the rebels had suffered numerous deaths. Additionally, they claimed that Sánchez had been captured and that a "large quantity of weaponry and important documents" had been confiscated. Batista knew that this news would shake the M-26-7, and it indeed caused alarm in the Sierra. Reflecting on those turbulent times, Guevara wrote in his diary that Sánchez was "our only known and safe contact . . . her detention would mean isolation for us."[13]

The rumors were only partially true. Rebel forces were indeed battling government troops near El Turquino, but there had been relatively few deaths. Sánchez had indeed been captured again while scouting for additional arms in the llano, but she secured her own release on 5 June by claiming that she was a servant in a house in Vista Alegre and was going to visit her family. Castro finally heard on 15 June of Sánchez's safe return, and wrote her a letter stating, "you and 'David' [Frank País] are our basic pillars. If you are well, then we are well. How can I explain to you the anguish and sadness we all experienced when we heard that you had been detained?"[14]

Shortly after hearing of Sánchez's release, the rebel forces received the disheartening news that País had been captured and was being held in Santiago de Cuba. Fully recuperated from her own brief imprisonment, Sánchez decided to take the initiative to search for him. Realizing that she must take added precautions in order to pass through the city undetected, Sánchez decided to travel in disguise. She hid a small cushion under her skirt, pretending to be pregnant, cut her hair short and sold it for twenty-five pesos, and grabbed the Colt .45 pistol her father sent with his plea that she not be taken alive. The pistol—with the initials "MSS" (Manuel Sánchez Silveira) on the handle—now sits in a glass case in her childhood home museum in Media Luna, as does the cushion she used to feign pregnancy.[15] Disguised in this way, and accompanied by "Gena" Verdecia, Sánchez was able to avoid another military entanglement. Sadly, she soon learned that on 30 July, País had been shot dead by the police. Castro biographer Robert Quirk states that in his last letter to Sánchez, País articulated a sense of foreboding, stating, "we have been very fortunate, but I don't know how long my luck will last."[16]

There are many mysteries surrounding País's death. It has been said that from the beginning País challenged Castro and contradicted him unhesitatingly on strategy and organization, even criticizing him within his own movement, and that it was only a matter of time before the two men clashed. This rumored rivalry has led some historians of the Cuban Revolution to question whether an insider in the M-26-7 facilitated País's death. Agustín País contends that Vilma Espín—acting as an "instrument of Fidel"—participated in the plot against his brother. The morning of his death, Espín placed a call to the residence where País was hiding. Agustín País believes that since it was common knowledge that his brother did not make or receive calls from private phones except in an emergency, it is odd that Espín called him only to ask, "Why have you not called me? What has happened?" Within ten minutes of her call, País's safe house was surrounded by government agents, he was apprehended, and was soon assassinated.

Agustín País believes that Espín might have had personal reasons for participating in his brother's assassination, as she had tried to become his girlfriend or mistress, always with the thought of being a power behind the throne. País put her off, and named others—like Sánchez—to serve as his most trusted emissaries. País's indifference bothered Espín tremendously, according to Agustín. Whether Espín's phone call was connected to the police discovery of País's hiding place may never be fully known, but the possibility hangs in the air around her story still today.[17] Friends and family of Espín chalk the accusations up to lingering bitterness directed toward the revolutionary leadership among Cuban exiles living in the United States and roundly deny that she had any hand in the assassination.

News of País's death was a source of both sadness and anger for the members of the rebel forces. As a public display of outrage, Sánchez and Espín organized a demonstration of mourners at Céspedes Park in Santiago de Cuba to greet U.S. Ambassador Earl Smith and his wife during their visit to the area. A scuffle broke out between the women and the police, and the police turned water hoses on the women. Espín later recalled,

"The ambassador's wife, who was not accustomed to witnessing these things at such close range, was affected by seeing police hit women while the women shouted 'Assassins!'"

The news of País's death was especially difficult for Sánchez. Those who had the opportunity to listen to her speak of País testify to the affection she felt for him. In a letter to Haydée Santamaría written the day after País's death, Sánchez stated that "Frank's absence had affected me so deeply, but why even tell you this when I know that we are all grieving?"[18] The two had worked together during the most intense months of organization and preparation in the *llano*, and, side by side, became a unifying force for the troops. They were a team and were recognized as such. A few months before his death, Sánchez stated that "in order to speak of Frank, one would have to mention above all his absolute loyalty to Fidel, comparable only with that of Raúl, Camilo, and Che." She never questioned his orders. When País sent a delegation from Santiago de Cuba to reorganize and supervise her operations in Manzanillo, she collaborated fully with the members of the delegation, submitting to their detailed inquiries into her monetary and supply holdings without complaint, because País had ordered it.

Castro biographer Quirk states that Castro's reaction to País's death was somewhat mixed, and even perplexing. Initially he seemed "strangely unmoved" by the news, feasting exuberantly at a baptism at which he had agreed to act as godfather.[19] The next day, however, he wrote Sánchez an emotional letter calling País "the most valiant, capable, and extraordinary of our combatants." He went on to state that "it is hard to believe the news. I cannot express to you the bitterness, the indignation, and the infinite pain that has overcome us. What barbarity! The cowards caught him in the street armed with all the advantages they have for chasing a clandestine fighter. How monstrous! They do not know the intelligence, the character, and the integrity that they have assassinated. Now, the people of Cuba will never fully understand who Frank País was—the great and promising qualities he had. It hurts to think of him that way, killed at twenty-five years of age—just when he was giving the best of himself to the Revolution. . . . The death of Frank País should mark a new phase of our fight."

The incongruity between Castro's perceived initial indifference to the news of País's death and the passionate grief expressed in his letter to Sánchez fuels rumors that the assassination eliminated one of Castro's primary rivals for power within the movement, whether or not he directly plotted País's murder. Despite these rumors, the revolution has commemorated País as a revolutionary hero. He was buried in his M-26-7 uniform in Santiago de

Cuba's Santa Ifigenia Cemetery and Raúl Castro's guerrilla unit was renamed the Frank País Second Front. Today the international airport in Holguín, an orthopedic hospital in Havana, and several schools bear his name.

Aside from the emotional effects País's death had on Sánchez, it also brought her a significant increase in responsibility within the revolution. In the same letter to Sánchez, Castro asked her to assume many of País's responsibilities, certain that she was the most capable of completing that work. He wrote, "For the moment you will have to assume a large part of Frank's duties, a task you are more qualified for than anyone else. I know that you will not lack the strength necessary to add these obligations to those that already push you to the limit of your mental and physical capabilities. But, these are extraordinary moments in which determination and energies must be multiplied."[20]

Sánchez shared this view of the Cuban struggle. An ultimate victory over the dictatorship necessarily required that each combatant push herself beyond her limits. In a letter to Elsa Castro Mestre written in November 1957, Sánchez admonished her friend "not to cease to help as you were before I [left for the Sierra]. Now you must double your efforts and tell the few who remain with you to do the same. All of the sacrifices made so that the revolution can triumph are worth it. I have watched so many young people give their lives to this cause and they have died with a smile, proud to die for this just cause."[21] Sánchez's sister, Acacia, stated that "for Celia, nothing was impossible if Fidel wanted it. Celia trusted Fidel completely. Not only did she complete his orders to the letter, but she also planned the form in which they should be carried out. As Fidel wanted things, that's how it always was."[22]

Final Days in Manzanillo

In addition to her numerous other duties, Sánchez was now also in charge of communications and correspondence in Manzanillo. She also continued selling bonds, often coordinating with one of the noncombat wings of the movement known as Resistencia Cívica (Civic Resistance), a covert professional organization with a reach beyond the island that channeled funds to the M-26-7. Sánchez was able to help generate an impressive revenue stream by calling on Civic Resistance collaborators operating in Miami and New York, who published newspapers with titles like *Sierra Maestra: Official Organ of the 26th of July Movement in Exile* in which they urged supporters to "make contact with the men of the Civic Resistance and those of the 26th of July and give them your weekly support; help end the Batista dictatorship so that your brothers won't continue to be assassinated in the streets and in their own homes."[23] The Acción Cívica (Civic Action) group in New York also sold bonds in values ranging from $5 to $25 in support of the rebels.[24] Receipts signed by Sánchez reveal bond sales as high as 4,230 pesos in a single day.[25]

Recognizing the greater risks associated with her new responsibilities, Sánchez adopted a new alias in the wake of País's assassination. Although she had used various pseudonyms already, such as Lilian, Carmen, and Caridad, she had been using the name Norma—her youngest sister Acacia's middle name—for some time. In mid-July 1957, however, she decided to change her alias a final time, adopting the name Aly. In a letter to Haydée Santamaría dated 2 August, Sánchez explained the change stating: "Even the dogs know who 'Norma' is."[26] Castro's nom de guerre was "Alejandro" in the early years of the revolution, evoking the historic conqueror Alexander the Great. He later changed his nom de guerre to the shortened form, "Alex."

Although she was well aware of the important role she played in Manzanillo, Sánchez's primary goal during those several weeks was to reincorporate herself, in a more permanent way, into the rebel troops in the Sierra. She was elated, therefore, to receive a message from Castro in mid-August in which he stated: "Why don't you make the short trip here? Please consider this possibility as these days of observation and expectation are passing so quickly." Sánchez thus began preparations to return to the Sierra.

On the night of 1 September, however, Rafael Castro arrived at the house where Sánchez was hiding to tell her that Castro wanted her to leave immediately and come to the Sierra Maestra. Sánchez faced a difficult decision, as only hours before she had received word that the Rural Guard had arrested her father at his home in Pilón with the hope that his arrest would lure her out of hiding to rescue him. Sánchez was in the frantic process of planning an escape for her father when Rafael Castro arrived. Her decision was characteristic; she left for the Sierra the next morning. Four days later, upon arrival in the Sierra, Sánchez explained to Castro that she "thought it more important that [she] come to the aid of her *compañeros*, rather than stay to defend the life of [her] father." Family friend Bécquer Céspedes informed me in an interview that "it was a terrible fight between her conscience and her feelings. In the end, the former won."[27]

On 22 September, Sánchez learned that her father had been released, thanks to letters sent by his colleagues all over the region. Sánchez pleaded with him to relocate to Havana, as she feared for his life more than her own. "Dearest Father," she wrote, "again I must plead with you . . . things are worse here every day. These people do everything in their power to destroy us, but it is impossible to destroy the people or Cuba. . . . Don't worry about me. I am safer than you all are." She did, however, ask that he reach out to all of his contacts in Havana to ask for "*plata*" (money), because "it costs more now to keep ourselves supplied, as everything runs out more quickly." She trusted that any money he could collect from friends in the capital would find its way to her, noting that "everyone there knows who to give money to so that it makes its way to the movement."[28]

Sánchez was not able to remain in the Sierra for long on this trip as she soon received word that she was needed in Manzanillo again. She left the rebel headquarters on 27 September and returned to her duties in Granma Province. Upon arrival in Manzanillo, Sánchez immediately became aware of the heightened climate of repression in that city. On 30 September, Sánchez wrote to a *compañero*, stating, "With the first foot that I placed in Manzanillo, they knew of my arrival and were looking for me daily. Two jeeps and two trucks full of soldiers arrived at my sister's house. How astonishing! In these last few days, they have buried me alive, and after my having spent so many days running."

Taunted by this woman who was such a powerful political presence in the city, Captain Caridad Fernández, chief of the military in Manzanillo, ordered his troops to capture Sánchez at whatever cost—even if they had to go house to house and street to street. He tightened security at the entrances to the city and brought more troops to the area. Despite the heightened threat of arrest, Sánchez continued to look for resources for the rebels, which, in turn, necessitated her leaving the security of her friends' homes to enter streets filled with soldiers looking for her. Sánchez's presence in Manzanillo was never a secret from Batista's troops. More than a dozen homes in the city were offered as refuges for Sánchez and her *compañeros*, and each now bears a historical marker.

The situation in Manzanillo became increasingly difficult for Sánchez, and her life was threatened on a daily basis. On 15 October 1957, therefore, Sánchez began to make preparations to leave Manzanillo again and return to the Sierra Maestra. Little did she know that this would be her last trip to the mountains until the triumph of the revolution, nearly fifteen months later. On 17 October she arrived at Castro's camp, thus putting an end to her clandestine life. Although the original plan was that Sánchez would stay only briefly and then return directly to the *llano*, Castro decided that Sánchez should stay in the Sierra until the climate of repression in Manzanillo improved.

In a letter to her brother Manuel Enrique ("Quique"), written on 4 November 1957, Sánchez stated, "I'm doing very well here . . . never thought that they would discover my whereabouts, but ultimately they did. After that persecution and insecurity, I find myself so calm and secure that hopefully I won't have to return right away."[29] Her goal to remain in the Sierra was achieved, perhaps more quickly than she herself could have imagined. Sánchez became indispensable to the guerrilla troops in the Sierra and in mid-November she wrote a letter to Elsa Castro Mestre stating, "I don't think I will leave here unless it is something extremely important that only I can take care of and I don't think that situation will arise. Here I work, too, but I am happy and peaceful. Nobody is chasing me."[30]

Sánchez never forgot the loyalty of local collaborators in Manzanillo who assisted and protected her during her eleven months living in clandestinity. Although there were no guarantees that the farmers, business people, professionals, and other people that she approached for aid would not turn her over to the police, Manzanillo was loyal to Sánchez, and continued to be throughout her life. In our interview, Mirtha Hernández recalled proudly that after the success of the revolution Sánchez's visits to Manzanillo always caused a tremendous stir and people eager to see her formed long lines in front of the assembly hall located on Manzanillo's Céspedes Park. "People were so impertinent, always wanting, pleading, asking her for stuff . . . houses, food, but not us . . . we never went there," she recalled. She could never have imagined, she said, that Sánchez would make a surprise visit to her home years later to thank her for offering her home as a safe house. "I would do anything for her and for this revolution. . . . I still get invited to official receptions [at the assembly hall]. At the last reception, I was even asked to be the one to place the flowers at the red chair where she sat," Hernández beamed as she recalled the details of the moment. "I was handed the bouquet of flowers and carefully walked toward the vase where I was to place them—rows of government officials, members of the party, and heroes of the revolution were watching me—and I was so worried that I would knock something over," she chuckled.

At Hernández's urging, my friends from the Manzanillo archive secured permission for me to enter the assembly hall and see the red-cushioned chair from her story. The simple wooden chair now sits to one side of the hall's center stage under a large portrait of Sánchez and a pair of commemorative plaques that identify the chair as the one Sánchez used on the day she was elected to the National Assembly of Popular Power (2 November 1976). Dilver Reyes Peña, president of Manzanillo's Municipal Assembly of Popular

Power, remarked in a January 1980 interview that "Celia will always be for Manzanillo our deputy and the true example of the Cuban woman."[31]

Sierra Realities

Upon her arrival in the Sierra Maestra, Sánchez immediately became involved in supporting the revolutionary effort. There were soldiers to outfit, medical supplies to organize, weapons to distribute, and training sessions to facilitate. Photos on display at her childhood home museum in Media Luna even show Sánchez acting as godmother at the baptism of a baby born in the Sierra Maestra. Sánchez and Castro also served as witnesses at weddings conducted in the Sierra and received requests to serve as godparents to children whose parents sought refuge from violence in their war-torn rural towns and villages.[32] In a letter to a friend, Anselmo de los Santos, asking for his assistance gathering supplies, Sánchez reflected on the scope of the project before her, stating, "we need everything, everything is useful here. Our territory is growing every day, as are our needs and our work. While some are fighting with weapons and give their life and their blood to Cuba others are industrializing, others give classes, others cultivate crops, and others help with communication."[33]

Sánchez's efforts to meet the needs of the troops, as well as the campesinos living in the Sierra or who traveled there seeking protection, spread her energies across a vast array of projects and initiatives. In a letter to her father she wrote with a mixture of pride and apprehension that "they come to me with all of their problems and all of their joys for everything they flock to me. . . . I feel the weight of work and responsibilities."[34] To her sister Acacia, she confessed, "I don't even know how I am writing this, [as] we are surrounded by farmers. They have me crazy. . . . I don't even know what they are saying to me."[35]

Her primary and constant concern was with providing enough food to sustain the troops and to alleviate the suffering of local civilian populations affected by the war. In a memo dated 18 May 1958, Sánchez notes that "everything is necessary and useful to us, nothing is ever enough, [as] there are more of us each day."[36] The greatest percentage of memos she sent and received centered on cattle.[37] Castro mandated that rebel troops could only seize cattle from ranchers with more than 200 head and ordered the execution of anyone who participated in unsanctioned seizures of cattle, as happened in at least one case.[38] Sánchez kept detailed records of the number of cattle seized from each ranch, as the ranchers were promised a reparation payment at the end of the war.[39] Sánchez then managed the redistribution of these cattle to the various military units and villages scattered throughout the mountains. In her own words, "these redistributed heads of cattle are sent to zones that have never even had milk. For families that have as many as eleven children, this helps with a serious problem."[40]

Many of the foodstuffs that arrived into the Sierra—especially in the early months of the revolution—were purchased in lowland shops and transported to the Sierra in twice-daily shipments carried by foot or by mules or horses.[41] Sánchez was, however, eager to organize self-sustaining gardens and farming operations in the mountains to produce corn, rice, and vegetables, as well as eggs and butter.[42] She ordered sent up from the towns below regular shipments of seeds as well as pigs, chickens, turkeys, and ducks. She referred to the resulting menagerie of animals as a "Noah's Ark" in the Sierra Maestra.[43] The most difficult foodstuff to acquire was salt, and Sánchez vexed often about how difficult it was to procure.[44] The rebel army eventually devised a solution. Sánchez noted in a communiqué to Haydée Santamaría that "we have resolved the grave salt problem by sending noncombatants to the beach to make salt for the troops and the campesinos."[45] She also had to ration sugar, prioritizing troops on the front as recipients of the prized resource.[46]

In the same way that many of the early foodstuffs that arrived into the Sierra were purchased in towns below and transported, so, too, were the grenades, bombs, bullets, and rifles needed to arm the rebel troops.[47] Scarcity drove the rebels to begin manufacturing their own weapons, and even to develop and manufacture their own rifle, the M-26, named for the M-26-7.[48] In an April 1958 memo, Sánchez declared that "when they write this part of the history, nobody will believe it. We have defended ourselves with the M-26."[49]

In addition to outfitting the troops with weapons, Sánchez was in charge of acquiring sufficient clothing and uniforms for the troops. As with all things in the Sierra, scarcity drove innovation. In order to provide sufficient clothing for the rebels, Sánchez facilitated the creation of a small factory where a team of twelve seamstresses under the direction of Olga Lara Riera sewed uniforms, hats, backpacks, bandanas, and hammocks for the rebels.[50] She established another workshop for the production of shoes and boots.[51] Not all clothing needs were met in the Sierra, however, especially those for women. Sánchez sent word to her sisters when she, or another woman in camp, needed bras or feminine hygiene products.[52]

Sánchez also dedicated special attention to the needs of the male rebel commanders. When Guevara needed a vehicle, for example, Sánchez found him a jeep that, she remarked, "made him happier than a kid on Three Kings Day."[53] She also attended with great care to Castro's personal needs and comforts, securing for him toothbrushes and toothpaste, condensed milk, tobacco, candy, wine, and books and sending his watch and eyeglasses for repair when they broke.[54] Sánchez would maintain this kind of caretaking role for the rebel commander throughout her life.

Sánchez was also instrumental in coordinating the arrival of medical supplies to the Sierra to treat wounded rebel soldiers or distribute to local communities.[55] The troops battled ailments ranging from malaria to hemorrhoids that required Sánchez to maintain a steady flow of medications into the mountains.[56] She also secured the funds to construct a hospital under the direction of rebel physician René Vallejo, who later served as Castro's personal physician after the triumph of the revolution.[57] The hospital featured a surgical ward and a lab, which Sánchez stocked with the necessary anesthesia, bandages, syringes, and lanterns.[58] In a letter to her father, Sánchez remarked that "the hospitals are full lately, as there are a lot of wounded civilians, guards, and soldiers," and reported that she had recently witnessed the first surgery conducted in the Sierra. A lieutenant with a serious abdominal wound was attended to at the rebel hospital and had survived. "He is already walking and has even come to visit me on horseback," Sánchez reported.[59]

Sánchez also assisted in the establishment of several schools throughout the rebel-controlled zone. In a letter to her father, Sánchez said, "in our territory we have seven schools functioning with forty students in the mornings and another forty in the afternoon and with night classes for the older students. [We also have] a revolutionary school [and] nobody can join the rebel forces if they have not graduated from the school. It has a capacity for 300 students."[60] She described for her father the layout of the school building with its dormitories, classrooms, lunch room, library, and sports field. She raved in her correspondence with friends and family about these advancements, telling her father that "nobody could imagine what the Sierra looks like now, every day we are more civilized," and to her sister Acacia she wrote of how "shocking it is [to see] how we are living now compared to how we were living before."[61]

All of these projects required funds to complete, and Sánchez was entrusted by Castro with managing the revolutionary finances. Sánchez maintained a detailed record of all supplies that moved through the rebel headquarters and collected every receipt. A great many of the memos she sent to fellow rebels ended with the words "Keep records of your expenses."[62]

Money remained a constant source of apprehension for Sánchez, and in one letter to her sister Acacia she confessed, "we only have $7 and this is incredible. Don't tell anyone because they won't believe it. All that seems like so much is always too little."[63] Castro eventually sent Haydée Santamaría to fund-raise in Miami in the wake of the failed April 1958 strike—a task that did not please her but which she completed. She ended up traveling widely across the United States and later reported gathering as much as $12,000 to $15,000 dollars per month.[64] One photo of Sánchez shows her seated on the ground with Santamaría counting money (figure 4). Donations made either through the purchase of M-26-7 bonds, direct cash contributions, or gifts in kind provided the principal revenue stream for the rebels. Sánchez met with bankers in lowland towns and cities to secure larger financial contributions. In a memo dated 29 April 1958, she informed Castro that she "had received a message from two bankers in Manzanillo who—along with some doctors—want to meet with me about what I asked them for because they want to be very organized in terms of getting us all those things that we need. I am going to see if I can go down tomorrow."[65]

The most fascinating financial document I reviewed during my time at the Office of Historical Affairs was an anonymous letter to Sánchez informing her about the status of a bank account called the "Aid Fund for the Sierra Maestra" in Havana's Chase Bank in the Vedado neighborhood. According to the letter, the account was used to collect donated funds to support the rebel army, which were then distributed to Sánchez in the form of $21,862.30 in cash contributions and 3,042 boxes of supplies. A note at the bottom of the document indicates that M-26-7 treasurer, Raúl Chibás—whose famous brother had founded the Orthodox Party and later shot himself on live radio—was the primary contact for the account. Raúl Chibás eventually retracted his support for the Cuban Revolution. In 1960 he boarded a motorboat for Miami and defected to the United States.[66]

According to Sánchez, the most unsavory part of her job was dealing with the "long parade of journalists" who arrived in the Sierra and who "drive us all crazy."[67] In a letter to her father she complained that the constant presence of the global press "was a bit overwhelming because we have so much to do and attending to them takes a lot of time." She also confessed that "those are the most stressful days for me because they are no longer satisfied with an interview with Castro and photos, but rather [they] want to conduct lots of interviews asking everyone the same questions and I just detest it. I will only tolerate journalists until this is all over and then I may even change my name. I have told you about my phobia with this and I tell everyone

FIGURE 4 Counting money in the Sierra Maestra, 1958. Author's collection.

here the same thing and what most annoys me is that it makes no difference."[68] In a letter to her sister Acacia, Sánchez instructed her to "tell everyone
who knows me and make sure Quique [her brother] knows, too, that this
journalist Enrique wants my biography. . . . Make sure that nobody gives
him even one fact about me. You know that I hate that and that I can't tolerate it. I am so uncomfortable every time I see my name in print."[69]

Despite her discomfort with media attention, Sánchez acknowledged the
historical significance of events unfolding around her. She began her only
known diary in March 1958, but abandoned the project that same month after
penning only a few entries. The original diary is entirely illegible, but Sánchez fortunately left a transcription of the contents in the Office of Historical Affairs. Writing with a broad external audience in mind, Sánchez—always
protective of her privacy—does not delve into personal reflections about
rebel life in her diary. Her entries instead recount the minute details of daily
life in the Sierra Maestra ("We woke up at 6 o'clock A.M. and by 6:30 we were
already marching toward Jeringa"). She briefly remarks on the human cost
of war, stating, "Every day the acts of sabotage are more intense and every

day there are more murders of young people and children," and states emphatically that the rebels "would not accept anything with Batista in power." She also defended the Sierra Maestra as a "decisive front in the war" and "not merely a symbol of the revolution."[70] The content, however, does not generally provide an intimate glimpse into her emotions and thoughts during her months in the Sierra.

Sánchez's letters to friends and family are quite different. They recount major developments in the revolutionary process, but also provided a space for her to express her vision for the future and to encourage her loved ones to remain resilient in the face of hardships. They reveal moments of deep homesickness and loneliness in which she lamented that "with this fight here we are so disconnected even from our own families."[71] She also confessed her own mistakes in her letters. Writing to her sister Acacia, Sánchez confessed that she had inadvertently placed several people's lives at risk when she sent a secret communiqué with Hart Dávalos that contained the names and contact information for several collaborators, including Acacia. When Hart Dávalos was detained, that information fell into enemy hands. Sánchez frantically informed her sister to "not get caught" and confessed that "Alex [Castro's nom de guerre] is outraged about what I did."[72]

Her letters also provided a forum for her to share the horrors of the violence happening around her. She lamented especially the civilian deaths—reportedly totaling over 20,000—associated with military bombings in lowland villages and towns presumed to be supplying the rebel army. The human cost of war and her despair are palpable when, for example, she describes the devastation that followed a bombing in which Sánchez and her fellow guerrillas "spent the night removing dead and wounded bodies of the families that have emigrated [into the Sierra]. It was so horrible. We didn't enter a single house that had not been shot up. There was a five-year-old boy and a gravely wounded woman of eighty years. The little town of El Cerro was totally burned, around 32 houses. The other town, San Juan, was also burned, and there had been 36 houses there. These were all families that traveled to the mountains with nothing." An 8 November 1958 memo to Sánchez spoke of the need to build a cemetery in the lowland town of Zarzal for the bodies of those killed in the war.[73]

She repeated in several letters one of the most heart-wrenching moments in the aftermath of these bombings, in which a seventeen-year-old girl presented herself at the command center with a terrible gunshot wound. The young mother had been shot by a Batista soldier while holding her infant daughter. The bullet killed the baby and entered the young woman's breast. She appeared in the rebel camp distraught and disoriented and in search of her husband. After relating the tragic tale, Sánchez remarked only, "There are so many cases like this that I cannot even cite them all."[74] In another reflection on the violence of war, Sánchez noted in a letter to her sister Acacia that "one can never really celebrate a victory," because the loss of a fellow soldier and the "crying of all the members of the soldier's unit" ensured that "any happiness about the success evaporates and we leave to march through the mountains."[75]

I found within the holdings of the Office of Historical Affairs the last letter Sánchez wrote to her father, dated 15 May 1958. At the time of the letter Sánchez had not seen her father in more than a year. She knew he was gravely ill, and I imagine she knew that this might be her last contact with him. Not surprisingly, it is the longest letter I ever read from her and the most personal. Writing over the course of ten days, Sánchez tells her father, "you are with me always, in ways that you cannot imagine. Every day more so. Every advance of the revolution reminds me of you and how often you worried about the problems faced by campesinos and by all Cubans. This is all moving in leaps and bounds. I stop to remember the 'beginning' of this war sometimes and all the memories I have and it seems that ten years must have passed for all that we have done and all that we have won."[76] Following a long description of the rebels' accomplishments in the war and of life in the Sierra, she signed off with the following words: "I don't worry about you father, as I know that Acacia and Griselda are taking care of you. I am always at your side and now more than ever. We will surely all be back together soon. Take care of yourself. I love you and send a kiss. Celia."[77]

Dr. Sánchez had not felt well for many months. In February 1957 he wrote a letter to Humbelina Alarcón stating, "I am still doing badly with pain in my legs. . . . I think this is a circulation issue. . . . We arrive at our maximum age and soon I will be in the cemetery."[78] Frightened by her father's rapidly declining health, Acacia had transported Dr. Sánchez to Havana's Calixto García hospital, where he remained through the end of his life. When Sánchez received the news of her father's hospitalization, she shared her fears in a letter to the medical team in the Sierra, stating, "I learned just eight days ago that my father is gravely ill, but have not heard anything further since that time, nor do I want to know. I have lost weight and am terrified to receive further word . . . when they told me it was CANCER . . . there are no words to describe. . . . I am consoled only by the fact that I know how to fulfill my duty to my father and to my country."[79]

Dr. Sánchez died on 24 June 1958 at the age of seventy-one of lung cancer, as had his brother before him, and Sánchez would after him.[80] Heavy government security placed outside the hospital room with orders to arrest Sánchez on sight denied the father and daughter a final reunion. Family friend and fellow revolutionary Lydia Doce, who had learned of Dr. Sánchez's death while in Havana, returned to the Sierra to deliver the sad news to Sánchez. Funeral attendees remember that the funeral home was filled with government agents who insulted the family members in attendance and eagerly awaited Sánchez's arrival to pay her last respects to her father. Sánchez knew she could not attend. A large flower arrangement with a silk ribbon and the words "With love from the M-26-7 Movement" sat near her father's casket. When he heard the news of her father's passing, Guevara sent Sánchez a personal letter of condolence, stating: "Celia, you will have learned of your father's death. I would not want to be the messenger of such news. There is no room between us for formal condolences; just know that you can always count on me."[81]

Two months after her father's death, Sánchez wrote her sisters Acacia and Griselda telling them that the news of their father's ill health had "completely paralyzed her." "I was very cowardly and had no idea what to say to you, nor what to do, nor what consolation I could offer you," she wrote. Addressing her decision not to come to the funeral or to the hospital, Sánchez noted that she "felt pleased from the moment I learned of his illness that I was not selfish. I only hoped that his death would be quick even if that meant I would never see him again. That never mattered to me. I only thought about his pain." Recognizing that her decision not to attend the funeral had been the source of some disappointment, she asserted, "I know that everyone still doubts me, but what others think of me does not interest me at all. I feel at peace about the fact that you all took good care of him and that he did not want for anything. That is all that mattered to me."[82]

Memories of Dr. Sánchez as a humble man who loved Cuban history and served his community with generosity continue to figure prominently in his daughter's life story. Dr. Augusto Fernández Conde—who attended to Dr. Sánchez in his final days and also delivered his funeral eulogy—concluded a 27 June letter to Sánchez by relaying that "[your father's] last steps toward his final rest were truly a testament to all of the love and friendship he had cultivated over the course of his life. The long line of *piloneros* [people from Pilón] of every background was his harvest."[83] In condolence letters sent to Sánchez and her siblings, family friends lamented that Dr. Sánchez had passed away "at this of all times when he longed to witness our country's democratic exit from this situation of crisis and crime."[84] Bécquer Céspedes shared with me in our interview that "Dr. Sánchez died believing that the revolution would triumph. He was very proud of Celia."[85] She then repeated one of the most common anecdotes told about Dr. Sánchez's final days, in which he proudly told his daughter Silvia that he could never have imagined that he would eventually "lose his former identity and become known as the father of Celia."[86]

For the remainder of the summer and into the fall, Sánchez occupied herself with her various projects in the Sierra, but she changed after the death of her father. The effervescence that had characterized the communications dating between her final ascent into the Sierra in November 1957 until her father's death in June 1958 gives way to palpable exhaustion and worry about the future. She told her sisters Acacia and Griselda that "the future has changed for the three of us. With father's death everything is now gone. When I thought about this all being over I thought about father and his normal life at home waiting for his children and grandchildren and about all that our life used to be. Now everything is empty. I don't know what is coming after all of this is over, everything is changed. Although I will never abandon the revolution, this war will end."[87] Months later, in December 1958, Sánchez continued to express her grief to her niece, writing, "you probably know now of the very sad days that we have had, first with grandfather's illness and secondly with his death. I know that you all have shared my pain, [and] I don't know if you yet comprehend how terrible all of this is, but I hope you know that my separation from father was not abandonment, but rather a duty which he, as a patriot, understood."[88]

Her communications after June 1958 are also heavy with reflections about the ravages of war. In a letter to her sisters, she wrote that "the person who is not accustomed to these planes would go crazy, I think. Even though they are ineffectual against us, when they know where we are they fire upon us like they are trying to end the world."[89] A few of her communications with Castro express her distress when she had not received word from him— "Today we have had no news from you. What is happening there?"[90] When possible, Sánchez planned celebrations and entertainment for the troops to combat the grim realities of mountain life. In a 14 July 1958 memo to Guevara, Sánchez requested he send the Rebel Quintet to play at a party in the Sierra, asking them to "come immediately with all of their instruments."[91] The following day, however, in a letter to her friend Delsa Puebla Vitrales, Sánchez noted dolefully that "around here it's a party with planes firing on us like crazy."[92]

While she continued to dedicate the majority of her energy to gathering food, medical supplies, and money for the M-26-7, her job became increasingly difficult as the months of fighting dragged on and the size of the rebel army grew.[93] She pleaded with friends to help gather funds to meet the rebel army's "imperious need for money."[94] To Olvein Manuel Botello Ávila, she wrote in July 1958 "we are in the mountains and hungry because we arrive without anything."[95] The burden of having to outfit and feed prospective troops who arrived in the Sierra became so burdensome that she had to order that "if they don't bring their own hammock and blanket, they are not allowed to come up. Nobody!"[96] In an 8 July 1958 memo to Mercedes de Varona Betancourt, Sánchez declared that "we need everything URGENTLY!" Remarking on the specific and pressing need for weapons, she lamented that existing weapons "have cost us so much money, so much blood. Were it not for the great and patriotic people of our nation who have helped us with supplies in the Sierra, we would not have this piece of freedom that we defend and which will bring freedom to all."[97]

Military victories held the promise of seized weapons and other goods.[98] Victories also meant caring for the medical and food needs of prisoners of war. In a communiqué dated 3 July 1958, Sánchez instructed Enrique Erasmus González to inform some prisoners who were complaining about the quality of the food they were receiving that "we are in the middle of a war and that Fidel requested that the Red Cross come and get them, but Batista would not allow it. Tell them to write to Batista and we will publish their letter."[99] Sánchez also received requests from parents desperate to secure the release of their children."[100]

Triumph on the Horizon

In the final months of 1958, a renewed energy and spirit enters Sánchez's communications. The end of the war seemed to be coming into view, and a new euphoria settled over the rebel force. An arms embargo imposed by the United States on 14 March in response to state military attacks on civilian populations and a major rebel victory at the Battle of La Plata (11–21 July) had weakened Bastista's forces considerably. Sánchez wrote to her sister Acacia on 10 September 1958 stating that "everything is improving every day and you will soon see all of the surprises of the future."[101] In a note to Mario "Guatemala" Carranza Rivero written on 18 October, she states confidently that "our war is the beginning of a Latin American revolution and our M-26-7 is already continental. We are fighting for Cuba and for the Americas."[102]

One critical contribution to the revolution during these final months in the mountains was the role Sánchez played in organizing the revolution's first unit of female soldiers, the Mariana Grajales Brigade, named after the heroic mother of Cuban independence.[103] The brigade was officially inaugurated in September 1958. Though consisting of only fourteen women, the Marianas took part in at least ten encounters with Batista's army. After their first skirmish in an assault on the Cerro Pelado base, a guerrilla commander wrote to Castro: "I must tell you that after being one of the main opponents to having women in our troop, I congratulate you once again because you are never wrong. I wish you could see, if only on film, the behavior of Teté [Puebla] and also of the other women comrades who, when ordered to advance, and while some of the men lagged behind, were out in front with a degree of courage and cool headedness worthy of the respect and recognition of all the rebels and everybody else." Women were finally being invited to take up weapons—if only the lighter M-1—and their new military role encouraged other Cuban women to join the revolution.

Despite praise for their efforts from male combatants, Isabela Rielo, the commander of the brigade, recalled that the Marianas continued to perform more traditional tasks such as cooking and sewing in the rebel camps. A picture of Sánchez published in the 19 May 1959 issue of the Cuban periodical *Diario de la Marina*—one of the few images of her to appear in the Cuban press during her life—shows her standing in the rebel command center in the Sierra Maestra over a wood-burning stove. The caption to the photo reads: "With great ability Celia Sánchez cooks with the rudimentary oven inside the General Command Barracks for the Rebel Army, as she did so many times during the revolutionary feat."[104] Sánchez is wearing fatigues in the photo, but there is no reference to her military contributions to the war. She is portrayed as domestic support staff to the rebel army, rather than as a key leader. Gendered imagery depicting life in the Sierra Maestra as one that balanced on the fulcrum of traditional notions of masculine and feminine behaviors continued to influence depictions of both the male and female rebel leaders long after the triumph of the revolution.

A final key contribution to the revolution made by Sánchez during the final months of the war reflects her historical sensibilities. She made diligent efforts to retain copies of all communiqués sent between the rebel commanders, understanding their importance "for the future."[105] She enlisted Castro as a key ally in her efforts. He ordered that certain objects relating to the revolutionary war should be delivered to Sánchez "as they might be helpful for a future museum."[106] Sánchez protected these letters, communiqués, and important objects — later supplementing the initial collection with additional items requested from combatants — and used them as the basis for the Office of Historical Affairs in Havana.[107]

Sánchez remained in the Sierra until 13 November 1958, when Castro and the other members of Column #1 left for Santiago de Cuba and the final revolutionary offensive. Before departing, Sánchez delegated her quartermaster responsibilities to another member of the movement, Aristedes Guerra Paz.[108] She noted in a letter to Melba Hernández that "we have left some responsibilities — thousands of them — to others but as our territory continues to grow, so do our responsibilities."[109] To her friend Aldo Santamaría, Sánchez wrote, "what more can I tell you, Aldo . . . we are headed to Santiago."[110]

The final offensive turned the tide of the war in the rebels' favor when Castro's column secured a decisive victory against Batista's forces at Guisa on 30 November. During an interview with reporters from *Moncada*, a member of the Mariana Grajales Brigade who fought at Guisa spoke of Sánchez's role in the battle: "No one ever saw her complain of the mud, the rain, the cold, or the other risks that the life of a guerrilla brings. Celia was such an example . . . and, in the middle of such privations, her first concern was always our security. When we entered into Guisa, the population acted as if they had known her all their lives and they assisted her. She gathered more than 13,000 pesos from local businesses in order to feed and clothe our troops, and, in exchange, she ordered us to aid those who were most in need in the pueblo."

La Riconada, which had served as a refuge to Major General Calixto García during the wars of independence, also served as a refuge for the M-26-7 after the triumph at Guisa. Sánchez and the other rebels remained there from 5 December through 20 December. On 12 December she wrote fellow revolutionary and friend Aldo Santamaría one of her final letters before the triumph of the revolution. She sounds both tired of war and hopeful for the future. She paints a vivid picture of the human costs of the war, recounting that "the highways are full of burned and overturned cars, a tank exploded by a mine, the body of guards at every step, a piece of a human being wherever you look and a smell of death everywhere. War is so terrible!" In the same letter, however, she marvels at the reaction of people in the towns they entered. "We entered Las Minas at seven at night in total silence, but it didn't matter. The whole town poured into the streets. It was impossible to walk or move, [because] the whole world wants to meet Fidel, they all want to hug him and everyone invites him to their house . . . everyone brings gifts. . . . The people are fanatical about Fidel." She acknowledged that this outpouring of support was "wonderful but also tiring [because] it keeps us from working," but she also found it inspiring. "All of this sacrifice every day; I see more clearly the Cuba that we desire."[111]

On 18 December, Fidel and Raúl Castro were reunited after nine months of separation—Raúl had opened a second front (the "Frank País Front") in the Sierra Cristal near Mayarí—and the rebel commanders began to plan the final steps of the revolution.[112] On 20 December, the rebel command unit moved to the nearby América sugar mill—known as América Libre (Free America) today—where they stayed until the 1 January victory of the revolution. This site guaranteed safety from enemy air strikes, as the generals of Batista's army preferred to avoid any conflict with the magnates of Cuba's sugar industry. Sánchez's mood lifted considerably when her sisters, who had joined her in the Sierra Maestra for a time after their father's death, returned definitively.[113]

The final weeks of 1958 were a whirlwind of revolutionary activity. Guevara and Cienfuegos advanced rapidly across the *llano*, capturing the key railhead of Santa Clara and the nearby town of Yaguajay in late December. News of the rebel victories shocked Batista. Without military support from the United States and in the face of an encroaching rebel army, he had few options. Batista called a meeting of his closest friends and advisers on New Year's Eve and then boarded a plane for the Dominican Republic at 2 A.M. the next morning. Havana was now open to the rebels.

Arriving from the eastern end of the island, the men and women of the M-26-7 rode into Havana atop captured tanks as the revolutionary caravan entered the capital city. Witnesses remember that the entire city was in the streets, and the tanks and trucks advanced under a rain of flowers. As the Marianas swept past, men yelled up to them, "Look! Here are the most beautiful women in Cuba!" Rebel combatant Rita García found that women's comments were the most moving: "The women asked 'You fought? You shot?' And when we said 'yes' many of them embraced us crying. I tell you those hugs conveyed an emotion and affection that I will never forget." With this triumphal entry into the capital, a struggle that began nearly six years earlier came to an end.

Aided greatly by U.S. press coverage, Cuba's new mountain rebels quickly became a pop sensation that captured the imaginations of U.S. citizens across gender and generational lines. In April 1959, *Life* magazine ran an article titled "Castro-Bearded Babes in the Woods," depicting a group of young boys and girls "taking to the woods like born guerrillas" in their New Jersey neighborhood.[114] The children wore commercially produced "Castro Cap" costumes complete with a beret embellished with the M-26-7 insignia, a toy rifle, and an attachable beard.[115] The article notes that the manufacturer of the costumes "expects soon to see every childish chin in the U.S. festooned" with the "latest novelty for moppets."[116] Even the girls are shown wearing the beards in order to fully exemplify the most fêted (male) version of the Cuban rebel. The costumes transmitted a normalized, romanticized version of a rebel identity so harmless that U.S. parents could incorporate it into their children's playtime. An image of the boys playing baseball in their costumes reminded readers of the two nations' shared affinity for America's favorite pastime.[117]

The majority of the major biographies of Cuba's revolutionary leaders were published decades after the triumph of the revolution. Early media coverage by U.S. journalists like Matthews and Taber, and Edward R. Murrow's *Person to Person* television special introduced the American public to Cuba's rebel commander.[118] On 6 February 1959 Murrow joined Castro via satellite in his postrevolutionary headquarters in a glamorous penthouse suite in the Habana Hilton hotel (now the Habana Libre). Far from his mountaintop command center and forgoing his customary fatigues, Castro dressed in pajamas and sat on a couch in his living room. His young son Fidel Castro Jr. joined him during the interview, speaking perfect English (a result of attending school in Queens, New York) and carrying a puppy that someone had gifted his father.

Murrow avoided any substantive policy questions, and the interview ventured only briefly into political territory. Asked about his now-famous beard, Castro explained that he planned to maintain it until the new revolutionary government had "fulfilled [its] promise of good government." Charming, relaxed, and easy to relate to, Castro fielded questions with a heavily accented English and coquettishly tilted head. He smiled sheepishly when addressing his emotional reunion with his mother after the triumph of the revolution. Murrow even (uncharacteristically) smiled at one point during the exchange and asked Castro when he planned to visit the United States. Castro responded affably: "I think when I have the chance." The show ultimately presented Castro as a sympathetic ally, a family man, and a patriot with dreams for the future that fell squarely in line with American values and ideals. The honeymoon period between the United States and Cuba would, however, prove brief.

Consolidating the Revolution

For the makers of the revolution, the rebel victory was a defining moment that positioned them as the political, economic, and social leaders of the country. They would become the architects of Cuba's new reality. Turning a guerrilla army into a government would prove both a daunting challenge and an exhilarating opportunity to institutionalize the promises made in the Sierra. Reflecting on the conversion of dreams into policies, Sánchez told Herbert Matthews that "we could not know during that period that when victory came we and the 26th of the July Movement would be so strong and so popular. We thought we would have to form a government with Auténticos, Ortodoxos, and so forth. Instead we found that we could be the masters of Cuba. That was when we began to put policies into effect that we always had in mind but thought would have to be postponed. There was no need to lose any time."[119]

Institutionalization also brought role changes. Fidel Castro became prime minister of Cuba; he was too young to serve as president, according to the terms of the Cuban constitution. Fellow rebel Manuel Urrutía was made president, though not via public elections, and the majority of his cabinet members were former M-26-7 combatants. By July 1959, Urrutía had already agreed to resign his post due to tensions over Castro's increasingly socialist reform agenda. The new Council of Ministers then appointed Osvaldo Dorticós Torrado (1959–76) as the revolution's second president. Dorticós had participated in the Civic Resistance, helping to channel supplies to the Sierra Maestra, and served as minister of laws after the revolution's triumph. That Dorticós was a Marxist and helped draft a May 1959 agrarian reform law seemed to confirm for Castro's critics his socialist sympathies and aspirations. Dorticós served as president until Castro became head of state under a new Cuban constitution implemented in 1976. Dorticós committed suicide in 1983. Castro would go on to become the longest-serving non-royal head of state in the twentieth and twenty-first centuries and founder of the first communist government in the Western hemisphere. He also survived hundreds of assassination attempts by the CIA to become one of the world's most polarizing political figures.

Other key revolutionary leaders also moved into official government positions. Raúl Castro became minister of defense, a position he held until assuming the presidency from his ailing older brother in 2008. He served two terms as president (2008–18) before stepping down in April 2018 in favor of the first non-Castro head of state since 1959, former vice president Miguel

Díaz-Canel. Camilo Cienfuegos—the only revolutionary leader born in Havana—was named head of Cuba's armed forces in 1959, but was presumed dead by October of that year when the Cessna 310 he was piloting disappeared mysteriously over the Straits of Florida on a routine flight from Camagüey to Havana. Rumors continue to swirl about the death of the handsome and popular leader, ranging from foul play by either the U.S. or Cuban governments to Cienfuegos faking his disappearance in order to relocate to Florida and escape the revolutionary government's communist turn. Cienfuegos's image dominates Havana's Plaza of the Revolution, and schoolchildren still throw flowers into the ocean on the anniversary of his death (28 October).

Guevara was initially appointed commander of the La Cabaña fortress prison near Havana and charged with overseeing a sweeping purge of the Batista army. Tribunals inflicted swift "revolutionary justice" upon accused traitors and war criminals, some of whom were executed by firing squad. Supporters of the purges took up the cry "¡Al paredón!" [To the wall] as hundreds of Batista associates were sentenced to death. Critics railed against both the method and the pace of the campaign, accusing the tribunals of human rights abuses, including the torture of prisoners, and for failing to respect the principle of due process. Following the five-month purge, Guevara became governor of the central bank and then minister of industries in charge of overseeing the National Institute of Agrarian Reform (INRA). He maintained that position until he left Cuba in 1965 to carry the message of continental revolution to Bolivia. Guevara was executed in La Higuera, Bolivia, in 1967 and his remains, and those of several fellow combatants, were repatriated to Cuba in October 1997 and laid to rest in a mausoleum in Santa Clara.

The triumph of the revolution brought with it the end of many women's participation in Cuban politics. Most of the women who participated in the guerrilla struggle disappeared from public view after 1959, and only a few went on to hold positions in the postrevolutionary Cuban government. Of 100 central committee members in the Cuban government in 1965, only five were women.[120] Isabela Rielo, leader of the Mariana Grajales Brigade, founded the Lidia Doce School for Militias in 1961. In the 1980s she was head of pharmaceutical services at a leading Havana hospital and conducted an internationalist mission to Vietnam. She died in 1989. Haydée Santamaría founded Casa de las Américas, which became Cuba's most important cultural institution. She married fellow M-26-7 member Armando Hart Dávalos, who became minister of education and then minister of culture. She committed suicide in 1980 on the twenty-seventh anniversary of the Moncada attack.

Melba Hernández, who died in 2014, served as a founding member of the Federation of Cuban Women (FMC) and was chairwoman of the Cuban Committee of Solidarity with Vietnam, Cambodia, and Laos. Vilma Espín and Raúl Castro married soon after the triumph of the revolution. Castro appointed Espín director of the FMC in 1960, a position she held until her death in 2007. For many years she was an alternate member and briefly a full member of the Politburo of the Communist Party.

Sánchez became Cuba's highest-ranking female official, privy to the most critical conversations that the revolutionary government would engage in over the next twenty years. Though she rarely appeared in the Cuban media, she was widely revered and respected as an authentic war hero. She earned both praise and position. Sánchez was purposeful in the construction of her postrevolutionary persona, presenting herself as historically grounded, politically engaged, attuned to the daily needs of the Cuban people, and committed to the creation of meaningful public works projects. While her life, especially as it related to Castro, drew considerable speculative attention—especially from the U.S. press—Sánchez maneuvered strategically to define a place of influence for herself in a postrevolutionary state in which few women operated at the highest rungs of authority. As such, she helped define Cuba's new socialist landscape and became the face of the revolution's New Woman.

CHAPTER FIVE

Like the Invisible Salt

The Making of a Revolutionary Stateswoman

> The people knew that she was there, where she should be,
> like the invisible salt in the immense sea of the Revolution.
>
> —GRANMA, 12 January 1980

> The female political official is forced to legitimate her role as
> that of a mother in the larger "house" of the municipality or even
> the nation.
>
> —ELSA CHANEY, *Supermadre: Women and Politics in Latin America*

The Apartment on 11th Street

Sánchez's apartment in Havana's Vedado neighborhood sits just off one of the city's principal arteries, Línea Street. The street is a river of people and vehicles at every hour of the day. Six lanes of traffic move in opposite directions on either side of a patchy grass median carrying people and goods toward the Miramar neighborhood to the west or toward the Malecón to the east. Lined with apartments, small businesses, elementary schools, and government offices, it is the oldest street in the Vedado neighborhood.

I have walked many times the nineteen blocks along Línea that lead to the Havana apartment where Sánchez resided from the time of the Cuban Revolution's triumph until her death. The apartment sits behind the Office of Historical Affairs within a *zona militar* (military zone) and once served as the nerve center of the Cuban Revolution. The apartment is completely inaccessible to individuals without authorization, a fact I discovered when I wandered too close to the zone. A guard in olive-green fatigues emerged from a checkpoint office requesting credentials to enter. I still have never secured permission to enter and view the apartment, but it is rumored to have remained untouched since Castro ordered it sealed shortly after Sánchez's death. A family member shared with me during an interview that "Castro stayed in the apartment on 11th [Street] until she died and then he moved out and he never came back."[1]

A few photographs taken by reporters and other media representatives over the years provide single-frame glimpses into the apartment.

Photographs of the entrance to the building reveal a simple, white, art-deco structure with a bank of low concrete benches in front and flower beds full of palm trees and ferns. The children that she adopted over the years, as well as siblings and friends, considered the apartment a safe haven where they could come to relax, enjoy Sánchez's famed hospitality, and escape the hustle and bustle of city life. With Sánchez's approval, the "apartment on *Once*" (11th Street) also welcomed a veritable parade of celebrated journalists, artists, and actors. If there was a center to the revolutionary government in Havana, "Celia's Place" served that function.[2] Castro maintained an apartment in the same building and received foreign dignitaries there when privacy and security were imperative. A series of diplomatic negotiations regarding the release of Bay of Pigs prisoners took place on the balcony of Sánchez's apartment.[3]

Sánchez's apartment in Havana sat at the crossroads of her two postrevolutionary worlds. It was both a headquarters for diplomatic negotiations and the center of her private world. For those eager to understand the nature of her authority and influence within the broader postrevolutionary power structure, it became a locus of media scrutiny and speculation. As a woman in government office, Sánchez's personal life was always subject to a kind of gender-based scrutiny. Insinuations that Sánchez received her power position due to her male connections swirled around her from her earliest incorporation into the revolutionary movement.[4]

Garlick, Dixon, and Allen maintain that the "implicit assumptions that women close to power must be exerting undue and inappropriate influence arises from the view that the political woman is a paradox. Her desire for such power is unnatural, her means dubious—probably behavior that has a place in male–female relations in the private world (sexuality, maternal ambition) but not in the Boys' Own world of public power and prestige."[5] The assumption is that in order to act in the public sphere, women must operate under the tutelage of a man. By extension, her ability to remain in an influential position depends less on her talents than on her ability to cultivate a patron.

Cuba's female revolutionary leaders never fully escaped speculation, evaluation, and judgment about their personal lives, while male leaders were rarely subject to such intense personal scrutiny. No aspect of Sánchez's life received more attention than her relationship with Castro. In fact, this is frequently the only context in which general histories of the Cuban Revolution mention her. It is clear that Sánchez wielded a considerable amount of personal and political power in her capacity as secretary to the president. What is less clear is whether her relationship with Castro was purely professional, and neither of them ever publicly addressed that question. U.S. journalist Herbert Matthews, who spent time with the rebels in the Sierra Maestra mountains, noted that "the relations between Celia and Fidel are one of the intriguing mysteries of the Cuban Revolution."[6] Speaking of Sánchez, Matthews noted only that "she is the soul of discretion and never divulges confidences."[7] A tour of Castro's command center in the Sierra Maestra—now a tourist destination—reveals the presence of a double bed in his two-room cabin. The living quarters raise the eyebrows of visitors familiar with the speculation surrounding the two leaders.

Within Cuba, people most often address the question of their relationship status at the level of rumor: "*se dice que eran amantes*" (they say they were lovers). A Havana taxi driver once told me that "everyone knew Celia had a boyfriend and we all assumed it was Fidel." Other Cubans dismiss outright any insinuation of a romantic connection between the two leaders claiming that Sánchez never married in order that she might fully devote herself to the needs of the Cuban people. Imaginings of Sánchez's private life (or perceived lack thereof) thus transfer to the public sphere as her image or profile.

Writers and journalists who visited Cuba frequently described Sánchez as Castro's personal assistant and house manager rather than a political leader, noting that "her home . . . continues to serve as one hideaway for Cuba's dictator."[8] They further noted that Sánchez exercised "iron control over Castro's headquarters and household."[9] Sally Quinn claimed that during her interview with Castro at Sánchez's apartment, Sánchez hovered over him "like a Jewish mother," fussing over his shirts and meals.[10] Herbert Matthews noted in 1969 that "it has been [Castro's] fate . . . to be living in a house in Havana that Celia Sánchez sees to it is kept spotlessly clean."[11] In his 24 July 1959 testimony to a Senate internal security subcommittee tasked with investigating potential communist threats to the United States, the disaffected former director general of the Office of the Prime Minister, Juan Orta—who was later recruited to assassinate Castro—stated that "every trip Castro took abroad, she was the one that not only accompanied him but even packed his suitcases and put his underwear in." When asked if Sánchez lived with Castro, he responded with a noncommittal "I think so."[12] In a 6 July 1964 article written for the *New York Times*, journalist Richard Eder noted that "Dr. Castro's apartment is a walk-up on the fifth floor of a building in a heavily guarded street in the Vedado section. His housekeeping is done by Celia Sánchez, his assistant who lives below."[13]

Writing about memory and Cuba's collective history, Quiroga reminds us that "any scholar interested in Cuba has to ponder whether one can write a history of the island without understanding that there are at least two histories, and that the history of the revolution can now be comfortably divided into an 'official' and a 'dissident' view."[14] The Cuban exile community in the United States has proven a major source of counter-memories of Sánchez's relationship with Castro. During a phone interview with me, a family member lamented: "In Miami they change her history or are not sympathetic. We really need a realistic depiction of her."[15] Several of the histories of the Cuban Revolution published in the United States derisively refer to Sánchez as the "proverbial lion at [Castro's] door" who also happened to be "sharing his double bed," or as "Fidel's long-term companion."[16]

Estranged friends and family members have also proven a source of speculation about the nature of Sánchez's relationship with Castro. Huber Matos was a former major in the M-26-7 who was sentenced to twenty years in prison on charges of sedition and treason shortly after the triumph of the revolution. He moved to Miami after serving his full sentence. In a 2008 interview, he claimed, "Yes, I don't have any doubt that they were intimate. . . . I have no doubt that he subjugated her and I believe that in the end Celia was a poor hostage of Fidel. Even after he rose to power . . . she was there—but later, years later, he dominated her tremendously, he marginalized her and looked for another." In the same interview he related an instance in which a blond teacher enthusiastically offered to help Castro perfect his English. According to Matos, Sánchez had been listening to the conversation. She approached the teacher and quietly pinched her, causing the woman to wince in pain and retreat quickly. The exchange—which Castro pretended not to notice—confirmed for Matos the nature of the relationship between the two leaders. "If I ever had a doubt, which I didn't," Matos noted, "they disappeared in that moment."[17]

Castro's daughter, Alina Fernández (born to his married lover, Natalia Revuelta), states in her book Castro's Daughter that "Celia Sánchez, La Venenosa (Poisonous One), exerted an irreverent power. . . . Widely known as Fidel's chief of staff and for having 'fought alongside him in the Sierra,' she was less well known as official witchcraft counsel in charge of the Comandante's personal clothes as well as his occult paraphernalia. She was a witch with style of sorts." Throughout her book, Fernández accuses Sánchez of "dark machinations" to keep her mother from achieving power within the Communist Party. She reveals the fullness of her contempt in her final reference to Sánchez: "[her] harassment and evil intentions lasted as long as she lived. She continued to be as hard as flint, until the malignancy that attacked her lungs and reached up to her tongue left her punier and more vermicular than she had ever been before."[18]

Former Cuban war correspondent Norberto Fuentes—who defected from Cuba and now lives in the United States—claims that Castro and Sánchez maintained a "quasi-marital" relationship in the Sierra Maestra despite the fact that Sánchez was actually *una lesbiana dura* (a tough dyke).[19] Fuentes claims that when friends began to advocate for the couple to formalize their relationship with a wedding, Castro sought—and was ultimately denied— an endorsement of the union from the leadership of the Popular Socialist Party. According to Fuentes, Sánchez's "petty bourgeois" background made her an "inconvenient" marital choice for a new revolutionary leader seeking to strengthen ties with the Soviet Union in the face of rising tensions with the United States. Fuentes claims that Castro accepted the party's recommendation and never married Sánchez, choosing instead to maintain the kind of quasi-marital relationship they had forged in the mountains.[20] At least one family member staunchly rejected this version of their relationship, claiming that there were never plans for the two to marry.

Castro biographers claim that Sánchez was nostalgic about the time in the Sierra Maestra, and Quirk even implies that she greeted the end of the war "morosely," looking as though "at any moment she would weep."[21] Other biographers claim that Sánchez noted wistfully years later, "Oh, but those were the best of times, weren't they? We were all so happy, then. *Really*. We will never be so happy again, will we? *Never*."[22] Quirk reads Sánchez's sense of loss, however, as tied primarily to the fear that she would now "be forced to share her charge [Castro] with the rest of the world."[23] Quirk's statement, published in 1993, proves the durability of gendered readings of Sánchez's role in the revolution, in which her presumed relationship with Castro overshadows all other aspects of her historical significance.

The subject of a possible romantic relationship between Sánchez and Castro still carries a political charge almost forty years after her death. In the summer of 2016 I attended a dinner party with friends in Cienfuegos that became strained when one guest began sharing his father's observations on the subject (his father had fought in the Sierra Maestra), only to be shut down by an older male member of the group. I noted then, as in other situations, a generational dynamic whereby older Cubans in a group steered conversations about her away from topics deemed off limits or sensitive. Considering that critics have used insinuations of a sexual relationship between

Sánchez and Castro to undermine or impugn their political commitment to the revolutionary project, I can understand these protective instincts. Ultimately, I do not know if Sánchez and Castro were lovers, nor do I consider such intimate knowledge necessary to my work. What does interest me, however, is how often the subject enters the conversation. I simply cannot deny its place in imaginings of her life.

Sánchez's apartment in Vedado was the geographic center of her twenty-year career as a Cuban stateswoman. It was also a touchstone and safe haven for many friends and family members, including Castro. Castro moved in and out of the apartment with an informality that raised eyebrows and prompted speculation primarily because intimate male–female relationships are presumed to be sexual. Perhaps Sánchez and Castro shared a romantic connection, but there is another kind of intimacy between the two leaders that rarely, if ever, receives the attention it merits. While the phrase "war buddies" is typically reserved for male comrades-in-arms in ways that make normative the male experience of war and revolution and erase the critical role that women have played in these processes, understanding that Sánchez and Castro were first and foremost veterans of the same war frames their thirty-year relationship within an intimacy forged in the trenches, and not (or at least not merely) in the bedroom. One need only witness the life-long ties of friendship and solidarity expressed through veterans' reunion celebrations to grasp the power of those connections. Castro respected and trusted Sánchez because she had earned his trust and respect on the front lines.

The observable comradery between Sánchez and Castro also sprang from their common roots. Both grew up in relatively isolated rural communities at the eastern end of the island, Media Luna and Birán, respectively. Both families were landowners and part of a modest provincial elite. In spite of their relatively affluent economic status, both Castro and Sánchez were comfortable with many social strata as a result of their upbringing. As children, they also both witnessed worker exploitation at the hands of large capitalist enterprises. Castro grew up in the shadow of United Fruit Company operations and Sánchez grew up in a town controlled by a repressive sugar manufacturing family, the Beatties. Sánchez and Castro drew from a similar source of experiences, cultural references, and memories when they interacted. Recognizing these key elements of their relationship helps explain its depth and durability in ways that other speculative leaps cannot. They also underscore the centrality of Sánchez's identity as a combatant and "small town girl" to her postrevolutionary influence.

Cultivating a Revolutionary Aesthetic

While Cuban newspapers rarely ran feature stories about Sánchez while she was alive—her aversion to media attention being at least partially to blame—existing press photographs capture her postrevolutionary activities, as well as her shifting personal style. The Media Luna museum displays framed copies of many of these images. A photo from New York shows Sánchez talking on the phone with papers spread across the desk in front of her, and another taken in Washington shows her standing in front of the Lincoln Memorial. Photos showing her walking with children through Cuban fields or interacting with children in rural schools highlight her association with children. A rare photo of Sánchez at Caney de Las Mercedes in Granma Province on the anniversary of the assault on the Moncada Barracks (26 July 1960) shows her standing in front of a podium, rather than beside or behind it. Castro sits beside the podium in a large straw hat. The most commercial of the photos in the room depicts Sánchez and Castro exiting the revolutionary government's *Sierra Maestra* plane after a trip to the eastern provinces. I was struck by the almost staged, movie-star feel of the crisp photo; both Castro and Sánchez are wearing well-pressed fatigues and large smiles and Castro is waving to an off-camera crowd.

Beards, fatigues, and cigars became globally recognized symbols of Cuba's new brand of male revolutionary heroism by the late 1950s. There was nothing inadvertent or accidental about the brand of hypermasculine virility advanced by the rebel leadership. They were telegraphing a purposeful message about power and change to both a national and an international audience. Sánchez's decisions with regard to her personal aesthetic were no less purposeful than those of her male colleagues. Press photos document the consciously constructed authenticity of her personal style, which shifted over the course of her adult life. This attunement to fashion and attire extended into her life as a stateswoman. Her personal papers contain detailed design notes for children's school uniforms and shoes—including the exact height of the heel to be worn by girls aged two to twelve years—which set the standard for the uniforms Cuban schoolchildren still use today.[24] Celia Hart—daughter of Haydée Santamaría and Armando Hart Dávalos—recalled Sánchez's preoccupation with details and aesthetics, stating, "I have a clear memory of the Summit Meeting of Non-Aligned Nations in 1979. Celia displayed a fine sense of taste in the uniforms of the waitresses, the housing provided for the invited heads of state, the meals, the cocktails. Everything had a tropical flavor with light and clarity without excess, maintaining the strictest etiquette."[25]

Despite her famous disdain for the media, Sánchez was keenly aware that her position made total obscurity impossible. Even if the Cuban press published very few photos of her while she was alive, she knew that they were capturing her movements. Her attire was subject to national and international scrutiny, and she dressed accordingly. Herbert Matthews commented on her attire, noting that "she dresses fastidiously and elegantly. And this is the same young woman who lived in soiled military fatigues and fought with the guerrillas in the Sierra Maestra for almost the whole dangerous and grueling period."[26] Her goddaughter, Eugenia Palomares Ferrales, notes that Sánchez always wore simple makeup and translucent nail polish, but took special care lining and filling her eyebrows into dark, dramatic arches. She also applied regular egg white masks to her face and arms and maintained her weight at a strict 115 pounds.[27] She worked with a stylist, Eduardo Sánchez Pérez, who attended to her attire, especially for formal state events. Palomares Ferrales confesses that Sánchez could be a challenging client. She resisted wardrobe advice when she felt it contradicted her preference for simple, subdued styles.

One anecdote shared by Palomares Ferrales recounts a particularly tense exchange between Sánchez and her stylist in the wake of a formal state reception in honor of a German official visiting Cuba. Sánchez originally asked Sánchez Pérez to design a gown for the event from a silver fabric gifted to her by the president of Indonesia. When she saw the final design, however, she determined it was too elaborate. Sánchez Pérez pleaded with Sánchez to wear the gown and she eventually relented. The day after the event, however, Sánchez Pérez received orders to come to Sánchez's apartment. She presented him with an envelope and scolded him for talking her into the gown. The envelope contained two press photos of Sánchez and a note from the photographer proclaiming that she had "looked like an Indian princess" at the reception. Sánchez was scandalized. "She was the center of attention [that night], which she never wanted to be," recalled Palomares Ferrales.[28]

Sánchez's fashion choices reflected her awareness that her most powerful positioning as a female political official was at the crossroads of tradition and change. She cultivated a personal aesthetic that fused old and new symbols of Cuban womanhood in a way that was uniquely her own. Cubans often describe Sánchez's fashion choices during her postrevolutionary career as both feminine and "very Cuban" (*muy cubana*). In the early 1960s, Sánchez favored—especially when traveling—tailored skirt suits paired with pumps and a short bobbed hairstyle that evoked the kind of "first lady" style cultivated by Jacqueline Kennedy, with whom Sánchez is said to have felt a deep affinity and to have studied closely. Sánchez's status as a rebel leader required that she wear fatigues to certain state functions, especially into the mid-1960s. Like her male fellow combatants, Sánchez understood the symbolic power of her fatigues. Wearing them highlighted her status as a war veteran and "authentic" revolutionary, and not merely a political official. She almost always added a colorful or ornate accessory to the uniform, however, as her own feminine touch to the olive-green uniform.

By the 1970s, however, Sánchez appeared in fatigues with decreasing frequency—though the male leaders continued to sport them regularly—and began projecting a kind of bohemian-inspired *cubanidad* (Cuban identity). Certainly stylish for the times, her wardrobe choices also projected her deep nationalism. She adorned her flowing cotton dresses with local artisan jewelry and multicolored espadrilles, and even fashioned a dress from flour sacks, which she found to have a simple elegance. The dress is on display at the house museum in Media Luna. She grew her hair long down her back and swept it up with elegant shell and bone combs. Palomares Ferrales claims that Sánchez never went to the hairdresser or dyed her hair, preferring to keep it natural and simply pluck any gray hairs with tweezers.[29] In many photos she wears a white mariposa lily tucked behind one ear.

One woman interviewed by Guerra made special reference to Sánchez's hairstyle when explaining the popular post-1963 practice of wearing hair rollers in public. Cuban women embraced this practice as a rejection of previous generations' judgments about suitable attire for women when outside of the home. Guerra's interviewee noted the popularity of the roller hairstyle, but clarified that while "almost everyone" participated, "you never saw Celia [Sánchez] or Vilma [Espín] wearing rollers."[30] Sánchez and Espín were "highly educated women," she added, as a means to further explain their nonparticipation in the trend. Implicit in this statement is a framing of the interviewee's personal identity and experience as distinct from the two leaders, but it is unclear if that framing was offered as a critique, a compliment, or merely an observation.

The allusion to fashion choices as a reflection of enduring class (and perhaps even racial) divisions in Cuba—articulated here as women who wear hair rollers in public versus women who do not—signals that not all women saw Sánchez as "one of the people." Even though Sánchez's aesthetic always incorporated fabrics or accessories meant to communicate her version of an authentic revolutionary *cubanidad,* her status as a government official complicated how those fashion choices were read by others. Her attire was still viewed as a kind of "high" revolutionary fashion that marked her as distinct from other women, and the hair roller trend was one reflection of the distance between them.

Whether dressed in fatigues or in a tailored skirt suit, Sánchez understood the influence that her choice of attire, hairstyle, accessories, and makeup would have on how she was perceived by supporters and critics alike. She established a look that walked a careful line between the past and the future. It was neither old fashioned nor avant garde. Her personal aesthetic reflected, instead, her keen understanding that as the highest-ranking woman in a new revolutionary government bringing sweeping change to the island, she would need to bridge two eras of meaning to be effective. Her personal aesthetic thus fused the familiar with the novel—encapsulated in her iconic fatigues and flowers look—to demonstrate the simultaneity of her new role. Sánchez's fashion choices were never only about attire. They were also a means to model a version of the New Woman as both deeply rooted in national history and tradition and pressing forward for change.

The Making of a Revolutionary Stateswoman

With her new official status within the Cuban government, Sánchez immediately began to act on the ideas she had first formulated while in the Sierra Maestra. I have often marveled at the number of projects that Sánchez executed in the twenty years of her life as a revolutionary stateswoman. They are a testament to her ability to mobilize her earlier experiences working with her father on small public works projects and later building schools, hospitals, and workshops in the Sierra. An economist friend who lives in Havana, reflecting on the scope of these projects, noted that "Castro had full confidence in Sánchez, and she worked with a lot of autonomy. He did not stand over her, which allowed her to move quickly."[31] This thread runs through memories of Sánchez's life—efficiency and dedication to managing the details of projects that others might overlook or undervalue.

As a helpmate to her father during her clandestine life as well as in combat, and then later in her postrevolutionary career, Sánchez demonstrated a keen ability to execute the myriad micro-level actions necessary to support grand plans. She was also an adept and approachable manager of people, attuned to the details of human needs. Family friend Bécquer Céspedes frames this role in gendered terms, noting that "Fidel was a man of ideas,

Celia worked from the heart."[32] Sánchez was also a woman of tremendous creative energy. She operated spherically, moving in multiple directions and managing overlapping projects simultaneously. Remarking on the scope and scale of her endeavors, an anonymous article published in *Granma* (the official newspaper of the Central Committee of the Cuban Communist Party, named for the famous yacht) the day before the first anniversary of her death noted that "there was not a single significant event related to the Revolution from the months of preparation for the arrival of the *Granma* to the minute of her death in which—in one way or another—this national heroine was not involved."[33]

The projects Sánchez chose to pursue as secretary to the president reflect how she viewed the revolution's central purpose as well as her role within it. Castro granted her almost total autonomy to realize these projects because he trusted her vision. She chose projects that reflected her belief that the revolution should reimagine public spaces as expressions of the collective. From tourist hotels and urban parks to museums and convention centers, she assembled a diverse portfolio of projects meant to provide new spaces for mass leisure, for conveying national history, and for preserving native flora and fauna. Working with a team of architects and landscape designers, Sánchez helped shape a new architectural style suffused with nationalist symbolism and meaning. Her projects range in scale, but they are instantly recognizable for their unique combination of modernist design elements, local building materials, and native landscaping.

Like her own personal style, this combination feels simultaneously traditional and forward-looking, epic and intimate. I note in the projects she chose as a government official a direct link to her early adult years when she and her father created a public park in Pilón and climbed the Sierra Maestra to place the Martí bust atop Turquino Peak. Her projects are all deeply patriotic, historically grounded, and subtly nostalgic. They feel like projects her father would have chosen. The Demajagua National Park project in Granma Province was, in fact, one of his dream projects that she realized in his honor.

The first task on Sánchez's public works project list was to create an official archive of the revolution. Reflecting on the genesis of this project, former M-26-7 member Jorge Enrique Mendoza Reboredo remembered that Sánchez "frequently told [him] about how her father had always criticized the deformation of the true history of the glorious *mambises* [troops who fought in the war for Cuba's independence]." He went on to state that the "rebels who were in the Sierra Maestra during the earliest months of the revolution remember Celia with the large pockets of her fatigues visibly bulging with papers." From her earliest days in the Sierra, Sánchez was determined to preserve the history of the revolutionaries. She began to collect rebel documents, materials, and writings with the objective of conserving them for posterity. In September 1958, considering these papers a national treasure, Sánchez began guarding them in the famous knapsack her *compañeros* later christened Cuba's symbolic "coffer of memories." The bag is on permanent display at her childhood home museum in Media Luna. Álvarez Tabío, the former director of the Office of Historical Affairs, once referred to the archive as "an institution born in Celia's knapsack in the Sierra."

Sánchez explained the importance of this tedious task, stating, "There are many papers without importance today. For the future and for history, however, they will be of great value. My interest in this has been that when this history is written, it will represent the truth and not myths or tales. Nothing matters more than these documents. Later, all this will matter." Committed to not only collecting, but also preserving these important papers, Sánchez set about creating the revolutionary government's first official archive. For this undertaking, she solicited the aid of former combatants and their families as well as the leaders of the revolution. The Office of Historical Affairs is filled with the thank-you notes Sánchez wrote—she never had a personal assistant—to everyone who donated letters, photos, or other documents to the archive.

On 28 March 1959, Sánchez wrote a letter to Camilo Cienfuegos asking for his help in gathering more documents for the archive. She wrote, "I have begun to put the entire archive of the Revolution in plastic—that is to say, the originals. Later, I hope to place the entire contents of the archive on rolls of film, which will then be available for public use. If I am going to do this, I want to do it right, or rather, I want to begin with those documents dating even before Moncada. Therefore, I would like everything that belongs to Fidel—all of his speeches, his writings, his letters, down to the last paper. Will you help me with the gathering of all these things? This undertaking will benefit everyone. If you are willing, and seeing as you have little free time, you can give all of your papers to me. Agreed? All your papers interest me. Your writings and your letters are so fascinating because you write beautifully and because, well, everything is interesting. Don't put anything in order for me."[34]

Sánchez was not able to complete the process of gathering and organizing all the papers until 1963. The first challenge she encountered was that Castro and the others did not always note the date and time on the messages they sent. One of Sánchez's first tasks, therefore, was to try to put everything in chronological order and assign each communiqué a date, which she then hand wrote in the corner of each document. Second, each document had to be thoroughly cleaned of any mold, bacteria, or fungus that might lead to its deterioration over time. Third, in order to maintain the quality of the documents, the building had to be fitted with a climate control system to maintain a consistent temperature and humidity level. On 4 May 1964, after nearly six years of work, the Office of Historical Affairs in Havana opened, and over the years it has become an invaluable—if highly restricted—archive and research center. Castro once referred to the archive as a "living monument to the fecund and undying memory of Sánchez." Today the archive holds more than twenty thousand original documents from the Cuban Revolution, many of which are being digitized by the archival staff.

Sánchez's role as historian of the Cuban Revolution did not end there. In keeping with her father's desire to preserve Cuba's history, Sánchez began several long-term projects to reconstruct the various battles of the revolution, and to collect the personal testimonies of the men and women who had fought in them.[35] In a February 1978 memo, Sánchez argued that one of the principal responsibilities of the Office of Historical Affairs was to locate and preserve significant sites from the war, and noted that "it is our duty to reach the future generations of our country and time may impact radically the natural physiognomy of these historic sites, so we need to conserve them . . . and ensure a general harmony and coherence between the buildings and monuments established in these locations."[36]

Beginning in 1972, Sánchez directed the first project to reconstruct the historic Battle of Guisa.[37] Members of the M-26-7, including several women from the Mariana Grajales Brigade, accompanied Sánchez and her team of young historians to the battlefield at Guisa in order to show them where the rebel troops had positioned themselves, and even where the dead had been buried. The result of these detailed inquiries was a highly detailed relief map of the battle site, which is currently on display in the Museum of the Revolution in Havana.[38] Sánchez also organized groups of university students to travel throughout the island and interview the combatants and collaborators in the Sierra Maestra, as well as those men and women who had served as guides to members of the rebel army. The original copies of those interviews are stored within the holdings of the Office of Historical Affairs.

Sánchez's interest in conserving Cuba's native flora and fauna also deserves mention, especially her concern for protecting its crocodiles and certain species of birds. She helped greatly in the creation of the Botanical Gardens and Lenin Park in Havana. Lenin Park was an epic project in keeping with the revolution's inclination for the grandiose, and was one of Sánchez's most famous projects. Before it was a park, this area (approximately 745 hectares or 1,841 acres) contained seventeen large cattle farms. In 1969, Sánchez "assembled the crème de la crème of Cuban architects, engineers, and decorators, who were encouraged to give their fertile imaginations free reign in designing Lenin Park."

Fourteen architects, headed by Dr. Antonio Quintana and directed by Sánchez, began the project to convert the land into a national park. Her collaborators on the project recount stories of Sánchez riding on horseback through the rain to assess the progress of the massive endeavor. She also volunteered on Sundays to help gather and transport the rocks used to construct the park's five-star restaurant, Las Ruinas, housed within an old sugar mill. Work crews moved more than three million cubic meters of earth and planted 149,000 trees. On 22 April 1972, Lenin Park was officially inaugurated, and on 8 January 1984, the revolutionary government dedicated a monument to Vladimir Lenin, which now stands atop the highest hill in the park. According to the Visitor's Center, Lenin Park currently employees over 100 staff members.

Despite lacking any formal training in construction or design, Sánchez was instrumental in the creation of many other significant buildings, museums, and tourist sites across the island. Randall, reflecting on the vast number and variety of projects that Sánchez directed, stated that "she was a creative force after the revolution and her reputation facilitated carrying them out. There was definitely some magical realism involved."[39] Sánchez became known for her attention to detail and for establishing the architectural "style of the revolution [and] the image of the country."[40] Sánchez infused her projects with a kind of tropical modernism that combined indigenous building materials and native botanical motifs to communicate a "sense of cubanía" (Cuban identity) in architectural form.[41] She demanded that her landscape artists use only native plant species—ferns, flowers, palm trees—at her project sites and ordered that they transport and replant any vegetation uprooted over the course of a project.[42]

Although Hart Dávalos later attributed the inspiration for these various construction projects to Castro, stating that Sánchez executed projects "inspired by the program and ideas of Fidel," friends and family tout her lifelong talent for design.[43] One newspaper article praised Sánchez's contributions to twentieth-century Cuban architecture and even reprinted a copy of the silhouette—the Asian-inspired landscape that won her an art award in Media Luna—as evidence of her lifelong appreciation of the arts.

The same article also reminded readers that Sánchez had been instrumental in designing hospitals, schools, warehouses, and workshops in the Sierra Maestra during the armed phase of the revolution.[44] Photos published after her death show her interacting with internationally celebrated Cuban artists like René Portocarrero and Wilfredo Lam.[45]

Sánchez was the project lead on the design and construction of the Pionero Palace in Santiago de Cuba, the Revolution Palace, the Congressional Palace, the Convention Palace, the Cosmonaut House in Varadero, the Ruins restaurant in Lenin Park, the Cochinito restaurant and the famed Coppelia ice cream park on 23rd Street in Havana, and the Prehistoric Mural in Viñales, among many other projects. Of special personal importance was her work to create the national monument in Granma Province, the Demajagua National Park, at the site where sugar mill owner Carlos Manuel de Céspedes freed his slaves and proclaimed Cuba's independence from Spain on 10 October 1868. Dr. Sánchez first called for the former plantation to become a national monument during a 1946 speech to Manzanillo's chapter of the Lions Club.[46] Following his death, Sánchez — in her capacity as secretary to the president — helped fulfill her father's wish, exactly one hundred years after Céspedes's initial uprising.

Sánchez was also the driving force behind the Guamá ecotourism resort in the Zapata Swamp, which was once a popular honeymoon destination for Cubans. She also established a ceramics workshop, the Taller Guamá, in March 1960, where sculptor Rita Longa oversaw the production of hundreds of sculptural monuments to Cuba's native Taíno population.[47] The hotel grounds at the Guamá resort still display a selection of those sculptures. Finally, Sánchez oversaw the rehabilitation — and conversion into embassies — of a number of historic mansions in Havana's Miramar neighborhood west of Havana.[48]

There is an element of Sánchez's projects that strikes me each time I visit one of them. For a woman whose image is so grounded in humility, I find the sheer number of Sánchez's large-scale projects fascinating. How do we reconcile her behind-the-scenes persona with the scope of her public works portfolio? Why would a woman who loathed the spotlight build multi-thousand-square-foot buildings? The number of "palaces" that she designed or renovated — the Convention Palace, the Presidential Palace, and the Pioneer Palace — for example, lends a certain monumentality to her portfolio. Lenin Park remains Havana's largest recreational area, covering a massive 1,600 acres. Sánchez's projects communicate her personal vision of what the revolution should strive to promote and achieve. She envisioned them as expressions of the new collective, repositioning, for example, the category "palace" within an architecture of socialist cause and "park" within the landscape of (urban) mass leisure. They are conceived as projects for "the people."

Without negating Sánchez's intentions, I also see her project choices as strategic. All of her large-scale works slotted nicely within the gendered category of "social projects" in ways that posed no threat to her male colleagues. Sánchez did not design military bases, roads, or dams because those were considered projects for men. Educational centers and sites of mass leisure were closely enough associated with maternal duties and concerns to not raise eyebrows or cause conflict. Never mind that the actual work of designing and executing the projects required Sánchez to acquire many of the same skills and establish the same collaborative relationships with engineers and architects as would be required to build a highway. As she did in so many other aspects of her professional career, I believe Sánchez maneuvered through the terrain of public works projects with a canny sense of the power of traditional gender roles.

I also see in the selection and execution of her public works projects an opportunity to extend her influence within the revolution beyond the limits of her own life. Sánchez's official biography frames all of her contributions to the revolutionary project within a framework of humility and self-sacrifice. To be sure, none of the sites bear her name, and any on-site imagery of her was placed there after she died. They are less memorials to her person—though several would acquire that status posthumously—than monuments to her values. They form part of her legacy, and I believe she understood that element of the endeavor better than her official state biography captures or allows. Lenin Park was created *for* the people, but it was also *about* Sánchez. Recognizing this component of her work does not nullify or negate her intention to execute socially meaningful projects, but it does add nuance to our understanding of how she imagined her role. There is space within our discussions of Sánchez's professional life for us to recognize both her civic mindedness and the magnitude of her own vision.

Sánchez's goals were ambitious because she understood the role of the New Woman in those terms. While she selected projects that did not overtly challenge traditional gender norms, we might find in the very scope and scale of her projects a subtle reframing of those norms. Her projects highlighted both the amplitude of the Cuban people's social needs and the ability of the New Woman to respond to them in strategic and meaningful ways. She also elevated that kind of work to the status enjoyed by male colleagues charged with attending to political or economic needs through road or dam building—traditional "men's projects." In so doing, she provided a new stage for women to shape the revolutionary state-making process and elevated the value attributed to that work.

Celia in Office

Throughout her life, Sánchez held numerous political offices within the revolutionary government, and received countless awards. Garnering positions of influence, as well as many of the country's top accolades, marked Sánchez as a political insider with a secure seat at the most influential tables on the island. The range of the awards she received also certified her accomplishments as an elite veteran of the revolutionary war. Despite dismissive portrayals of her as merely Castro's housekeeper, secretary, or lover, Sánchez was an indisputable political heavyweight within a highly centralized government structure that permitted only a handful of individuals—and very few women—access to core decision-making power. In addition to serving as secretary to the president, Sánchez was elected as a member of the Central Committee of the Communist Party of Cuba on 1 October 1965, and again in 1975. In 1976 she became secretary of the Council of State and a delegate to Cuba's legislative parliament and its supreme body of state power, the National Assembly of Popular Power. She received a commemorative medal from the FAR on the twentieth anniversary of the Moncada attack (figure 5).

Sánchez also served her country in a diplomatic capacity. In 1996 I had the opportunity to interview historian Nydia Sarabia—a collaborator on Sánchez's Office of Historical Affairs project—and she described Sánchez as a "passionate internationalist." She recalls that during the Vietnam War, Sánchez was active in "gathering food, medicines, clothing for children, and above all, helping the Vietnamese people maintain the faith that they would win the war even though they were fighting against the most militarily sophisticated army in the world." In 1960 alone Sánchez traveled to the United States, Canada, Brazil, Argentina, and Uruguay. She also traveled to Angola, Ethiopia, Nicaragua, El Salvador, Romania, Hungary, Algeria, Poland, Czechoslovakia, and Bulgaria. The Media Luna museum displays Sánchez's collection of diplomatic gifts, which includes clothing and jewelry from the countries she visited. As early as 1959, Sánchez accompanied Castro to New York. She accompanied him to New York in 1960 for the United Nations General Assembly when he famously left the Shelburne Hotel amid accusations of harassment and unfair treatment of his entourage by hotel staff and

FIGURE 5   Climbing Turquino Peak for medical graduation ceremony, 1965. Author's collection.

relocated to the Hotel Theresa in Harlem. A photo shows her sitting in the front seat of the car he traveled in that night (figure 6). She was at his side in New York again in 1979 when he made his famous address to the nonaligned countries at the United Nations.

Sánchez was also a decorated member of the FMC, an organization established in 1960 to craft the official discourse and concrete policies needed to address gender inequality and bring Cuba's New Woman firmly into the revolutionary coalition.[49] In his 1966 address to the assembled members of the fifth FMC national plenum in Santa Clara, Castro charged the organization with overseeing the "revolution within the Revolution," which should liberate women from gender subordination and capitalist exploitation.[50] Cuba's socialist revolution would provide for this liberation through education, worker training programs, day care centers, and—beginning in 1975 with the "Family Code"—new social legislation meant to redefine marital roles in more egalitarian terms. In so doing, the FMC would establish the necessary social base to alleviate the burdens of childrearing and domestic work so that women could be incorporated more fully into the national labor force. Participation in the FMC became compulsory for women in 1968, which boosted the number of official members to almost a million.

Despite the high numbers of official FMC members, critics of the organization—and even some female revolutionary leaders—noted that while the Cuban Revolution might offer the promise of advances for the New Woman in the realms of education, work, and domestic life, one of her biggest obstacles just might be the New Man.[51] U.S. journalist Georgie Ann Geyer quoted Cuban revolutionary leader Haydée Santamaría who, in reflecting on obstacles to female advancement in Cuba, noted that "ideologically, the man is advanced. But when he arrives at home, he wants his wife there, preparing dinner."[52] Journalist Marlise Simons quoted a Cuban female architect she interviewed as stating that thirteen years after the revolution she "now [has] a double life . . . when I get home, he sits down and I cook dinner."[53] An *El Mundo* (Oakland) article reported that "many women stay in the home despite pressures from the Committees for the Defense of the Revolution and the League of Young Communists [because] the greatest resistance comes from the men who find it difficult to purge themselves of their feelings of superiority."[54] Castro confessed his own lingering machismo in a 1977 interview with U.S. journalist Sally Quinn. When asked if he still considered himself "macho," Castro responded: "*Síííí*, I will have to admit I still have a little machismo myself" before launching into a lengthy history lesson on the Spanish-Arabic roots of Cuban machismo.[55]

FIGURE 6 Leaving the Shelburne Hotel en route to Harlem, New York, 1960. Author's collection.

The FMC is not a feminist organization and Sánchez never identified as a feminist. Like FMC President Vilma Espín, Sánchez was critical of what she viewed as bourgeois feminism, with its reformist approach to social change. At the same time, she embraced an ideal of revolutionary womanhood that stressed the uplift and incorporation of popular class women and the sacrifice and dedication of more educated women. There is an inherent "othering" in this approach to women's liberation that has brought criticism of the FMC platform from radical and socialist feminists. Scholars and activists point to the organization's historically limited engagement with feminism or issues of racial and sexuality-based discrimination as critical limitations to its impact.[56] They also note that the FMC remains the only legally sanctioned women's organization on the island, which the government enforces via a "nonduplication" law that forbids the charter of new organizations deemed to overlap existing organizations. Critics of the revolutionary government argue that these kinds of control mechanisms constrain the conversation around women's shifting needs and maintain an outdated status quo that serves only the top echelon of political insiders.

A handful of Cuban press photos show Sánchez attending FMC events, and she received the FMC's "Ana Betancourt" medal in August 1975 for displaying "unbreakable faithfulness to revolutionary and internationalist ideals."[57] Sánchez also sat on the FMC's organizing council and attended congress meetings. Despite the titles and accolades that she received from the FMC, however, Sánchez seemed to maintain a certain distance from that organization, especially relative to her other affiliations. While she never addressed the decision on her part, it seems important to ask if Sánchez saw some benefit to not tying herself and her image too closely to the FMC. Sánchez's image was deeply embedded in her status as a woman of the people. Perhaps aligning herself with an agenda that was too women-specific might have compromised her work. Sánchez's broad portfolio of projects often required her to work closely with men. Maintaining a kind of gender neutrality in terms of her affiliation may well have contributed to her administrative effectiveness.

She may also have maintained some distance because the FMC was Espín's sphere of influence and she wanted to avoid any potential conflict on that front. In terms of spheres of authority, the postrevolutionary government was indeed characterized by some level of institutional atomization of its highest-ranking female leaders. Sánchez became secretary to the president, Haydée Santamaría presided over the prestigious Casa de las Américas cultural institution, and Espín became president of the FMC. One family member hinted in an interview that the decision to maintain some distance from the FMC was personal, noting that "Haydée was [Celia's] close friend, but not Vilma Espín. Celia frequently ignored Vilma, and Vilma did not like to be ignored. In one particular incident, Vilma came to Acacia's [Sánchez's younger sister] house and Celia escaped into the street through the back door to avoid talking to Vilma. Theirs was not really a rivalry, though. Vilma wanted the power and Celia didn't."[58]

Though she never centered her political career on women's issues, Sánchez's life might easily be cast as one premised on the rejection of conventional femininity. While Sánchez did take in several children over the years, many of whom were orphaned by the revolutionary war, she was not a biological mother and she never married in an era when those were standard expectations for women both inside and outside of Cuba. The Cuban Revolution's ideology of revolutionary womanhood—the "revolution within the Revolution"—created only so much room for a woman with political aspirations to maneuver. Speculation as to why Sánchez never married range from the tragic loss of a rumored teenage love, to her belief that marriage limited a woman's personal freedom, to assumptions that she and Castro were romantically involved, to rumors that she was a lesbian. Sánchez never addressed the question in the few interviews she granted, nor in her surviving personal correspondence.

Sánchez never bore children of her own, but she was bound to the physical, material, and emotive sacrifices and duties of motherhood through the children she took into her home. The fact that she was not a biological mother also allowed her maternal role to extend to all the children of Cuba. The loss of Sánchez's own mother at a young age finds its place within this maternalist narrative—the motherless child becomes the mother to all. In spite of her high rank within the revolutionary government, many Cubans viewed Sánchez as both approachable and concerned with their personal and familial needs. Sánchez's decision to open her home to children orphaned by the revolutionary war undoubtedly reinforced that perception. Palomares Ferrales, who eventually came to live with Sánchez at the apartment on 11th Street, was the daughter of rebel collaborator Pastor Palomares, who was killed at Palma Mocha.[59] She published a 2015 book about her relationship with Sánchez, titled *Celia: Mi mejor regalo* (Celia: My Greatest Gift), that describes Sánchez's tender care for her health, nutrition, education, and social formation from the moment she arrived in Havana with anemia, a deformed spine, and intestinal parasites.[60]

Sánchez also coordinated with Castro to establish the José Martí School in Tarará (east of Havana), which offered full scholarships to children orphaned by the war.[61] In an interview with French journalist Deena Stryker, conducted in February 1964, Sánchez commented on the regular movement of children through her home, stating, "As soon as the war was over, Fidel sent for all those kids to whom he'd promised that, one day, they would go to school. We brought them to Havana as scholarship students, and they're doing fine. One is already in pilot training school. And since their families are [in the Sierra Maestra], they got in the habit of coming here Saturday and Sunday, and we give them their spending money [which amounts to] five pesos a week times twenty." When Stryker questioned Sánchez about the funding source to support these children, Sánchez replied, "What column would we put this money in? . . . Of course, my salary isn't enough, so what do you think? I take it from the Presidential Palace, of course."[62]

Thousands of requests flowed into Sánchez's office from petitioners seeking help with problems as significant as a child's illness, the need to secure housing after a hurricane, or help with job placement.[63] More minor requests included petitions for access to photos held within the Office of Historical

Affairs.[64] In one memo she notes that she sent a watch to a doctor when she learned that he did not own one.[65] The requests are dizzying in both their volume and their variety and are almost always laced with effusive apologies for bothering someone "so burdened with work."[66] Sánchez also received many requests for aid from former revolutionary combatants, or solicitations made on their behalf. One letter dated 29 August 1969 informs Sánchez that one of Guevara's former messengers in the Sierra Maestra was found "living in conditions which required immediate action."[67] A veteran of the Battle of Uvero sought her assistance with "problems relating to his retirement."[68] A few families—being always careful to cite their steadfast support of the revolution—requested assistance with issues of a diplomatic nature. One such family wrote Sánchez in April 1977 asking for her help to return to Cuba after they had traveled (presumably illegally) to the United States seeking medical assistance for a sick child.[69]

Despite their bureaucratic appearance, the small notepads Sánchez carried in her purse provide a surprisingly intimate view into how she understood and performed the philanthropic aspects of her identity as the New Woman. Each notebook is filled with scribbled reminders about requests from individuals she encountered during the course of her day. I was struck to discover that her father made similar notations in the pads he carried on his medical rounds.[70] Sánchez jotted down the name of each petitioner's spouse, details about the extended family, notations about the size of their house or farm, and the names and ages of each child, often with a note to send them a special toy.[71] She carefully noted the amount of money distributed to each family member (e.g., "Ciro's cousin: $100"), and when a widow of a military veteran approached her for assistance, she noted carefully the deceased combatant's contributions to the revolutionary war effort.[72] Hart Dávalos noted that this element of her work reflected her self-identification as a fellow veteran, claiming that "she had lived intensely the clandestine life in Oriente and was closely acquainted with the feelings and problems . . . she was one of them! From the Sierra she fulfilled the role of *compañera* to all and offered her fraternal help. She worried about the smallest details and personal concerns we faced."[73]

The concern with daily needs reflected and recorded in Sánchez's notebooks was not only a function of her character traits, family background, and combat activities. Expectations about how women in leadership roles should operate shaped the kinds of requests many Cubans felt comfortable presenting to Sánchez. They were not sending hundreds of letters to Castro's office seeking help with housing and employment issues, because they understood those as concerns of the New Woman. Cubans expected Sánchez to fill a role as an accessible, approachable mother figure, more concerned with daily needs than were her male colleagues. One former government insider referred to Sánchez as Castro's "human face."[74] Sánchez embraced her role within this important sphere of influence, both because it was familiar to her and because it allowed her to exercise a considerable, quiet power within the Cuban Revolution with minimal resistance or conflict.

Godmother of the New Cuba

> From Palma Soriano a combatant
> Dedicates a poem to the diamond of the Sierra and the llano.
> Her name, Celia Sánchez Manduley.
> Mother, vanguard mother,
> Immortal mother,
> Heroic mother.
>
> —EUGENIO RODRÍGUEZ, "Kinafru"[75]

When asked about Sánchez's contributions to the Cuban state subsequent to the triumph of the revolution, it is not her titles or her involvement in the construction of national monuments, museums, parks, and hospitals that most Cubans remember. Rather, it is her dedication to answering the most fundamental questions facing the Cuban people that Cubans recall most vividly. Smith and Padula have likewise commented on Sánchez's attentiveness to the daily needs of the Cuban people, stating that Sánchez "served as a national benefactress, a socialist Eva Perón, who through the years responded to personal appeals for assistance and investigated complaints of injustice from thousands of Cubans."[76]

Lourdes Sang recalled that "Celia never really worked within the FMC or in the other large governmental bureaucracies, and she was rarely seated behind a desk. She worked from wherever she was . . . that became her office. She was never seen with a chauffeur; instead she drove her own jeep. Celia was a campesina, and was never seen enjoying the smallest privilege. Instead, she concentrated on the Cuban people's most basic needs. In fact, when she heard that my father-in-law died, she even came to our house to be with us in our time of need. That's how she was."[77]

Nilda Porot, an employee at the José Martí National Library who lived across the street from Sánchez for several years, recalls that "Celia gave houses and cars to people, she even fixed people's roofs. If she couldn't help you, she sent someone who could."[78] Porot linked Sánchez's benevolence to her status as a "believer" who placed fresh flowers at the foot of a small altar dedicated to the Virgen de la Caridad (Virgin of Charity) that stood at the entrance to her apartment. Nirma Cartón recalled both Sánchez's generosity and her graciousness, stating that "everyone came to [Sánchez's] office to talk to her . . . there was always a line at least a mile long. And when she would go to visit the homes of the peasants in the countryside to attend to their problems, she wouldn't scratch herself when fleas bit her for fear of insulting the people who lived there."

Sánchez's elementary school teacher and family friend, Cossío, recalled in an interview that "one time Celia heard that I was having a small issue with my [blood] pressure. It was nothing serious, but without consulting me she sent a specialist to examine me. How was she able to remain so attentive to such small issues when she had so much on her shoulders? When she heard that my mother could no longer walk [and] that we had to drag her in a chair around the house to be able to move her, I opened the front door one day to [find] a wheelchair." Stories of Sánchez's commitment to finding solutions to the daily problems of her fellow Cubans became bedrock for her legacy of quasi-maternal self-sacrifice and connection to the people.

Each of these oral testimonies depicts Sánchez as a sensitive, caring, and humble woman who prioritized the daily needs of the Cuban people. Not only did Sánchez take the time to visit individual Cubans during their time of need, but she also lived a life of relative austerity herself—a further sign of her solidarity with the people. There are also discrepancies between the testimonies, however. First, Sang's comment contains an ambiguous reference to Sánchez not having an office, whereas Cartón makes special mention of Sánchez's office as the center of her popular outreach programs. While there are several known photographs depicting Sánchez working from her office in the Plaza of the Revolution, what is important is that these two women used the existence or absence of Sánchez's office to make the same point about the nature of her connection to the Cuban people.[68]

Another intriguing component of Sang's testimony is her reference to Sánchez as a "campesina." In terms of class, Sánchez was not a campesina, as Sang indicates; rather, she was from a relatively affluent family. Sang may well have evoked the term to refer to Sánchez's childhood roots in the provincial towns of eastern Cuba, but it seems likely that she chose the term campesina more as a way of indicating Sánchez's solidarity with Cubans of humbler origins than as an indicator of her social class. Reframing the revolutionary leaders as members of the rural working class is not uncommon, even though many of them—including Fidel and Raúl Castro, Espín, and even Guevara—came from prosperous families. Imagining them in this way positions them more comfortably within a national mythology that still centers the revolutionary epicenter in the Cuban countryside.

Finally, Porot's reference to Sánchez's dedication to the Virgin of Charity highlights a facet of her life that is often spoken of in a whisper, if it is mentioned at all. The revolutionary government's complicated position on religion shapes conversations about spiritual belief and practice, especially in reference to its leadership. For every person I spoke with who mentioned that Sánchez practiced Catholicism, another informed me that, like her father, she was not religious. Palomares Ferrales recalls that when she came from the Sierra Maestra as a child to live with Sánchez in Havana, she was instructed to discontinue her use of the phrase "Be blessed," when greeting friends and family.

Sánchez's nephew informed me that the statue of the Virgin of Charity cited by Porot actually stood in a different family member's home and not in Sánchez's apartment.[79] Perhaps Porot, who wore the beaded necklace and bracelet of a devotee of Santería to her interview with me, referenced Sánchez's religious identity as a way to link herself to Sánchez through a shared spirituality, or as a means to validate her own religious identity. Whatever the reasons for its inclusion in her testimony it was important for Porot to share with me this element of her own imagining of Sánchez.

In many ways Sánchez's personal life and professional career fused into one role—godmother of the new Cuba. Chaney notes that women in professional and public office "are generally confined to tasks analogous to those they perform in the home. The female political official is forced to legitimate her role as that of a mother in the larger 'house' of the municipality or even the nation."[80] The expectation is that they will continue "carrying out the nurturant and affectional tasks society assigns to women, rather than in the instrumental male role, which is defined as more aggressive, authoritarian, and achievement-oriented."[81] Amy Richlin calls this sentimental stereotype the "First Lady" icon—a "benevolent super-mother, bestowing largesse and concern on her subjects . . . [a] lady of impeccable virtue."[82]

Chase warns that this maternalism has had contradictory effects, by "rationalizing the entry of women into the public sphere while also reinforcing their association with the private and domestic sphere. It tends to present women's activism as something exceptional, necessary only in times of crisis, motivated by disturbances to the sanctity of the home."[83] At the same time, the image of the New Woman as someone who could balance international travel, regular volunteer labor, and political office with (symbolic and material) caregiving duties created a measuring stick for women's contributions to the revolutionary cause that was unachievable to most Cuban women. Cuban women complained that the "double burden"—which Castro described as the dual class- and gender-based exploitations that women suffered under capitalism—was only augmented when the New Woman was asked to shoulder the triple burden of duty to home, work, and party.[84] Constructions of Sánchez as the New Woman that were meant to inspire women to evaluate, affirm, and expand their commitment to the revolution could, and were perhaps intended to, shame those who were unwilling or unable to follow her example.

Many Cubans remember Sánchez as deferential, private, domesticated, and maternal, not because she felt compelled to conform to contemporary sexual mores or the expectations of a macho male leadership, but because that was her authentic nature. Her ability to rise to the highest ranks of power in Cuban government stands for them as proof of the revolution's progressiveness, despite increased scholarly attention to the government's limited advancements toward true gender equality. Unexamined is the possibility that Sánchez's personal ambition and ability to perform a kind of acceptable domesticity, even as she took her place as the highest-ranking woman in the revolutionary government, shaped her access to power.

I believe that Sánchez accepted the terms of her maternalist role and even performed it in ways that worked to her advantage. To say that Sánchez performed a role as a kind of national godmother is not to suggest that it was merely a guise. I view it as something closer to what Alice Wexler has termed a woman's "own heroic self-presentation."[85] Sánchez tapped into and mobilized her authentic sensibilities and skills in a way that resonated with many Cubans and thereby enhanced her political effectiveness. Her presence within the world of Cuban politics gave little cause for alarm, as she did not frame her activities in ways that looked like power seeking to her comrades.

To be sure, not everyone I interviewed was a fan of her maternal style of leadership. One senior faculty member at the University of Havana who fought alongside Sánchez in the Sierra Maestra described her to me as "too mothering" and even "smothering." Yet Sánchez was both perceptive and purposeful in the way she constructed her public persona. She occupied an official government post, yet she exercised her most powerful influence in extra-bureaucratic, informal ways not bound by the limits of formal politics. These choices granted an elasticity and expansiveness to her role in Cuban politics that made her position unique. One family member noted in an interview with me that "Celia was not a romantic figure. She was a complex character . . . a political creature."[86]

Imagining the New Woman

Sánchez was the highest-ranking woman in the Cuban government for more than twenty years, yet never claimed to represent the New Woman. I believe, however, that she realized fully her power to shape what that idea meant. Sánchez's official biography casts her as primarily humble and loyal—which I believe she was—but she was also strategic. Her public persona linked the traditions and history of her father's generation of political activists and the radical politics of the revolutionary generation. She was both a *martiana* and a *fidelista*, borrowing symbols and mobilizing meanings from both eras in ways meant to communicate her authenticity, patriotism, and femininity. From her choice of attire to the projects she developed, Sánchez communicated her understanding of women's roles in postrevolutionary Cuba. She wore a mariposa flower with her fatigues and oversaw the dedication of Céspedes's Demajagua plantation as a new national monument because she understood the New Woman as a bridge connecting two eras of her nation's political, social, and economic history. The New Woman was a creative force engaged in an imaginative enterprise to honor the past and build the future.

Sánchez understood that her position on the front lines of this imaginative project would draw attention from a U.S. press eager to weigh the successes and failures of the Cuban Revolution and its leaders. She went to great lengths to avoid the press, but knew she never could completely. Until 1960, the U.S. media depicted Cuba's new generation of revolutionary women in a positive light. When diplomatic relations between the two countries began to founder as Cuba's new revolutionary government shifted its discursive focus from republican nationalism to radical reform, however, depictions of the Cuban leadership—both male and female—changed dramatically. As the woman most closely associated with the revolution's supreme leader, Sánchez came under heavy fire. From a brilliant and influential political leader in her own right, she was transformed at the hands of the U.S. press into a calculating power-seeker who used her sexuality to control Castro. In the hand of the U.S. press, Cuba's New Woman was thus reimagined as a potential threat to national and international security.

CHAPTER SIX

Who Is Celia Sánchez?

Image, Politics, and Sexuality in the U.S. Media

> Jokes about Fidel's romantic prowess are spurred by the fact that
> the one woman in his public life is Celia Sánchez, who seems to
> love only Communism.
>
> —STANLEY ROSS, "We Were Wrong about Castro," 12 June 1960

> Any scholar interested in Cuba has to ponder whether one can write
> a history of the island without understanding that there are at least
> two histories.
>
> —JOSÉ QUIROGA, *Cuban Palimpsests*

Dinner at Versailles

As my Uber pulled up alongside Miami's famous Versailles restaurant, I found
scattered tourists snapping selfies and weaving their way between groups of
gray-haired Cuban men drinking hot Cuban cafecitos over animated political discussions. In spite of the early hour, a line of customers awaited their
turn to enter the bustling restaurant. The bright lights of the restaurant's
green and red sign cast a festive glow over the scene as I passed through the
front door. I had learned—like the many tourists, scholars, and journalists
gathered around the restaurant's linen-topped tables—that no trip to the city
was complete without a plate of *ropa vieja* (meat stew) and some spirited debate at Versailles. The hostess directed me to a table at the center of the
room and I sat to await my dinner companion, whom I had never met.

Ten minutes later, a dapper man dressed in a wool trench coat and neck-
tie approached my table with a smile. Although he appeared to be in his late
sixties, his niece—a dear friend who had connected us—had already informed me that at almost ninety years old he still lifted weights daily and
only indulged in a bowl of soup during his nightly outings to the restaurant.
She had also informed me that her uncle was somewhat of a local celebrity
so as to prepare me for the attention he would draw at the restaurant. Following a few moments of lighthearted small talk, we ordered our meals and
settled in for our chat.

The animated two-hour interview with my charismatic dinner companion drifted between stories of his childhood in Cuba to his adult years as a high-ranking agent of the United States government assigned to carry out secret missions to overthrow or assassinate Castro. In heavily accented English he wove a tale of intrigue and drama that could easily sell a million copies on a bookstand. When I asked him why he had never written a memoir, he remarked with a shrug, "My life is not a success story. Fidel is still alive." The parade of well-wishers who streamed by our table wanting to shake his hand expressed a different sentiment. Assuming I was a journalist writing a story on their famous friend, they heaped their praise upon him and patted me appreciatively on the hand or shoulder. I noted that he did not correct them about my identity.

When the conversation finally turned to Sánchez, the tone of the interview shifted. I recounted the long history of my work on Sánchez's biography as he sat listening quietly. He nodded slowly at the mention of a familiar place or name, but otherwise refrained from responding. I was struck by the change in his manner and wondered if he had misunderstood the primary purpose of the interview. Just as I was about to shift the subject away from Sánchez, he reached across the table and touched my hand. Beckoning me to lean forward, he half-whispered: "You know, around here, they say that she killed Camilo Cienfuegos in order to protect Fidel. Camilo's plane didn't really disappear, you know. That was the story they made up to cover for her." I pressed for details, but he was already standing to put on his coat. He generously paid the bill and escorted me out the front door, where he waited with me until my Uber arrived. With a parting wave he began charting a course to the restaurant's adjoining bakery. As I drove away I noted that he had already been stopped by a group of admirers.

From the moment of her official incorporation into the Cuban Revolution, Sánchez was either eulogized or villainized. Consequently, most treatments of her life are either polemical or hagiographic. For many Cubans, Sánchez is the embodiment of the New Woman—the mythic, even iconic, image of a female revolutionary ideal. For others, her story is grounded in her identity as a small-town girl who rose to power but never forgot her roots. For still others, especially some Cubans living in Miami, she represents a power structure associated with loss and betrayal. She has been the focus of both veneration and disdain. Whether expressed by the global press, by supporters and critics on or off the island, or by the Cuban government, imaginings of Sánchez's significance have always pointed beyond themselves. Sánchez's life story is a prism through which pass deeper assessments and judgments of the revolutionary project writ large.

Treatments of Sánchez's life and legacy published in the U.S. press between 1958 and her death in 1980 were also refracted through complex visual and discursive negotiations about shifting gender roles on the domestic and global stages. Not surprisingly, discussions of her position within the Cuban Revolution's power structure consistently cast her in either maternalistic, self-sacrificial terms or as a manipulative climber who used her sexuality to secure personal power. The one constant in U.S. press coverage of Sánchez was that journalists never decoupled her from their discussions of Castro. When she is not merely relegated to the literal or metaphorical footnotes of Castro's life, she is referred to either as his mother/sister or as his lover.

The assumption that Sánchez, as secretary to the president, had achieved and was able to maintain her official position within the revolutionary government because she cultivated an intimate, personal relationship with Castro shifted the focus away from Sánchez's political contributions to the revolution and onto her gender and sexuality.[1] Only six years after the triumph of the Cuban Revolution, U.S. journalist and photographer Andrew St. George titled his *Parade* magazine article on Sánchez "The Woman behind Castro." Her name does not even appear in the title—her identity is tied entirely to Castro's.[2]

Meet the Press

In April 1965, Andrew St. George began his article for *Parade* with a rhetorical question: "Who is Celia Sánchez?" St. George went on to claim that "it is a reasonable if regrettable guess that, as this is written, not one American in a thousand knows. In fact, neither did President John F. Kennedy when the name, typed on blue CIA stationery under a red-striped TOP SECRET cover, was first shown him during a tense National Security Council meeting." St. George reports that President Kennedy frowned upon seeing the unfamiliar name and asked: "But who is Celia Sánchez?" Ambassador A. A. Berle purportedly answered the president, stating: "Sánchez seems to be . . . the most influential person in Havana."[3]

If the American public knew relatively little about Castro in 1959, they knew even less about the woman they would come to know as his "constant companion" and "beardless right hand man."[4] The American public learned about Castro and Sánchez simultaneously, and they were presented as inextricably linked from the start. Sánchez's first contact with the U.S. press actually occurred many months before the triumph of the revolution when she escorted U.S. journalists into the Sierra Maestra to interview Castro. U.S. journalist Bob Taber apparently remarked later that "Celia Sánchez is the most intriguing figure in Havana . . . she's the only person for whom Castro shows an unashamed *need* [emphasis in original]."[5]

The first photo of Sánchez to appear in the mainstream U.S. press was in a 5 January 1959 Associated Press wire image of Castro enjoying a "victory lunch" while listening to news of Batista's flight from the island. Sánchez is shown—as she would be for the next two decades—seated at Castro's side and wearing her M-26-7 fatigues.[6] Four days later, the *New York Times* coverage of the rebels' triumphant entry into Havana visually eliminated Sánchez when the photo of the jeep she was riding in was cropped so as to draw focus to the male leaders. She was referenced within the text of the article, however, as the "best-known woman of the Revolution."[7] Eager to understand the source, nature, and extent of her power in Cuba, the first dedicated article about Sánchez appeared by 14 January 1959.[8]

Sánchez never existed in a space separate from Castro in the U.S. media, and while her power was not wholly derivative, it did not exist independently of Castro. Unsure of where to slot Sánchez within the field of political leadership in Cuba, the U.S. press approached her identity as a mystery to be solved. Was she a First Lady? Castro's secret lover? Had the revolution created a new type of Cuban female leader who defied easy (read traditional) categorization? Sánchez's aversion to publicity only bolstered the sense of mystery around her life. Jay Mallin, writing for the *Boston Herald*, noted that "over the years she has shunned the limelight, but nevertheless has been one of the two persons closest to Castro."[9] Journalists writing about Sánchez noted that even Cubans rarely saw her, as she conducted most of her daily business by telephone and stayed off the center stage of Cuban revolutionary politics.[10] Those rare journalists who observed her personally, or who spoke with her, described her as uniquely modest, humble, and even deferential. Journalist Phyllis Battelle noted that when she asked Sánchez to reflect on a political matter, she responded (through an interpreter) with three words: "Talk to Fidel."[11] Sánchez almost never granted interviews, which was a source of perennial frustration for journalists and scholars.[12]

Even if they were unable to categorize her role, U.S. journalists never questioned Sánchez's power. Castro's own (albeit rare) public invocations of Sánchez's name underscored the singularity of her influence. When Castro traveled to Washington, D.C., in February 1959, a reporter asked if Sánchez was traveling with him. He responded tersely: "Of course she is here."[13] The emphatic nature of Castro's response caught the reporter's attention to such a degree that he used the response as a subtitle within his article. Journalists were also generally willing to accept that the title "secretary" did not fully or accurately encapsulate her position in the revolutionary government. Already by January 1959, a *Dallas Morning News* report noted that "captains and lieutenants followed [Sánchez's] orders as if Castro himself had given them."[14] The U.S. press cited her diplomatic travels with Castro and the fact that she received foreign dignitaries as proof of her status as a stakeholder in the revolutionary government.[15] When the story of Frank País Fiorini — an American-born supporter of Castro who later shifted alliances and played a prominent role in the Bay of Pigs landings — hit the U.S. press in 1961, País Fiorini noted that he once intercepted a telegram intended for a Cuban agent in Miami who was spying on him. The coded message was signed by Sánchez.[16] The *Boston Record American* reported that Sánchez "has about the same importance in Castro's inner circle as Henry Kissinger enjoys in Nixon's."[17]

One journalist noted with interest that Sánchez was charged with reviewing the contents of Castro's pockets at the end of the day.[18] Scribbled ideas for Castro's new pet projects, requests for aid, and phone numbers passed through her fingers to be categorized or discarded as she deemed fit. She was very simply the gateway to reach Castro. Journalist Paul Hoffman wrote, "Today, ministers and diplomats defer to her and her telephone number — unlisted like those of everybody who is anybody in Cuba — is a precious piece of information, for Sánchez is the indispensable link between Castro's breast pocket and the Cuban state machinery."[19] When Castro wanted to see someone, that person often only received a last-minute call from Sánchez.[20] When the *New York Times* caught wind of a possible Castro assassination in 1964, the editorial staff phoned Sánchez for a response. She denied the story, reporting only that the "city [was] very quiet." Her word sufficed to discount the rumor.[21]

The precise nature of Sánchez's relationship with Castro was always the primary source of U.S. press speculation and interest about her life. The *Fort Worth Star-Telegram* labeled one early picture of Sánchez and Castro seated together with the words, "Nothing Personal," as if answering a question on everyone's mind.[22] Labeling the photo in that way prompted the question: If they were not romantically involved, who *were* they sleeping with? A flurry of "Who Is Fidel?" exposés speculated about his romantic involvements, and their assessments of his status ran the gamut. Echoing the earliest imaginings of the chaste *barbudo*, some reporters cast Castro as a domesticated family man. Sally Quinn claimed that since his divorce in the 1950s, he had been faithful to Sánchez and the two kept their marriage secret for security reasons.[23]

Other journalists debated whether Castro made room in his life for romantic relationships at all.[24] Casting him as a "monastic" hermit with no permanent residence, they theorized that he avoided romance for security reasons, that he simply had no time for personal relationships, or that he purposely cultivated a "mystery" around his love life in order to maintain international intrigue.[25] Hoffman noted only that "Fidel's private life, if he has one, is impenetrable."[26] Another reporter suggested that he might be gay.[27] At the other extreme, some journalists cast Castro as a Latin playboy who entertained the world's most beautiful actresses and socialites. Photos of him standing surrounded by adoring female fans evoked contemporary images of pop icons like the Beatles and Elvis Presley.[28] The most Castro ever said on the subject occurred during a 1977 televised interview with Barbara Walters in which he stated that he was not married in the "bourgeois sense."[29] This response only fueled speculation about his romantic life.

Sánchez, like Castro, remained famously silent on the subject of her personal life, which bolstered press interest in the subject. Reporters were puzzled that Sánchez and Castro often acted as a unit in ways that blurred the line between colleagues and consorts, even serving as godparents to U.S. journalist and photographer Andrew St. George's son.[30] Eager to weave a love story for the two revolutionary leaders, some journalists presented Sánchez as a woman who once enjoyed an intimate, albeit ill-fated, relationship with Castro. They described it as a romance born of the tense and isolated life of the Sierra Maestra, where rebels lived for years without regular contact with family and friends back home. They claimed that Sánchez pined for a return to those days, but had settled for the role as secretary to the president in order to remain close to Castro. St. George quoted one of Sánchez's (unnamed) childhood friends as stating, "She stayed on as Castro's chief of staff and discussed with him all the country's needs, without ever so much as hinting at her own—a husband."[31] Her own sister Acacia, a married mother of two children, was quoted in St. George's *Parade* article as saying, "If you could ask my proud sister Celia if she wanted to relive her life again in a different way, she might tell you 'yes, Acacia's way.'"[32]

The U.S. press seemed almost wholly incapable of dealing with a woman who was powerful and influential but who might not actually be married to, or at least sleeping with, a male leader. The press returned perennially to speculation about the sexual nature of their relationship. The other female revolutionary leaders with this kind of (at least perceived) influence on the island—Espín and Santamaría, for example—were married to influential male leaders (Raúl Castro and Hart Dávalos, respectively). The status of these women as wives provided an easy explanation for their influence while also allowing the U.S. press to largely dismiss them as leaders in their own right.[33]

Sánchez was not such an easy case, and the struggle to categorize her pre-occupied the U.S. press for more than two decades. Only one U.S. article published during this period refers to Sánchez's rumored teenage boyfriend, Salvador Sadurní, who died following surgery, and to her rumored love for the tragic reform leader Eduardo Chibás, who shot himself in 1951 during his weekly radio program and later died.[34] Sánchez was thus presented as a woman without a significant romantic past or present outside of her relationship with Castro.

In the same way that she was a romantic blank slate, U.S. journalists rarely discussed Sánchez's life before the revolution, which implied that it was either unknown or unimportant to the story that the press wanted to tell about her. Few articles focused on her family background or childhood, except to emphasize how and where it connected her to the revolutionary cause and to Castro. In most cases she was described simply as the "moderately wealthy daughter of a rural doctor."[35] Her life mattered most where it was tied to Castro and to the revolution. Journalists thus repeatedly noted that Sánchez and Castro both grew up in the island's easternmost Oriente Province. As a product of "his beloved mountains," journalists claimed that she understood Castro and the people he claimed to represent. She was a home-town girl who kept him connected to his roots, which helped explain their apparent mutual trust.

One early story that appeared in several newspapers across the United States in February 1959 underscored the power of these shared roots. During the years of fighting, Castro had promised the people of Bayamo that when the war was over he would return with Christmas gifts for the children living in that area. Making good on his promise, Sánchez organized an air drop of an estimated sixty tons of toys, food, and clothing over thousands of agricultural workers, farmers, and their families who came for the celebration.[36] According to the story, each red and black box (the colors of the M-26-7) featured a note: "To the real Cuban people, the families of the Sierra, collected throughout Cuba by Celia. Patriots, brothers, share this with your neighbor." There was no need to include Sánchez's last name on the notes, as she was already known to them as "Cuba's most famous woman," and as one of their own.[37]

Without knowing about Sánchez's long history of giving toys to rural children, this story broadcast Sánchez's positive influence on Castro and the revolution in several ways. Not only did it declare that she had the power to hold him to his promises, but that she understood the importance of maintaining his rural base of support in the Sierra. Press coverage of this project provided a vision of Sánchez not only as "Castro's devoted assistant," but also as a strategist. That she shared deep roots with Castro's childhood and to the mythologized origin of the revolution made her a special asset to Cubans.

The U.S. media initially offered a fairly adulatory, even romanticized, portrait of Sánchez, her relationship with Castro, and her strategic importance for the Cuban Revolution.[38] In all cases, early U.S. press coverage of Sánchez collapsed the political dimensions of her position within the revolutionary apparatus, which made her image easy to manipulate. Without details about her life, her background, or her accomplishments, the American public could easily accept any recasting of her persona. When the tenor of U.S-Cuban relations deteriorated beginning in early 1960, the U.S. press refracted depictions of Sánchez through the lens of growing disenchantment with the Cuban Revolution and its leadership. The result was a new and increasingly negative assessment of her position. Depictions of both Sánchez and Castro, like the entire revolutionary project, underwent a dramatic change during this period. The "woman behind Castro" was cast as a potentially dangerous influence on Cuban state policy in general, and on Castro in particular.

El Barbudo and La Sardina

The December 1958 entry into Havana of the victorious rebel army is one of the watershed moments of modern world history. In its wake, both the future of Cuba and the landscape of global diplomacy were profoundly reimagined. U.S. political and corporate interests watched expectantly in the initial months following the rebel triumph to see what course Castro would set for the island. They had no way of knowing how quickly the two countries would stand at the brink of nuclear war with the missile crisis of October 1962.[39] Filtered through the lens of broader Cold War tensions, Castro's audacious move toward agrarian reform, the expropriation of foreign-owned properties, and the nationalization of industry beginning in May 1959 sent shock waves through the Western hemisphere and beyond. Though he continued to deny until the eve of the Bay of Pigs invasion (17 April 1961) that he was pursuing the creation of a socialist revolution, Castro's critics were increasingly dubious about the island's accelerated radicalization.

For the Kennedy administration, Castro's new policies threatened to undermine the future of democracy and private enterprise, the dual imperatives of post–World War II U.S. political discourse. For an emerging global New Left seeking social revolution, Cuba's radical new policies—which Castro framed as necessary to secure a "Cuba for Cubans' sake"—provided a model for securing true political sovereignty and economic self-sufficiency in the face of American imperialism.[40] For many Cubans, especially those whose own economic interests were threatened by these new policies, Castro had betrayed the revolution and the country. Plane loads of wealthy families carrying suitcases bulging with precious family heirlooms fled the island to wait for the Castro regime's collapse. Most of those families never returned to the island.

Depictions of Sánchez's relationship with Castro, her influence within the Cuban revolutionary state more generally, and even her looks were refracted through the lens of these broader (faltering) geopolitics. Just as she was linked to Castro's power, influence, and masculine virility in 1959, she became linked to his perceived weakness, degeneration, and "impotence" after 1960. On 12 January 1960, several U.S. newspapers ran an article titled "We Were Wrong about Castro."[41] The tag line for the piece read "Cuba's bearded boy wonder came in on a wave of rosy promises, but now his disillusioned countrymen are starting to laugh at him."[42] The lead photo captured one of the most dramatic and iconic moments following the triumph of the Cuban Revolution. While delivering a victory speech to a large crowd of Cubans gathered at Camp Columbia on 8 January 1959, someone released three white doves, one of which landed on Castro's shoulder.[43] Supporters of the revolution saw the dove's landing as a sign that the Cuban Revolution (and its principal leader) had received the blessing of the Afro-Cuban deity Obatalá.[44]

The photo of Castro with the dove, which detractors asserted was staged, became a key piece in the visual iconography of the Cuban Revolution. It represented the early hope and euphoria experienced by many Cubans eager for reassurances of a promising future ahead. The decision to lead the article with this particular photo was both strategic and powerful. The author, Stanley Ross, warned that, like Cuban supporters on the island, the U.S. public had been duped by the imagery, rhetoric, and fanfare surrounding the rebels. Caught up in a wave of romance and hero worship, the U.S. public had been conned by the "idol of Latin America" who "set masculine pulses racing and feminine hearts pounding."[45]

Just one year following his exuberant entry into Havana, Ross proclaimed, the truth about Castro had been revealed. Not only was Castro "not the brave military hero" that he had presented himself as, he had actually "bought victories." Furthermore, he was not even the great Latin lover that his supporters had depicted. Much to the disappointment of "the volatile Cubans who make a fetish of being he-men machos," Castro was reportedly a "lousy lover" and a total "failure in the boudoir." Ross noted with disgust that "Fidel's reputed failure in the boudoir can be almost as serious as his irresponsible economic and political acts which have wrenched Cuban-American relations and taken Cuba almost to the fringe of the Iron Curtain." Since Ross believed that Castro's masculine failures were at least as problematic as his menacing new policies, he discussed them before providing a laundry list of Castro's (ten) unkept political and economic promises. That Castro had failed to make good on his promises of freedom of the press, free elections, and cooperation with the United States mattered, to be sure, but so did the fact that Castro had failed to live up to his macho image. The author linked these failures to reports of declining attendance at public rallies since the heady days of the dove landing one year earlier.

The only other Cuban revolutionary leader referenced by name or depicted visually in the article was Sánchez. Ross chose to include an image of her that was taken on her first trip to the United States as part of Castro's diplomatic entourage, and shows her dressed for a formal evening event. The caption to the image reads "Jokes about Fidel's romantic prowess are spurred by the fact that the one woman in his public life is Celia Sánchez, who seems to love only Communism."[46] Within the text of the article, Ross provides his singularly unflattering description of Sánchez as a "willowy, pinch-faced, sallow woman with sparkling eyes, yellow teeth, and a steel trap for a brain, which can rattle off the exact number of bales of cotton produced in any of the Soviet Union's provinces. Sánchez, an 18-karat Communist who recently made her third trip to the Red Mecca, is not Cuba's idea of the kind of mistress its handsome leader should sport. Yet, much of his disastrously pro-Red, anti-American policies can be traced to her." Foregrounding her failure to conform to Ross's conception of ideal feminine beauty, in the same way that he had foregrounded Castro's sexual failures, he concedes that Sánchez is brilliant. Ross warns, however, that the real threat to U.S.-Cuban relations may not be Cuba's controversial prime minister, but rather his mysterious secretary-mistress.

The "We Were Wrong" article, which was reproduced in a number of U.S. periodicals in January 1960, emerged at a pivotal moment in the complex history of U.S.-Cuban relations. Not only did the article reflect a broader decline in U.S.-Cuban political relations that soon led to a complete severing of economic and diplomatic ties; it also offered a reimagined discourse on two of Cuba's most visible leaders. The article undercut Castro's sexual, military, and intellectual prowess—hallmarks of the imagery surrounding the male rebel leadership that had previously circulated in the United States—with insinuations of impotence on all fronts.

That Sánchez's influence over Castro was cast in both intellectual and sexual terms underscored her power while simultaneously questioning Castro's own. Mocking, almost grotesque, descriptions of her physical appearance, however, were clearly intended to demean Sánchez as a woman—a common weapon used to undercut the authority of political women—and create a chink in her otherwise formidable armor. Caricaturing the two revolutionary leaders in gendered, sexual terms was an attempt to destabilize the dominant, romanticized imagery surrounding the revolution. If the U.S. public had initially been duped by imagery depicting the revolution as one aligned with American values and helmed by admirable and sympathetic leaders, this article, and the hundreds like it to come, excused American—and even Cuban—readers for being collectively hoodwinked ("We Were Wrong"). At the same time, the author urged Americans to immediately reorient and reformulate their imaginings of the Cuban Revolution so as to be ready for the conflicts ahead.

The brand of revolutionary femininity that U.S. journalists had applauded in their early assessments of life in the Sierra Maestra proved a double-edged sword for Cuban women, and Sánchez especially, when U.S.-Cuban relations began to cool in early 1960. Journalists quickly began to revisit and retool the narrative of female revolutionary participation to reflect the United States' revised stance on its island neighbor. If the original reading of the revolution was erroneous, the original casting of the rebels as moderate and like-minded allies was also false. Sánchez emerged in the U.S. press over the course of 1959 as the most visible female revolutionary leader. She was thus first in the discursive line of fire after 1960.[47] As in the January 1960 "We Were Wrong" article, journalists stressed the precarious nature of her influence over the revolutionary project and its principal leader. They questioned her political motivations and ideological commitment while mocking her physical appearance in ways that inverted the earlier language and imagery used to describe women rebels operating in the Sierra Maestra. The result was the recasting of the Cuban revolutionary woman, and especially Sánchez, as someone to distrust and even fear, just as Americans were encouraged to fear and reject the revolution as a whole.

The most noticeable change related to descriptions of Sánchez following the shift in U.S.-Cuba relations related to her physical appearance. Journalists focused increasing attention on Sánchez's looks, eager to connect her appearance to her power and influence. Sánchez was, of course, not the only female political figure in Cuba whose looks garnered press interest. When three women—Teresa Casuso, Conchita Fernández, and Sánchez— accompanied Castro to Washington, D.C., following the triumph of the revolution, published commentary made special note that the women were all "well-dressed and trim."[48] In Robert Berrellez's 27 November 1960 *Morning Advocate* article titled "Women Perform Vital Tasks in Castro's Government," he made special mention of how the "tight-fitting blue shirt and tighter-fitting olive drab slacks" worn by female members of Cuba's civilian militia drew a "symphony of wolf whistles from the usually irrepressible Cuban."[49]

While the U.S. press had never described Sánchez as beautiful, the most generous descriptions of her features prior to 1960 described her as "trim and handsome." Errol Flynn's physical description of her in February 1959 was more eroticizing and misogynistic than complimentary. Flynn had visited the Sierra in December of the previous year and included his "clinical Hollywood eye" estimation of Sánchez's measurements in order to make the point that she was too thin to represent the Cuban ideal of beauty.[50] The language used to describe Sánchez's physical appearance became markedly harsher as the general opinion of the Castro regime shifted after 1960. From a trim and handsome woman, she becomes a pinch-faced shrew with yellow teeth caused by years of smoking.[51] Journalists began to reference a rumored nickname for her, "*La Sardina*" (sardine), which contrasted her with the stereotypical Cuban curvaceous ideal as "colorless and without curves."[52] Many reporters noted that they were perplexed that Castro would choose to associate so closely with a woman they deemed unattractive when he had access to any number of adoring young women. The "We Were Wrong" article proclaimed that "Sánchez . . . is not the kind of mistress its handsome leader should sport."[53]

One of the key images for highlighting the shift in the perception of Sánchez's physical appearance is a photo that appeared in the U.S. press numerous times over the years. In fact, it appeared more often than any other single photo of her. The photo (of unknown origin) depicts Sánchez wearing fatigues and a beret and applying lipstick (figure 7).[54] The first appearance of the photo in the 27 November 1960 edition of the *Milwaukee*

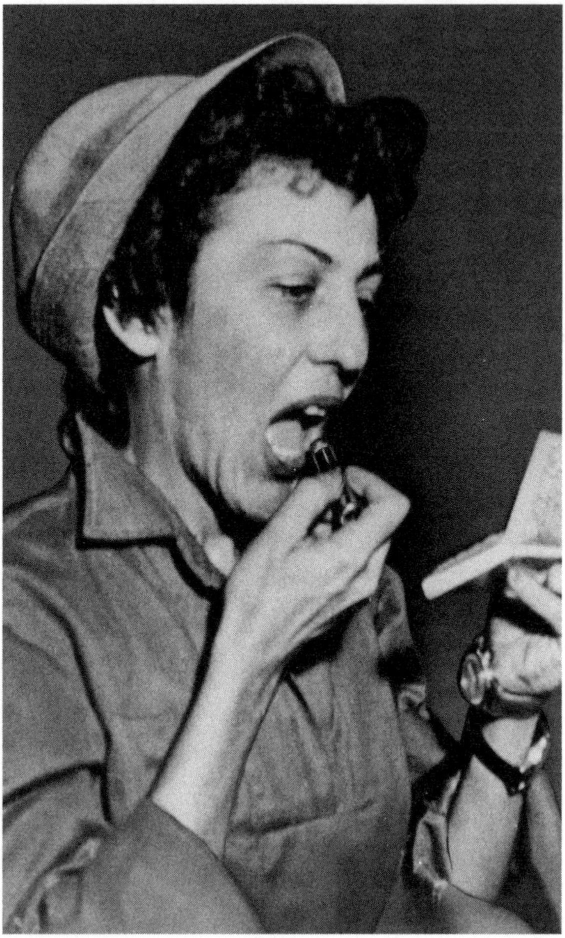

FIGURE 7 *Fatigues and Lipstick*. © AP Photo.

Journal Sentinel echoed early depictions of women operating in the Sierra Maestra as eager to maintain their femininity despite the privations of war. Attending to her appearance even when dressed in green drab, the new Cuban woman was cast as both rebellious and feminine. Commentary on Sánchez's attention to her appearance were not new. In her January 1959 article titled "The Woman in Fidel's Life," journalist Phyllis Battelle noted that within thirty-six hours of the rebels' triumphal entry into Havana, Sánchez had changed clothes and was wearing an "orange knitted dress and huge crescent-shaped gold and pearl earrings . . . she was a lady again."[55]

After 1960, however, the fatigues-and-lipstick photo became the standard image to include in articles that mocked and disparaged Sánchez.

Reading the image alongside the text of the articles in which it was used reveals that journalists intended to imply that Sánchez was completely self-absorbed and disconnected from the problems of the Castro regime. Desperate to secure the affections of a man (Castro) who did not love her, she allowed her vanity to cloud her judgment as a political figure. The *Milwaukee Journal* ran the image above a text line citing the "number of women [who] hold key posts in Castro's regime" and alongside the subheading: "Sánchez Is No Charmer."[56] The Miami newspaper *La Verdad* ran the image on its 15 January 1980 cover to herald Sánchez's death. The magnified image ran under inflammatory, dual headings: "Lover, Bodyguard, and 'Advisor' to the Executioner, Celia Sánchez" and "Conflict in Cuba: Was Celia Sánchez Assassinated?"[57] Notably, this particular Sánchez image never appeared in Cuban newspapers—it was entirely the product of U.S.-produced imaginings of her.

The heavily circulated image of Sánchez in fatigues applying lipstick initially suggested a kind of marriage of femininity and power before 1960, but thereafter became a means to undercut the sanctity of her commitment to the revolution. Attacking Sánchez's femininity became a means to mock and belittle her, even as reporters never questioned her power and influence. Negative descriptions of Sánchez's physical appearance after 1960 pointed to a question that remained unanswered for many journalists: If the source of her influence over Castro did not reside in her physical appearance or sexuality, then what exactly *was* the source of her influence? Furthermore, journalists questioned whether that influence was beneficial or detrimental to the Cuban Revolution.

The Woman behind Castro

While pre-1960 reports tended to portray Sánchez as a supportive and generally positive presence in Castro's life, after 1960 reporters increasingly cast her as wily, manipulative, and even dangerous. One anecdote that appeared several times over the years—but never in Cuba—posited that Sánchez had single-handedly subverted an important military maneuver in the Sierra Maestra. As the story was told, Castro had ordered the troops in the Sierra Maestra to march to a new location, but Sánchez intervened stating that "dinner was cooking." Rather than continue with the march as planned, Castro chose to delay the operation. The late departure left the troops stranded in the mountains mid-trek, forcing them to make camp in the dark. Journalists noted the folly of Castro's decision to heed a woman's bad counsel.[58] That he followed her orders to the detriment of his own raised the question of whether or not Castro was capable of making his own decisions. An inversion of the positive role U.S. journalists attributed to women in the Sierra Maestra prior to 1960, this anecdote, and others like it, cast Sánchez as a domesticated danger to the revolution.

There were also suggestions that Sánchez was not above getting rid of women whom she feared might usurp her position in Castro's life. While she might have tolerated his one-night stands, she moved quickly to remove serious female threats.[59] On the opening page of his article "The Woman behind Castro," St. George captioned a photo of Sánchez standing behind Castro in a room filled with staff members—where one female appears to be embracing Castro—with the line, "Cuba's woman in the background, Celia Sánchez (at door), coolly eyes aide's embrace of Castro."[60] Several U.S. journalists suggested that Cuban revolutionary Teresa Casuso and U.S. soldier of fortune June Cobb were both "banished" on Sánchez's order because they had grown too close to Castro.[61] Casuso received an appointment to the United Nations in 1960 and Cobb returned suddenly to the United States that same year after serving as a translator for Castro, initially at Sánchez's invitation. In his testimony before a Senate internal security subcommittee in 1959, when directly questioned on the matter by Senator Jules G. Sourwine, the former director general of the Office of the Prime Minister, Juan Orta, denied that Sánchez dismissed Cobb. Allegations continued to circulate, however, that Sánchez's jealousy shaped her administrative actions.[62]

The U.S. press further speculated that Sánchez's problems with other women extended to her fellow female revolutionary leaders. One article mentioned infighting between Sánchez and Espín, stating: "Now there is woman trouble in Cuba between Celia Sánchez, close companion of Castro, and Vilma Espín, wife of [Castro's] brother Raúl Castro. Both women are reported as jockeying for power in the Cuban communist hierarchy. . . . A third woman, Haydée Santamaría, has also risen to power in Cuba, but isn't involved in the feud."[63] Here again Sánchez is cast not as a dedicated civil servant—as she had been before the summer of 1960—but rather as strategic, conniving, and power hungry. Some journalists even suggested that her rumored affair with Castro in the Sierra Maestra was less about true affection on her part than about gaining access to power.

U.S. journalists never questioned Sánchez's intelligence, even when they disparaged the nature of her knowledge. On 16 April 1959, one U.S. journalist offered vaguely that Sánchez "acts and reacts like a Communist," without offering any explanation for that assertion.[64] The January 1960 "We Were

Wrong" article noted that she had a "steel trap for a brain . . . which can rattle off the exact number of bales of cotton produced in any of the Soviet Union's provinces."[65] Other journalists writing after 1960, however, began to challenge the sincerity of her professed commitment to communism.[66] This line of questioning may well have been influenced by a series of ongoing Senate internal security subcommittee hearings on "Communist Influence in the Caribbean" (1951–77) conducted by Senator Jules G. Sourwine.[67] In those hearings, which centered in large part on identifying the source of communist tendencies within the revolutionary state, Sánchez was the only leader whose status as a "true Communist" was ever questioned.

In one set of hearings conducted on 22–23 January 1960, Captain Alfonso Manuel Rojo Roche, former chief of parachute troops in Castro's army, listed her as an "insincere [suspect]" communist while confirming that the other leaders (Guevara, Raúl Castro, Espín, etc.) were all devoted, and dangerous, fanatics.[68] None of the members of the Senate committee, nor Sourwine himself, ever pushed for clarification as to why Sánchez was repeatedly singled out as potentially "insincere" in her political orientation. June Cobb offered a similar assessment of Sánchez's political leanings during her March 1962 deposition, claiming, "No, I was quite sure she could not be [a communist]." Senator Sourwine appeared satisfied with Cobb's response and did not request that she elaborate further.[69]

It is unclear to what extent the Senate hearings may have colored press assessments of Sánchez's ideological orientation, but several journalists writing after 1960 insinuated that Sánchez was only "pretending" to be a communist. These accusations, which ran directly counter to her portrayal within Cuba as a devoted communist, especially after her death, challenged Sánchez's personal integrity and loyalty to Castro while also calling into question Castro's ability to count on (or control) those closest to him. Was she merely a ruthless strategist capable of great manipulations in order to remain within Castro's inner circle? St. George reported that Sánchez's own sister, Graciela, questioned her sister's professed communist alignment. Sánchez's simulated compliance with communism, Graciela argued, provided a means to maintain a hold over Castro after the end of their love affair in the Sierra Maestra.[70] In short, her decision to adopt communism was considered more strategic than ideological.

Questions about the sincerity of Sánchez's ideological orientation persist in other evaluations of Cuba's revolutionary history. Historian Hugh Thomas rather dismissively counts Sánchez among the Castro loyalists who "would probably have followed whatever policy he decided on."[71] While Sánchez never addressed in writing or in an interview any questions about her personal politics, when I asked my interviewees over the years to rank the order of the various elements of her political ideology, they almost always provided the following assessment: (1) *fidelista*, (2) *martiana*, (3) socialist/communist. Interviewees shared their belief that Sánchez aligned herself with Castro's vision for Cuba—as embryonic as it was at that time—from her initial weeks in the Sierra Maestra, because his message resonated with José Martí's deep patriotic nationalism. Her faith in Castro's leadership was complete and unfailing, they argued, and her intellectual nature was elastic enough to accommodate the necessary shift toward socialism and communism as a means to secure Martí's failed dream of sovereignty. One family member assured me that, despite U.S. government reports to the contrary, Sánchez sincerely embraced both socialism and communism from its earliest appearance within the triumphant government's revolutionary discourse.

Without an explicit statement from Sánchez about the sincerity of her alignment with the revolution's radicalizing politics after 1959, it is difficult to prove or disprove her position. I believe, however, that Sánchez's ideology radicalized along the same trajectory as the other leaders who, as devout nationalists, turned to socialism and communism as powerful weapons to repudiate encroaching "Yankee imperialism" and define the terms of a new society in more egalitarian terms. Both socialism and communism had been, after all, on Sánchez's radar since her childhood exposure to Marx via her father's studies and through her cousin's work with Joven Cuba. They were not new concepts to her. As for the sincerity of her beliefs, we know only that her official capacity within the revolutionary government extended beyond her role as secretary to the president to include seats on the Communist Party's Central Committee and the National Assembly. Her position at the innermost core of revolutionary state power indicates that in both word and action she had demonstrated to Cuba's political elite her ideological compatibility.

The notion that Sánchez's communist identity might be feigned opened the door to other kinds of speculation about her political loyalties and alignments. Could she be cultivated, or indeed had she already been cultivated, as an asset by the U.S. government? On 28 July 1971, the *Boston Record American* published an uncorroborated story that Sánchez had traveled to a Boston hospital by way of Puerto Rico under an assumed identity and with the protection of the Nixon government. The article suggested that the White House had granted Sánchez safe passage to the United States to seek treatment for an inner-ear injury caused when she was "struck on the head by falling debris." The hospital director denied the report, as he surely would even if the story was true.[72] While the story is suspicious (the author does not cite his or her source), it did insinuate that Sánchez enjoyed special protection from the State Department. Her own sister Graciela Sánchez, who lived in Miami, hinted that sibling status granted her special protections by the U.S. government because it viewed her as a direct line to Sánchez and, presumably, to Castro.[73]

To be sure, depictions of Castro shifted after 1960 as well. If the U.S. press had originally described him as a promising visionary, after 1960 he was more frequently depicted as an immature, overweight, and even impotent (sexually, politically, and militarily) buffoon who bought his military victories and was "lousy in bed." In the same way that Sánchez's personal life and appearance came under heavy fire after 1960, U.S. journalists attacked Castro's sexuality in order to undercut his political authority. At stake was Castro's literal and metaphorical virility. Sánchez was implicated in this reforging of the *barbudo* image in the U.S. press. Earlier stories that she helped Castro pack his suitcases, clean his house, and organize his entire life — which were initially offered as proof of her devotion and organizational capacity — now stood as proof that Castro was incapable of handling his own business. Some U.S. journalists went so far as to speculate that she was, in fact, the real brains of Castro's operation.

In 1965 rumors even began to circulate that Sánchez was in consideration for the Cuban presidency after Osvaldo Dorticós Torrado stepped down.[74] Ironically titled articles claimed that the "Woman behind Castro" might soon step out of his shadow to "become the first female President of Cuba"[75] Geyer also offered in her 1966 article on the position of women in Cuba that "[Sánchez] has been spoken of as a possible President."[76] When I asked Sánchez's family and friends about the rumors of a presidency, they all adamantly denied any such possibility. Family friend Bécquer Céspedes stated that "Celia was never considered [for that position], nor would she have wanted to be. Castro was the person to realize her dreams for the revolution and she knew her strengths well."[77]

Whether or not Sánchez was ever considered for the presidency, speculation of that nature in the U.S. press underscored Sánchez's perceived power. It also called into question Castro's own capacity for leadership. If Sánchez was the real captain of the revolution, what was Castro's role? Was he somehow in over his head or not cut out for the job? In her 1977 *Washington Post* article, Quinn argued that Castro needed a woman's approval. "His posture changes when he talks to a woman. The confidence and assurance diminishes. . . . He needs approval from a woman."[78] Questions about Castro's dependence on Sánchez surged following her death in 1980 when friends and critics alike noted that Castro seemed disoriented and adrift during the Mariel Boatlift crisis. They reported that he appeared to be operating in a fog, even coming apart at the seams, and wondered if he was capable of governing without Sánchez.

Battles over Image and Meaning

Despite the scope and depth of Sánchez's influence in Cuba, the revolutionary government published only a few photos and brief notices about her public appearances between 1959 and 1980. The Cuban press—which falls under the purview of the national government—framed an image of the revolution as made and maintained by men. When Sánchez did appear in a newspaper, it was almost always a single image embedded in a photomontage, and never as the focus of a feature article. She is almost always shown standing directly at Castro's side, interacting with children, or within a group of other officials.

Sánchez was, however, included in a popular commemorative album of collectible cards published in 1959. The album was intended as a means to teach young audiences the history of the Cuban Revolution. Rendered in cartoon form, the 268 cards in the set give a chronology of basic events and highlight critical players. Only two of those cards include Sánchez, though a few other women are honored in the collection. One card dedicated to Sánchez shows the "first woman to join Castro's forces" in fatigues and carrying her rifle; the second card depicts her standing with a group of other female rebels, including Santamaría.[79] In both cards Sánchez's significance is relational, as it was in print press coverage. She is bound to either the supreme male leader of the revolution or to other women (figure 8).

In general, the Cuban government offered no real counter-narrative to U.S. depictions of Sánchez during this period. The global New Left—enamored though they were with Cuba's male revolutionary heroes—paid almost no attention to the female leaders. With so little published information about Sánchez's life, role, and influence coming out of Cuba or globally prior to her death in 1980, the U.S. press was largely dealing with a blank slate. Depictions of Sánchez operated in a kind of discursive echo chamber that promoted the heavy recycling of a few canned, stereotypical images.

85.—Para eludir el fuego de los aviones envia-
dos en su persecución, los revolucionarios se
dividen en grupos, tratando de llegar a la
Sierra Maestra.

88.—Celia Sánchez, es la primera mujer que
se une a las fuerzas de Fidel Castro coope-
rando intensamente en la organización y los
trabajos iniciales.

FIGURE 8 Collectible card in the *Albúm de la Revolución*, 1959. Cuban Miscellaneous Collection, Special and Area Studies Collections, George A. Smathers Libraries, University of Florida, Gainesville, Florida.

Sánchez also rarely appeared within the Miami-based print press for the period 1959–80, a silence likely intended to deny and deflate her importance within the revolutionary apparatus. References to Sánchez in the *Miami Herald* did increase briefly during the late 1970s alongside growing concern with the island's faltering economy. Critiques of extreme food shortages and a general lack of construction, especially of housing, were linked to a failure of leadership at the top. Journalists criticized what they perceived as a growing obliviousness to the daily hardships borne by average citizens on the part of the "super elite of the new class" of Cuba's career revolutionary politicians.[80]

In March 1977, the *Miami Herald* ran a pointed editorial that stated: "Neither Celia Sánchez, nor Vilma Espín, nor any of the lovers of the *sacatripas* [disemboweler] Castro, nor any of this new class that created the Communist regime, have to stand in lines, nor do they have to eat the same [as others]."[81] Even Sánchez's iconic Coppelia ice cream park came under fire, "The Coppelia ice cream park at 23 and L [Streets] stands as a portrait of Cuba and Castro with its enormous hunger lines, just like the 'pizzerias' and everywhere else that they sell 'something' to eat."[82] The press claimed that the situation in Cuba under Castro had become so intolerable that family members of the top leaders, including Sánchez's own siblings, "detest and censure what their family members are doing and when they are behind closed doors and under their covers they mock the official rhetoric of these hawks."[83]

The real surge in print references to Sánchez within Cuba occurred following her death in 1980. As they battled over image and meaning more broadly, Cubans living on the island and in Miami volleyed depictions of Sánchez as either a revolutionary heroine or as a dangerous force. Her death also coincided with a particularly precarious moment for the revolution in which it became imperative that the government find a way to reorient and rally the Cuban people. The timing of her death allowed for the creation of a new revolutionary iconography meant to instill a sense of renewed purpose and hope in a future that seemed increasingly uncertain. In a situation in which all of the key revolutionary leaders were either still living or had been dead for years (Guevara, Cienfuegos, etc.), the creation of a new icon—and its first *female* revolutionary icon—provided a unique opportunity to forge new meanings during an era of significant national and global challenges to socialism.

CHAPTER SEVEN

Toward the Gates of Eternity

Death of a Revolutionary Heroine

Silence! Celia has died!

—ALEIDA RIVERO SUÁREZ, "Celia de todos los días"

In our Plaza of mourning
The grief-stricken processed
But Celia has not gone
Because she is loved by all.

—EDENIA HERNÁNDEZ GARCÍA, "A la flor de la Revolución"

Havana's City of the Dead

Making a right turn off of Vedado's bustling 23rd Avenue in April 2018, I strolled one short block up 12th Street past a kaleidoscopic row of flower vendors with plastic buckets filled with roses and lilies. A few individuals held handmade cardboard signs offering to engrave stone plaques or grave markers for a fee. Weaving my way through these assorted vendors, I crossed the final street that separated me from the grandiose marble gate into Havana's Colón Cemetery. Considered the second most important cemetery in Latin America behind the Recoleta cemetery in Buenos Aires, Argentina, the Colón Cemetery was founded in 1876 and now covers forty acres and contains over 500 mausoleums and 800,000 graves. The cemetery's massive northern gate features a triple arch meant to evoke the Holy Trinity, and the cemetery itself is laid out like a crucifix with two broad, tree-lined avenues that intersect at an ornate chapel. I paid the entrance fee and made my way toward the opposite side of the cemetery.

Strolling down the main avenue, I passed the ornate marble mausoleums dedicated to Cuban independence war heroes Carlos Céspedes, Calixto García, and Máximo Gómez, as well as the tomb of the famous Afro-Cuban singer and musician Ibrahim Ferrer, best known for his collaborations with the internationally successful Buena Vista Social Club ensemble. When I reached the towering funeral statue honoring the twenty-five firemen killed in Havana's devastating 1890 fire, I cut left toward the most famous gravesite in the entire cemetery. I could see a handful of people gathering at the end of the row of graves. I shared a brief greeting with the attendant, whom I had met during a prior visit to the cemetery, and joined the short queue of individuals waiting to approach her grave. Amelia Goyri, or "La Milagrosa," is Havana's most beloved secular saint. Wrapped in mystery and romance, her grave is a pilgrimage site for thousands of Cubans and Cuban Americans each year. Born to an elite family, Goyri was a noted Havana beauty who married the love of her life at a young age and then died tragically in childbirth in May 1901. Her devastated husband buried his deceased wife and child together with the infant placed at Goyri's feet, as was customary. He visited the grave several times a day for the rest of his life and dutifully performed a complex ritual at each visit. He attached four metal rings to the corners of her burial vault, which he knocked in succession. Refusing to ever turn his back to his departed wife, he walked backward from her graveside. When her body was exhumed years later she was found—according to popular mythology—completely intact and with the baby now resting in her arms.[1]

The line of devotees at Goyri's grave on the day of my visit was made up entirely of women. Three young women were dressed completely in white, signaling their status as initiates into Santería, an Afro-Cuban syncretic religion combining Yoruba and Catholic customs and beliefs. Each woman prayed softly until it was her turn to approach the grave. She then performed the same circumambulatory ritual first crafted by Goyri's husband, knocking with each of the four rings, softly stroking the statue that now stands at the head of the grave—which features Goyri holding her infant in her arms—and slowly backing away from the grave without turning her back. Some of the women offered their prayers to Goyri aloud, asking for assistance with infertility or for an easy childbirth. One older woman laid an ornately embroidered robe over the statue and offered her gratitude for Goyri's help. Through tears she announced audibly that she had promised to return to Cuba and dress Goyri's baby if she would help her family get to Miami. She thanked Goyri repeatedly and told everyone in the line that she had now completed her "*promesa*" (promise).

The graves surrounding Goyri's are completely covered with small plaques, flowers, and other small offerings. The vast majority of the plaques offer gratitude to Goyri for the miracle of conceiving and delivering a healthy child—some of whom were named in her honor—but others offer thanks for cured illnesses, financial windfalls, and emigration out of Cuba. A small handmade dollhouse placed on a nearby grave featured a plaque stating: "This is the beautiful home in Miami that my family now owns. We are so thankful to you, Amelia, for this miracle." Nearby, a yellowed diploma in a frame celebrated the Miami Senior High School graduation of a woman with the middle name Amelia. After taking a few photographs and hugging the attendant goodbye, I made my way back to the cemetery's main avenue, passed the central chapel, and headed toward the mausoleum dedicated to Cuba's FAR, where Sánchez's remains rest.

As I walked I reflected on the connections between these two burial sites. Both Goyri and Sánchez are women who have been subject to a mythification process. The historical identity of both women is refracted through a set of ideals—sacrificial womanhood, maternal care, service to the Cuban people—that may or may not reflect the realities of who they really were. As the embodiment of these abstracted ideals, however, both women wield incredible power. Reflecting on Eva Perón's postmortem influence, Taylor noted that "her continuing importance and popularity may be attributed not only to her power as a woman but also to the power of the dead."[2] Operating outside the parameters of life, of fact, of rules—but not of meaning—both women have burst the subjective seams of their individual biographies. One family member asserted that "Celia was certainly no saint," yet truth may occupy little space within the realm of mythology.[3]

Both Goyri and Sánchez lived during times of seismic political and social change in Cuba—the war of independence and the Cuban Revolution, respectively—and both are treated with the kind of solemn, deferential reverence one might expect of a secular saint. Goyri's devotees seek her spiritual counsel and protection, while Sánchez's admirers venerate her as a political role model. The long lines of supplicants who now gather at Goyri's graveside beseeching an easy pregnancy mirrors the long lines who gathered to speak with Sánchez when she made public appearances or sent letters to her office. Goyri and Sánchez were both raised in economically privileged families, but Goyri was never famous in life. Sánchez was famous in life, but her personal life is not the center of her legacy as it is for Goyri. While Sánchez is associated with politics in ways that Goyri is not, it is not the high politics of diplomatic negotiation or policy making for which Sánchez is best known, but rather for the same kind of quasi-maternal care and concern that draws women to Goyri's grave. Both women are the subject of prayers, or poetry written in a prayerful voice, that elevates them to the status of secular saints within a broader female-centered popular religiosity positioned in the interstices of Catholicism and Santerísmo.[4]

I noted, however, a generational difference between the two women's admirers. Goyri's devotees are often young—still in their childbearing years—while most of Sánchez's most loyal fans bore witness to the triumph of the revolution. The comparison raises the question of how the inevitable death of Cuba's revolutionary generation will impact Sánchez's legacy. Cuban friends tell me that their school-aged children receive relatively little information about Sánchez in their history classes. Their textbooks focus only on Sánchez's role in the armed phase of the revolution, rather than on her later projects and accomplishments.[5] La Milagrosa appears to have endured the test of time (for now), but what story will future generations tell about Sánchez?

Approaching the south wall of the cemetery, I noted a familiar pair of royal palms towering on either side of an imposing rectangular mausoleum. Two bronze soldiers flank the entrance to the concrete structure. One soldier is saluting and the other stands at ease with his rifle. A large Cuban flag flutters on a flagpole nearby. Two double-sided wings of numbered cement crypts extend out from an archway, and Sánchez's crypt—one of the few that is permanently sealed—sits within the left wing. The only distinguishing markers on the otherwise nondescript crypt are the number "43" and a rose tucked behind the torch-shaped crypt knob (figure 9).

Funeral Rites for a Revolutionary Heroine

> The funeral procession for Celia Sánchez Manduley, member of the Central Committee of the Communist Party of Cuba, diplomat to the National Assembly of Popular Power, and Secretary to the Council of State, will depart today, Saturday, at 3:00 in the afternoon, from the base of the José Martí Monument in the Plaza of the Revolution where her body is currently on view.[6]

The furious pace of Sánchez's life began to slow in 1974, the year she was diagnosed with lung cancer. She was extremely ill between 1974 and 1980. A heavy smoker for most of her life, she had lost several members of her own family to the disease, including her beloved father. One family member I interviewed reported that Sánchez's inner circle always knew her true health status, though she did not want the news to circulate. He shared with me that "Celia was sick as early as 1973, but she tried to cover it up by claiming she had a 'fungus' in her lungs. It was really cancer."[7] Sánchez quietly underwent surgery on her lungs in July 1977; however, her goddaughter Eugenia Palomares Ferrales claims, "nobody, not even her doctors, was ever able to get her to stop smoking, especially when she drank coffee."[8]

The Cuban press remained silent on Sánchez's declining health until her death. Even then they resorted to the most customary, euphemistic way of

FIGURE 9 Crypt in Revolutionary Armed Forces Mausoleum in Colón Cemetery, Havana, 2018. Author's collection.

referring to death from cancer, stating only that she had lost her battle with a "painful illness." Radio and newspaper coverage still does not ever mention cancer specifically as the cause of her death. The silence on Sánchez's cause of death grants an almost mythical quality to her passing. She was not truly gone, she had merely laid down the burden of her illness and moved on to a place where she could continue to serve the revolution. The 11 January 1981 memorial feature on Sánchez published in *Juventud Rebelde* was titled simply, "Celia vive" (Celia Lives).[9]

Despite being quite ill between 1974 and 1980, Sánchez continued to work on her various civic and government projects. Her elementary school teacher and family friend, Cossío, worried that Sánchez sacrificed her personal health for her job. She relates that on one visit to Havana she made plans to visit Sánchez, but Sánchez was stuck in meetings all day without resting or eating, "only drinking coffee and smoking all day." When she was finally able to slip away to meet Cossío at 11 o'clock, Sánchez asked for some dinner.

Cossío was astonished and upset with the size of the meal: "Do you know what she ate? A plate with one tamale. I fussed at her for how little she eats. She was so thin and weak [*desmejorada*]. She only lived to work." Bécquer Céspedes likewise noted that "Celia hardly ever slept."[10] Former guerrilla combatant Luís Más Martin made a similar observation about Sánchez's work ethic in February 1959, stating that she "slept less than the person who slept least."[11] French journalist Deena Stryker remarked after interviewing Sánchez in February 1964 that "not much had changed in her life [since her time as a rebel fighter]: she drove around alone and survived on two or three hours of sleep, drinking coffee and being tired."[12]

On 30 November 1979, Sánchez participated in the ceremonies commemorating the first revolutionary uprising in Santiago de Cuba. A photo from the event shows a frail but smiling Sánchez. Every tendon in her wrist is visible as she pins a medal to an honoree's jacket. The Santiago de Cuba celebration was Sánchez's final public appearance. In her final days Sánchez requested to be moved to the Palace of the Revolution, where friends set up a small room for her. From that room, Sánchez continued to receive visitors daily and hosted study groups for her fellow social sciences classmates at La Escuela Superior del PCC "Ñico López."

Sánchez died in Havana at 11:50 A.M. on Thursday, 11 January 1980, just a few months shy of her sixtieth birthday. When Cossío learned later that Sánchez had secretly been gravely ill, she was shocked. "I was so alarmed when I learned of her illness. Silvia [Sánchez's sister] kept me updated," Cossío recalled in an interview. "Her death caught me by surprise. When the news arrived at my university in Santiago [de Cuba], nobody knew how to tell me. It impacted me immensely. I felt that I had lost something that was mine, very much my own. Something that was at the same time a support and guide. My very beloved and unforgettable Celia. My small and big Celia." When Sánchez passed, Castro is said to have entered her room at the Palace of the Revolution and stayed alone with her body for a full hour.

Sánchez's passing marked a unique moment in the history of the Cuban Revolution. She was the first revolutionary leader to die not as the result of an assassination (Guevara and País) or a disappearance (Cienfuegos).[13] Hers was also the first body of a leader that the revolutionary leadership had been able to bury since País in 1957. Guevara's remains were not returned to Cuba from Bolivia until the 1990s and Cienfuegos's body was never located. Sánchez's was also the first—and only for many years—state funeral for a female revolutionary leader. Santamaría died only six months after Sánchez, but she did not receive the same kind of adulatory farewell that her dear friend received.

Santamaría's tragic death was controversial. On the anniversary of the failed 26 July Moncada attack, she shot herself in the head in her bathroom. Friends and colleagues cited her ex-husband's (Hart Dávalos) decision to re-marry with a younger woman as an exacerbating factor in a long struggle with depression that began with the brutal murder of her brother and her fian-cée by agents of the Batista government.[14] Randall also cited in our phone interview the loss of Santamaría's close friend Sánchez as a factor in the de-cision to take her own life. Randall noted that "Celia understood Haydée. She was one of the few people who could get her out of bed when she was de-pressed."[15] Santamaría's daughter, Celia Hart (named for the famous revo-lutionary), classified her mother's friendship with Sánchez as a "revolutionary sisterhood," and noted that the only other time she had seen her mother so stricken was when Guevara was executed in 1967.[16] A Sánchez family mem-ber similarly told me that "Haydée and Celia were soulmates. Celia's death destroyed Haydée."[17] That Santamaría timed her suicide to coincide with the anniversary of the Moncada attack gave it an almost ritualistic weight.

Santamaría's action disqualified her from the kind of grandiose funeral that her status as a founding member and heroine of the revolution would otherwise have merited. Revolutionary leaders were expected to live for the people, and to commit suicide was to betray that cause. Santamaría's body never lay in state at the base of the José Martí statue in the Plaza of the Revo-lution, as did Sánchez's, and the public announcement of her death appeared a full two days after she killed herself.[18] She was buried quietly, with only her closest family and friends in attendance. Although the revolutionary leadership later created a space for Cubans to celebrate Santamaría's work and contributions to the revolutionary cause, her suicide was initially met with strong disapproval.

Santamaría's long-term friend and comrade General Juan Almeida Bosque was tasked with navigating in his eulogy some particularly turbulent politi-cal and emotional waters. His approach was to recast her suicide as a kind of psychological murder that had actually occurred in 1953 at Batista's hand. He noted that "as revolutionaries we cannot agree on principle with suicide. The life of a revolutionary belongs to his or her cause and people and should be devoted to serving them to the last ounce of energy and the last second of existence. But we cannot coldly judge comrade Haydée. That would not be just. Those of us who knew her well were aware that the wounds of the Moncada attack never managed to heal in her."[19] The text of his eulogy appeared on the front pages of the 29 July and 30 July issues of *Granma*. News of her death also appeared in the *New York Times* and the *Boston Herald*.[20]

If Santamaría's funeral was a solemn and semi-secret event, Sánchez's funeral was a public spectacle. As an event that set the standard for state funerals for Cuba's revolutionary heroes but also telegraphed a global message about the state of the nation more broadly, Sánchez's wake and funeral required the Cuban government to engage in what Quiroga refers to as "a funerary art of memorialization."[21] Aesthetics mattered, and every detail of her funeral—many of which Sánchez had herself organized prior to her death—was carefully orchestrated to evoke a deep sense of national unity and revolutionary nostalgia.

Sánchez's body lay in state at the José Martí monument in Havana's Revolutionary Square for a decreed twenty-four-hour period of mourning beginning Friday, 12 January. The receiving area within the base of the monument was draped in orchid-colored cloth to coordinate with the more than 600 orchids that filled the space. A spray of orchids atop her gray casket featured a silk banner with the words "To Celia from Fidel," and a small glass window granted a view of her face when it was closed. Sánchez was buried in her military fatigues, a reminder that she was an authentic revolutionary and not merely a political official. A rotating honor guard that included both male (Fidel and Raúl Castro) and female (Santamaría, Espín, and Hernández) revolutionary heroes stood solemn watch beside her casket. Nicaraguan leader and chief of the Sandinista Popular Army, Humberto Ortega, flew to Havana to stand guard as a show of his country's solidarity with Cuba.

A Cuban state funeral is—like any such event—an "orchestrated scene," which complicates its utility as a measure of genuine popular support for the person being memorialized.[22] Quiroga notes that participants in Cuban mass spectacle are invited to exercise their "at times free, at times coerced, at times implied, and at times suggested right to become one as a people."[23] Newspapers published notices that workers would be bused to the Plaza of the Revolution directly from their place of employment, just as they were for mass rallies.

The Cuban press combated any question about the authenticity of the crowd's emotion, however, with photos of women and children weeping and assertions that the crowds had gathered in a "spontaneous show of affection" for Sánchez. One newspaper article claimed that it "would be impossible to calculate how many filed past the base of the monument to Martí or congregated in the Plaza of the Revolution and along the funeral procession route.

Without doubt, however, they numbered in the hundreds of thousands . . . because that serpentine river of humanity that filled the Plaza on the afternoon of the 11th wanted to say their final farewell to the woman who had been and would forever be the image of the Revolution."[24] *Granma* released a poem by "El Indio Naborí" titled "I Ask Permission from Death." In his final line, the despairing poet tells the deceased Sánchez: "Permit me to say that Martí / Weeps for you today."[25]

Photos of the funeral show a long line of mourners stretching back to a bus terminal several blocks away. News that Santa Clara Province would observe a moment of silence and six other provinces were opening *libros de condolencia* (books of condolence) for individuals unable to make the trip to Havana provided a sense of national mourning. I was disappointed to learn during my time at the Office of Historical Affairs that the books and letters of condolence—many of them addressed to Castro—are not available to researchers, perhaps because they contain information considered too personal and intimate for circulation.

At precisely 3 o'clock on Saturday, the military-styled funeral procession—complete with uniformed troops carrying bayonets—moved slowly along Zapata Street. Witnesses claimed that the only sound anyone heard was "the thud of boots from the accompanying soldiers" who marched alongside her flag-draped casket. A stricken Castro followed immediately behind the olive-green jeep that carried her body. Raúl Castro walked along at his brother's side. One journalist reported that when the procession passed by him he was astonished by the look on Fidel Castro's face, writing "the hidden pain within his chest escaped through Fidel's face . . . it was there, deep inside, dropping in tears [and] stirring souls." Sánchez's goddaughter, Palomares Ferrales, recalls in her book, "I saw Fidel leaning over the coffin with both hands over the shroud, observing her carefully, with his face red and with tears he could not contain. I thought in that instant: 'This is the farewell of one guerrilla fighter to another.'"[26] Many of my interviewees echoed a similar version of this story, stating that Sánchez's funeral was the only time they ever saw Castro cry in public.

When the procession reached the gate of the Cólon Cemetery, the crowds were not allowed to enter. Only a select group of state officials and family members were allowed the final walk up the cemetery's central avenue toward the FAR mausoleum where the Cuban flag flew at half-staff. Though she never held a military rank, Sánchez was buried with full military honors.[27] Following a rifle volley, a lone bugler played "Taps" from atop the mausoleum, and the honor guard performed the flag-folding protocol. Sánchez's longtime friend and minister of culture, Hart Dávalos, then stood to deliver the eulogy.

Memory Trouble

How people imagine Sánchez depends heavily on who is doing the imagining, and the conflation of the political and the personal shapes the production of our knowledge about her life. Noakes offers a succinct definition of "public" and "private" memories and their interrelationship. She states that "private memories refer to memories that focus, at least in part, on the individual experience and memories of the war years; public memories refer to more general images of the war that appear in public sites of memory." Noakes is also quick to point out the interdependent nature of these two forms of memory, nothing that "in the practice of people's everyday lives, of course, public and private memory can be difficult to separate. Public and private memories are essentially interactive: private memories can be validated when they are shared by large numbers of people, thus gaining access to the public field of representation, while dominant public or popular memory has to have a purchase with most people's personal memories of the war years in order to become widely accepted."[28]

In the case of both private and public recollections of Sánchez's life story, I find that these imaginings are deeply gendered. The experience of the Cuban Revolution, more than any other national historical event, has influenced the discourse of masculinity and femininity in Cuban society at both the individual and collective levels. Noakes defines masculinity and femininity "as related cultural and social constructs. They are not living, breathing men and women but sets of ideas about how living, breathing men and women are expected to act."[29] According to Wandor, the "imperative of gender" is tied "not only to [a person's] biological sexual characteristics, but also implies imaginative and social assumptions about her/his personality, power, and place in the world."[30]

My interviews with women revealed that gender operates as a prism through which individual memories are refracted. Sánchez's legacy provided a framework within which these women could articulate their experience of the Cuban Revolution. Lourdes Sang joined the Cuban Revolution as a young girl and continued to participate actively in Cuban political life as an organizer of women's work in the FMC. As a young girl inspired by the dramatic changes occurring in her country, Sang began posting M-26-7 flags in her hometown of Santiago de Cuba. She recalls with pride the splinters she received from climbing posts and fences—a "small price for a great cause." Later, she also served as a clandestine messenger, and her commitment to the revolution took priority over the completion of a university degree. Her situation was common: "It was the young students who delivered the messages. The student masses have always been important in revolutionary movements."[31] Sang focused her testimony around Sánchez's similar reputation as a "woman of the people" who conducted official business from her jeep.[32]

In comparison, Nirma Cartón—a prominent lawyer in Havana who was highly involved in several of the large bureaucracies of the Cuban government—presented Sánchez as a political official who facilitated the construction of several key government-sponsored facilities. Similarly, Cartón was exceedingly proud of her participation in the early battles of the revolution and made repeated references to Sánchez's military role in the Sierra Maestra. At the age of eighteen, Cartón left the safety and comfort of her middle-class life and assumed a new identity. She became the third woman to officially join the ranks of the revolution, behind Sánchez and Teté Puebla. The only female combatant in Column #4, Nirma spent nine months in the Sierra Maestra alongside Guevara. She placed all of her medals on the table at the outset of our interview.[33]

Although none of my interviewees, nor any of Sánchez's contemporaries, ever expressly referred to Sánchez as the New Woman, I utilize this terminology to refer to an explicitly gendered formulation of the ideal female Cuban revolutionary that permeates her image. Prior to Sánchez's death, the Cuban Revolution had never presented Cubans with a contemporary role model for understanding what being a New Woman meant, at least certainly not in the way that Guevara was presented as the New Man. The FMC's magazine *Mujeres* offered general instruction on this matter and occasionally highlighted examples of women who made exemplary contributions to Cuba's independence struggle or to the revolution. Yet those sources did not elevate one specific woman to iconic status. The variety of commemorative acts and texts that emerged in the wake of Sánchez's death provided a primer on ideal female revolutionary behaviors and a course correction to the revolution. They also personalized the notion of the New Woman in ways that more general treatments of the subject had not. To be sure, not everyone understood what being a New Woman meant, or interpreted that notion in the same way.

Formal state discourse cast Sánchez's service to the revolution in a language of womanly modesty and quasi-maternal duty that reassured Cubans of her essential femininity. Guerra notes that revolutionary state agencies in Cuba "emphasized the importance of traditional femininity to the successful reproduction of the New Man."[34] The ideal New Woman embraced her role as both a motor for change and a conduit for channeling the energies of the New Men in her life—spouse, siblings, children, coworkers—toward the needs of the state. The maternal self-abnegation and devotion presumed to define a Cuban woman's private life prepared her to assume a public role as a symbolic mother for a new generation of dedicated revolutionaries. The scope of a revolutionary woman's maternal responsibilities extended out from the home and into streets, schools, and workplaces to benefit the nation as a whole.

This framing of motherhood as an act of patriotic sacrifice has deep roots in Cuban culture, extending back to the figure of Mariana Grajales Cuello (1808–93), the famed Afro-Cuban "Mother of Cuba" whose work to secure Cuban independence cost her several children, her property, and her personal safety. In recognition of her exceptional sacrifices for Cuba, Grajales is buried in the Santa Ifigenia cemetery in Santiago de Cuba alongside fellow national heroes José Martí, Carlos Manuel de Céspedes, and now Fidel Castro. Female rebels in the Sierra Maestra also formed their own platoon under the banner of her name—the Mariana Grajales Brigade—and their military competency prompted Castro to designate them as his personal security detail. Imaginings of the heroic New Woman as a devoted and sacrificial being thus resonated with an existing maternalist symbology on the island.[35]

In Sánchez's case, the fact that she was not a biological mother meant she could serve as a symbolic mother to Cubans. Her contributions to the birth of the revolution during the years in the Sierra Maestra connected her to Cuba's new origin story and certified her authenticity as a founding mother of the nation. Raúl Castro referred to Sánchez as the "official godmother of the military detachment" in a letter that he wrote her from the Sierra Maestra, and that phrase was thereafter incorporated into the discourse surrounding her life and legacy.[36] Photos of Sánchez attending ceremonies honoring the Pioneros (communist youth), interacting with and embracing small children, and attending baptisms—which appeared only occasionally during her life, but circulated widely after her death—linked her visually to the kind of maternal, feminine, and public activities expected of the New Woman. Several day care centers and schools across the island bear her name.[37]

It bears mentioning that despite her legendary status, Sánchez's image does not appear on any commercial merchandise anywhere in Cuba. Souvenir shops across the island overflow with T-shirts, tote bags, and keychains featuring the image of Guevara—and increasingly, since his death in 2016, of Fidel Castro. I spotted a number of vendors selling Castro T-shirts during my 2017 trips to Cuba. The use of Castro's image for commercial purposes seems surprising in light of his strict order, now codified in law, that no streets, schools, buildings, postage stamps, or forms of currency should bear his name. Castro publicly railed against world leaders who created cults of personality, and even ordered the removal of a statue erected in his honor at the Camp Columbia military base in 1959. His tombstone in Santiago de Cuba's Santa Ifigenia cemetery is a simple boulder—rumored to represent Martí's maxim that "all the glory in the world fits inside a grain of corn"—engraved with one word: Fidel. As Guevara biographer Michael J. Casey notes, "revolutionaries are supposed to frown upon idolizing the living."[38] Castro's image is, however, ubiquitous on billboards across the island and his framed portrait hangs in almost every government office. If the revolutionary government locates the distinction between a cult of personality and state propaganda somewhere in the space between postage stamps and billboards, critics of the revolution are skeptical. Tad Szulc noted in his 1986 biography of Castro that "The personality cult around Castro . . . is continually enhanced [and he] lives bathed in the absolute adulation orchestrated by the propaganda organs of his regime."[39]

Guevara was, of course, not Cuban (he was born in Argentina), and his image circulated globally prior to his death in 1967. Cast as a martyred hero, Guevara became even more famous in death than he was in life. Alberto Korda's renowned *Heroic Guerrilla* photograph (1960)—reportedly the world's most reproduced photograph—provided the genesis for the commercialized image that now adorns coffee mugs and bumper stickers. That same image also stands sentinel over the epicenter of the revolutionary government, Havana's Revolution Plaza. Rendered in steel and mounted to the façade of the Ministry of the Interior building, Guevara's stoic and determined visage attracts busloads of tourists, eager to take selfies with a revolutionary pop icon. His mausoleum complex in Santa Clara includes a twenty-two-foot-tall bronze statue, crypts for Guevara and twenty-nine of the soldiers who died with him in Bolivia, and a museum. A reported 4.5 million people have visited the complex over the last twenty years. The Cuban government allows, and even encourages, the proliferation of Guevara's image in full recognition of its visual power and popular appeal. Castro said that Cuba would never allow cults of personality for living revolutionary leaders. He made no mention of deceased leaders.

In contrast, the three principal female revolutionary leaders—Sánchez, Espín, and Santamaría (all now deceased)—appear exclusively in state-produced educational or commemorative materials, or in photographs. None of the women have ever had, in life or in death, anywhere near the same visual presence as the male leaders. I remember meeting an artist who displays her work in a gallery in Havana's Museum of the Revolution. She proudly showed me her painting of Guevara, but when I asked if she had one of Sánchez, she looked shocked: "No, never Celia." When I gently pressed for an explanation, she offered one word before walking away with a shrug: "Because."

The gendered difference in the reproduction and proliferation of images of the revolutionary leaders is telling. Would garnering economic gain from the image of the female leaders imply a kind of "prostitution" of their legacy that reproducing images of Guevara or Cienfuegos does not? Does the strong association between women and the sacred institution of motherhood in Latin American culture, and no less so in Cuba, make their image somehow sacrosanct? Maternalist images of Sánchez have indeed assumed, in many cases, an undeniably religious tone. Cast as a secular saint for the revolution and an intercessor who advocated for Cubans' daily needs, she continues to provide a quasi-spiritual link to *fidelismo*. Afro-Cuban poet Nancy Morejón depicts Sánchez as a Marian counterpart to a Christ-like Castro in her 1984 poem, "Elegía coral a Celia Sánchez" (Choral Elegy to Celia Sánchez).[40] The 1985 book *Celia nuestra y de las flores* (Our Celia of the Flowers) is the tale of a father and son who engage in a spiritual pilgrimage from the eastern end of the island to attend Sánchez's funeral in Havana.[41]

To be sure, Sánchez is not the only Cuban revolutionary leader apotheosized in this way. Anyone familiar with the voluminous imagery and artwork surrounding Guevara has undoubtedly encountered him exalted as the crucified "Chesucristo."[42] If Guevara's 1967 execution in Bolivia sealed his martyrdom to the cause of *continental* revolution, however, Cubans cast Sánchez's sacrifices in purely national terms. The cultural production surrounding her legacy—grounded in her honorary title as "the most native wildflower of the Cuban Revolution"—underscores her status as a native daughter of Cuba who lived and died serving her people. In exchange, her admirers refer to her as "our Celia."

Into the Sea of the People: Memory from Above

In their article titled "Captain of the People," published in *Bohemia* several days after Sánchez's death, Pedro Pablo Rodríguez and Manuel González Bello posed a rhetorical question to those Cubans still mourning the loss of their beloved compatriot: "For what better example is there of living after death than Celia? If, as a poet said, life is a river that gives itself unto the sea, which is death, Celia, the one who forever gives an image of strength and permanence beyond the short space of human life, has gone to the sea. Into the sea of the Revolution, into the sea of the people, into the sea of the Cuban nation . . . has disembarked the life of Celia."[43]

Quiroga invites us to view mass spectacles, like funerals and rallies, as "educational projects meant to remotivate the past."[44] These kinds of state-sponsored memory projects are not, he adds, about "simply using coercive mechanisms, but [rather] commanding a symbolic language that registered with the people, always addressed in the plural."[45] On 11 January 1980, Sánchez's life ended, only to then spark the beginning of a national project to resurrect her spirit in the name of rekindling Cuba's revolutionary fires. The timing of her death was significant. Two decades of escalating economic problems, caused by an increasing level of dependency on the Soviet Union, a failure to diversify Cuban exports, and the U.S. economic embargo, had left their mark on the nation in the form of mounting social and political tensions. Castro's failure to achieve his much-publicized sugar harvest goal during his *Zafra de los diez millones* (Ten Million Ton Sugar Harvest, 1964–70) was an embarrassment, as was Guevara's failed mission to Bolivia, which resulted in his assassination in 1967.

The Cuban government did not yet know that growing disillusionment and anxiety would eventually result in 10,000 Cubans seeking asylum in the Peruvian embassy in April 1980 or the mass exodus of 125,000 Cubans to the United States during the Mariel boatlift (April–October 1980). Increasing levels of worker absenteeism and the declining participation of women in work were, however, becoming cause for alarm.[46] Perhaps not surprisingly, in his 12 January eulogy to Sánchez—which was broadcast on the national radio station—Hart Dávalos stated, "Celia, with her valor, her constancy, her laborious nature, and her highly effective work next to Castro, entered definitively into history. In the Sierra, Celia was the heroine not only of the war, but also of work. In her, legend acquired real form and content."[47]

Only two days after her death, the revolutionary government's highest-ranking government officials were already constructing a nationalist memory of Sánchez as the quintessential symbol of work, dedication to Castro, and commitment to the revolutionary cause in Cuba. In turn, the revolutionary government pledged to serve as Sánchez's eternal torchbearer. A Cuban newspaper reported that "at her tomb [the revolutionary leadership] made a tacit pact, a promise to history and to themselves to be faithful followers of the virtues of this woman who had died: brave, optimistic, modest, always connected to the workers and the entire people. [She was] exacting, attentive to details, [and] loyal at every moment to the Maximum Commander." While Cubans could never repay what Pierre Nora refers to as the "impossible debt" of her generation's sacrifices for the nation, honoring Sánchez became an expression of alignment with the goals and values of the revolution and with pure *fidelismo*.[48]

Memory always functions as a two-way mirror in Cuba, however. The Miami-based press moved quickly to capitalize on Sánchez's death as a means to cast doubt upon both Castro's leadership and the revolutionary project more generally. A rumor emerged within days of Sánchez's death that she was actually killed as a result of gunfire that also killed Raúl Castro and wounded Fidel. The 15 January issue of the Miami-based *La Verdad* newspaper ran a cover story titled "Conflict in Cuba: Was Celia Sánchez Assassinated?" The lead image for the story was none other than the "lipstick and fatigues" image of Sánchez that had circulated for years in the Miami press. The news source captioned the image, "Lover, Bodyguard, and 'Advisor' to the Executioner, Celia Sánchez."

The accompanying article expressed doubt that Sánchez had, indeed, died of lung cancer. The anonymous author cited rumors that Raúl Castro had aligned himself with unspecified pro-Soviet forces intent on toppling Fidel and paving the way for the younger Castro brother to assume the reins of power in Cuba. The author found the timing of Sánchez's death suspicious in light of sources claiming that Fidel Castro and Sánchez knew about Raúl Castro's maneuverings and were mobilizing to thwart his efforts. The author sprinkled the story with unflattering references to Sánchez's physical appearance, labeling her "very skinny, very ugly, and VERY COMMUNIST." The author ended the short article prognosticating heartily that "if Sánchez was assassinated . . . her cadaver is the harbinger of the death of the Tyrant Castro . . . because the two Castro brothers can no longer fit on the same island."[49] The *Miami Herald* also picked up the story on 24 January.[50]

The Miami press labeled Sánchez's death the "most significant hit [Castro] had ever suffered" and gleefully predicted the precipitous decline of his political and personal fortitude. Labeling it as the "darkest moment in the blackest week of his rule," the *Miami Herald* reminded its readers on 13 January that Sánchez's death followed on the heels of Cuba being denied a seat on the United Nations Security Council for failing to denounce the Soviet Union's invasion of Afghanistan. Noting a recent major centralization of the Cuban government in which Castro assumed control of four ministries, the

Miami Herald article argued that "the implications of Sánchez's death are as important as the governmental restructuring efforts." On a more personal note, the article predicted that Sánchez's death would "create a vacuum for Castro [because] she organized his entire life."

The Miami-based press also used Sánchez's death as an opportunity to state what now seemed undeniable. Though the iconography of the revolution had always centered on self-sacrificial youth, Sánchez's death represented a moment when Cubans were forced to confront the aging of the revolutionary leadership. With only a "small nucleus of revolutionary veterans still able to hold Castro's confidence, many of whom are starting to die," the *Miami Herald* predicted that Castro's days in power were numbered. To combat any question about the capacity of the remaining leaders—and especially Castro—to continue directing the country in spite of their advancing age, the Cuban government used Sánchez's death as an opportunity to release a wave of visual reminders of the glory days in the Sierra Maestra. Photo montages of smiling rebels standing proud against the background of lush mountain foliage in the Sierra Maestra harkened back to the days of innocence and optimism when the razor-sharp dreams of youth had not yet been worn smooth by the grinding realities of institutionalized state-making. They were authentic revolutionaries present at the moment of the new nation's becoming—the original New Men and New Women.

In the week following Sánchez's death, two major Cuban periodicals, *Granma* and *Bohemia* (Cuba's longest-running magazine, established in 1908), dedicated full issues to mourning the loss of Cuba's revolutionary heroine. These initial commemorative acts mark critical moments in the creation of Cuban national memory, as they established the tone for what would become the official memory of Sánchez. She had so rarely appeared in Cuban newspapers or other media sources that I often wonder how many people were learning about Sánchez's life and work, at least in detail, for the first time at her death. One family member echoes this sentiment, stating, "I don't think people fully realized how influential she was until after she was gone."[51]

On 12 January, *Granma* published an assortment of editorials, photographs, and poetry reflecting on Sánchez's life and documenting the grief experienced by those who had known her directly or indirectly. Included also were official statements from the FMC, as well as statements from officials in each of Cuba's fourteen provinces.[52] While the former demarcated a gender-specific arena of mourning, the latter communicated a sense of national loss. Six days later, *Bohemia* likewise published an entire issue in commemoration of Sánchez's death, titled "Para siempre en el corazón del pueblo" (Forever in the Hearts of the People). The *Bohemia* issue, like the *Granma* issue a few days earlier, offered a collage of memories including dozens of photos, several editorials, a sampling of letters between Castro and Sánchez from their years in the Sierra Maestra, and a complete transcript of Hart Dávalos's eulogy at Sánchez's funeral. The use of photo montages — a holdover from the early years of the revolution when the government hoped to reach a still largely illiterate or semiliterate audience (40–50 percent of the population) — helped make the revolution accessible and appealing to Cubans and the outside world. Guerra has noted that "images allowed the state to represent, in an instant, the ways that citizens were supposed to interpret its policies and goals as well as their own reality."[53]

The selection of photos displayed in these issues attempt to re-create a basic chronology of Sánchez's life. The chronology begins with her trip to the highest peak in Cuba, Turquino Peak, in 1953 (at the age of thirty-three), where she, her father, and several colleagues installed the Martí bust. The final picture depicts Sánchez's casket being interred in the FAR mausoleum. Of the thirty-five photographs of Sánchez included in the issue, nineteen (a little over half) show her standing directly at Castro's side.

The first three decades of Sánchez's life are often omitted from the visual chronology of her life laid out by the Cuban press in the weeks, months, and even years after her death. Presumably those earliest years were considered unimportant to the story that the editors intended to tell about her. Conspicuously absent are photographs documenting her relatively affluent childhood, for example. Her life story centers instead on her sacrifice and dedication to the Cuban Revolution and to its leader. Positioned visually and symbolically at Castro's side, she becomes, quite literally, Castro's right-hand woman. Photos showing Castro teaching Sánchez to load a weapon underscored her deferential nature and teachability, while photos showing her offering him a glass of water or bandaging a wound on his hand highlighted her quasi-maternal generosity and caretaking skills.

While Sánchez maintained and operated her own M-1 — which is on display at the Media Luna museum — this imagery preserved the combatant and military strategist roles for the male leadership and cast Sánchez as the dutiful and devoted camp follower. Her authority was both relational and secondary to that of the man at her side. By comparison, the 19 October 1967 issue of *Granma* published ten days following Guevara's execution in Bolivia focused entirely on his status as a visionary and fallen hero.[54] Among the most admirable personal qualities attributed to Guevara were his status as an "insuperable soldier; an insuperable commander . . . an extraordinarily capable man, extraordinarily aggressive." Contrasted with the construction of Sánchez's image as a woman of modesty and simplicity, Guevara is described as representing the perfect union of "the man of ideas and the man of action."[55]

The text of the *Bohemia* and *Granma* issues that ran alongside the photos of Sánchez offered similar patterns in language, symbolism, and imagery. The text of the FMC's official statement on Sánchez's death, for example, asserted: "Today our people lost a glorious figure who elevated the name of women during the revolutionary struggle, one who knew how to win the love and respect of the sons of our country with her simplicity, modesty, exemplary attitude, and with her participation in every task necessary to the construction of a new society."[56] Another contributor to the issue, Marta Rojas, echoed this emphasis on love and respect as a reward for absolute devotion to the revolutionary cause. In a lengthy tribute to Sánchez titled "Hemos perdido un centinela a toda prueba" (We Have Lost a Proven Sentry), Rojas stated: "[Celia's] audacity, valor, and optimism; her discipline, modesty, and total devotion to the leadership of Fidel; her tact, discretion, and intelligence earned her the respect of the entire Revolutionary Army, of the troops of the Movement and of the rural people during the insurrection as with the triumph of the Revolution."[57] While describing her as "profoundly kind," Rojas was quick to note that Sánchez, in defense of her cause, could become an "insurmountable concrete wall against which those disloyal to the Revolution and the enemies of Cuba dashed themselves to bits."[58] This ideological toughness did not interfere with her fashion sense, however, as Sánchez was also described as being "made of one solid revolutionary piece, from her feet to the tips of her hair, which she so liked to adorn with flowers, ribbons, or combs."[59]

Finally, an anonymous editorial bearing the simple title "Celia" stated that while her name and image appeared only sporadically in public, she was never missed: "The people knew that she was there, where she should be, like the invisible salt in the immense sea of the Revolution. And thus, day after day, she entered more and more in the heart of the Cuban people, conquering that peak which is so hard to scale which is the affection, the admiration, and the respect of an entire people."[60] Reflecting on Sánchez's personal virtues, the author states simply, "rarely has such genuine glory marched hand in hand with similar modesty, human sensibility, and loyal and impartial devotion to the service of the revolutionary cause."[61]

While three different authors penned these examples from the *Granma* issue, there are similarities between the imaginings of Sánchez contained therein. A quick comparison of the adjectives utilized in the descriptions of Sánchez's personal attributes reveals that the words respect, modesty, and devotion appear in all three selections. Words like discipline, optimism, and simplicity are also prominent. Aside from the commonalities in language, all three selections present Sánchez as a woman who rigorously defended the cause yet sought no personal accolades for the tasks she performed. In fact, it was her status as an invisible element of the revolution—the invisible salt in the immense sea of the revolution—that earned her the love and respect of her compatriots. The statement by the FMC also grants Sánchez a maternal role, stressing her ability to earn the respect of Cuba's "sons" with her modesty and simplicity, and this type of imagery became even more pronounced over time.

Any subtle tensions between Sánchez's role as a public official and as a symbolic mother figure expressed in these early sources are perhaps indicative of broader ambiguities within Cuba's revolutionary project. As Sandra McGee Deutsch has noted, various Latin American revolutionary projects—specifically those that occurred in Cuba, Argentina, Mexico, and Chile—struggled over the definition of revolutionary womanhood and encountered difficulties when attempting to rectify the new image of the revolutionary woman with more traditional conceptualizations of gender roles.[62] Taylor likewise found in the case of Eva Perón that themes of sacrifice, maternal love, purity, and devotion were prominent, both before and after her death, primarily as they related to her image as the Lady of Hope.[63]

For her story to serve its intended purpose, Sánchez needed to become the embodiment of ideological toughness and fierce determination on the one hand, and femininity and superb aesthetic sensibilities on the other. On the first anniversary of her death, an anonymous article published in *Granma* noted that "while she was exceptionally sweet, tender, passionate, affectionate, and modest, Sánchez was firm and demanding when it came to questions of principles."[64] Reflecting on this depiction of Sánchez's personality and character, Bécquer Céspedes affirmed that "Sánchez had a way of sitting next to you and looking into your soul and knowing if you were lying. She had no patience with liars, and that was the quickest way to be removed from her life."[65]

The final pages of the issue are a complete transcription of Hart Dávalos's eulogy to Sánchez, which was titled "Celia's Example: Courage and Instruction to Continue the Journey and March Forward with Determination." At the height of his oratory fervor, Hart Dávalos proclaimed to the Cuban nation that Sánchez was "great in her heroic abnegation, her unconditional loyalty, great in her identification with the people, in her love for the revolutionary project, in her passionate interest in others. Great in her preoccupation with the concrete and decisive elements of every aspect of the Revolution. Great, perhaps, beyond every other virtue, in her modesty and simplicity. Among all her qualities we should certainly single out her rejection of all forms of ostentation and her fondness for simple manners and for the simplicities of life and work. This was, surely, one of her most moving virtues. Celia's character is reminiscent of the words of Martí: 'The rivulet of the mountain ridge pleases me more than the sea.'"[66]

Throughout his eulogy, Hart Dávalos highlights Sánchez's exceptional work ethic as a virtue to be emulated by all Cubans. It is this dedication to the advancement of the revolutionary project that provides the inspiration for the fiery conclusion of his speech. Switching abruptly from a lengthy enumeration of Sánchez's virtues, Hart Dávalos ends his speech by proclaiming that "a dignified homage to Celia is to . . . fortify the work of our mass organizations, improve the workings of the State and all the administrations in labor centers, and elevate the efficiency of our administrative, labor, and political organizations . . . with the noble purpose of advancing the Cuban Revolution."[67] This call to action was punctuated with shouts of "Victories against deficiencies! Victories against imperialism! Victories for socialism!"[68]

The many similarities in language and symbolism among the selections discussed above from the *Granma* and *Bohemia* commemorative issues merit our attention. Words such as loyalty, modesty, and simplicity appear in both. The *Bohemia* pieces take the commemorative act one step beyond mere praise to the realm of action. While the "Captain of the People" piece utilizes a much more symbolic language than Hart Dávalos's eulogy, there is a common theme. Both authors highlight Sánchez's intimate connection with the Cuban people, but both also stress the responsibility that relationship now carries. With Sánchez's passing, the burden to continue her life's work now falls on the "sea of the people" for whose benefit her labors were always intended. To this effect, Hart Dávalos quoted Julio Antonio Mella's phrase that "even after death we are useful!" explaining that "Celia should continue being useful, but this no longer depends on her. It will depend on every one of us being capable of understanding and applying the lesson of her life."[43] Hart Dávalos's eulogy thus ends on a highly practical note, in which the needs of the state are projected onto the Cuban people through Sánchez.

For a nation facing increasing economic and social difficulties and desperately in need of both uniting a fracturing society and spurring them toward collective labors, this oratory strategy proved both dramatic and functional.

Coincidentally, it reappeared frequently over the next years. In his 11 January 1985 memorial speech in honor or Sánchez, Faustino Pérez Hernández—member of the Central Committee of the Communist Party—noted that "together with [Celia] we will face today's battle victoriously. Each one of us in our workstations, in our trench. With Celia, we will win."[69] Anniversaries of Sánchez's death became critical moments for Cuban authorities to leverage her legacy in service to broader state imperatives. By connecting memories of wartime sacrifices to contemporary workplace sacrifices, officials hoped to bridge the gap between past and future victories through Sánchez's example.

On 16 January 1981, Castro recognized the first anniversary of Sánchez's death by dedicating a hospital in her name in Manzanillo. The dedication service for the large facility, which contained 630 beds, sixteen operating rooms, and cost 16 million pesos to construct, drew a large crowd.[70] In an exhaustive commemorative speech that was broadcast on both national television and radio stations, Castro outlined the history of medical services in the area and praised the work of all the individuals whose labors had made the construction of the hospital possible.[71] Aside from the obvious health benefits the hospital offered to the inhabitants of the region, Castro claimed a symbolic purpose for the facility. Encouraged by eager applause from the audience, he proclaimed that the Celia Sánchez Hospital was "an homage to our compatriot Celia Sánchez, on the first anniversary of her death . . . [APPLAUSE] . . . I truly believe that this is the best form of tribute to pay to someone who dedicated herself to duty, without resting for a moment, without forgetting one single detail; and I believe, sincerely, that this is the most heartfelt, profound, and revolutionary homage that one can give to a compatriot who gave her life for the Revolution [APPLAUSE]."[72]

In June of that same year, the periodical *Mujeres* published a short article titled "A Dignified Homage to Celia."[73] The article—whose title evokes Hart Dávalos's funeral eulogy the previous year—praises the work of the 2,900 female members of the "Celia Sánchez Manduley" volunteer labor brigade. The article's author, Gilberto Blanch, relied primarily on interviews and his personal observations in order to reflect on the women's work in the sugarcane fields of Ciego de Ávila. The multiple photos interspersed throughout the article's text depict smiling women proudly wearing the brigade's signature uniform—broad-brimmed palm frond hats and wristbands bearing the image of Sánchez—while driving tractors, cutting sugarcane, and carrying potatoes in large wooden crates.

While the women are clearly hard at work under the Cuban sun, the author of the article seemed particularly interested in the women's appearance. He wrote: "To see them in the fields is a feast for the eyes, because all are dressed elegantly in their uniforms." In reference to this commentary, Mirta Benedico, head of propaganda, stated that the women had been instructed that "all the members had to shine prettily, with hats, with the image of Celia Sánchez on our wristbands . . . and with blouses of different colors." The article concluded by proclaiming the honor of the brigade's contribution to the nation's productivity levels and the importance of their labors as a "dignified homage to our beloved Celia."[74]

In both the dedication of the hospital and in the establishment of the "Celia Sánchez Manduley" female volunteer labor brigade, evoking Sánchez's memory provided a means for encouraging social and economic development. The Celia Sánchez Hospital—a highly appropriate memorial to a woman associated with rural medicine since her childhood—fulfilled both practical and symbolic functions. The medical care provided by the individual doctors and nurses working at the facility became the symbolic extension of the caretaking Sánchez is remembered to have performed in life. The female labor brigade embodied other qualities associated with Sánchez, such as hard work and selflessness, and evoked images of Sánchez volunteering to cut sugarcane each harvest season. The focus on the women's appearance resonates with Rojas's description of Sánchez in the 1980 issue of *Granma*, in which she made special reference to Sánchez's penchant for adorning her hair with flowers and ribbons. Just like Sánchez, the women of the labor brigade are cast as both fiercely revolutionary and delightfully feminine.

The national mythology that emerged in the years following Sánchez's death was about much more than recalling the significant dates, honors, and accomplishments of one woman. Aside from representing the ideal Cuban revolutionary, Sánchez represented a distinctly female ideal. This role-model status was grounded in a list of imagined personal characteristics: simplicity, modesty, femininity, selflessness, austerity, and devotion. This fairly standardized list of personal virtues represented much more than references to a deceased individual. They provided a blueprint for Cuba's New Woman. For a country in desperate need of remobilizing its female labor sector, creating a vision of the ideal Cuban woman as someone who was capable of balancing physical labor with caretaking, strength with femininity, and leadership with modesty served a purpose above and beyond the mere commemoration of one woman (figure 10).

FIGURE 10 National Assembly of Popular Power in Manzanillo, 1976. Author's collection.

Stairways and Sunflowers: Celia in Popular Memory

> Celia, you have sung to me the song that I chose.
> You cradle me in your round breast,
> Which is a nest of feathers.
> You are the one who exalts me.
> You are the one who knows me.
>
> —NANCY MOREJÓN, "Elegía coral a Celia Sánchez"[75]

My driver picked me up and, in spite of the heavy rain, we made our way from Media Luna to Manzanillo to visit the Celia Sánchez Memorial Stairway. The stairway is a public art installation that was dedicated in 1990 and climbs two hilly blocks of central Manzanillo along Caridad Street. My driver parked near the base of the stairs and we began climbing the terra-cotta-tiled steps sandwiched between colorful wooden homes. Sunflowers and doves—meant to emphasize Sánchez's association with rural life, patriotic sacrifice, and human sensibility—provide a unifying visual language for the various murals scattered along the stairway. Only one of the murals features Sánchez's image. A towering installation at the top of the staircase presents Sánchez's face sitting atop a tall stand of sunflowers, as if she had sprouted from the ground. She is surrounded by flying doves. Another tiled vignette reproduces her signature.

The mural that sits at the midway point along the stairway features a poem written in Sánchez's honor by famed Afro-Cuban poet Nancy Morejón. The mural actually reproduces only a portion of a longer poem penned by Morejón titled "Celia: Amazing Daughter of the Orchid," which appeared in the January 1986 edition of the FMC's *Mujeres* magazine.[76] Echoing the same nature-centric theme presented in the stairway's nontextual installations, the poem reads:

La veíamos ayer en el patio de las picualas
Al regresar de la granja encendida
Con su uniforme verdeolivo
Y su estrella naciente
La veíamos ayer
Bajo el sol implacable
Recogiendo las flores de la melancolía
La veíamos ayer alta y velóz
Repartiéndonos balas néctares rosas

(We saw her yesterday on the patio with the picuala vines
Returning from the burning farm
In her olive green uniform
And her rising star.
We saw her yesterday
Under the relentless sun
Collecting the flowers of melancholy.
We saw her yesterday high and fast
Distributing to us bullets, nectars, roses.)

Weaving together references to flowers, flames, and fatigues, Morejón's poetry links to other memory texts produced in the wake of Sánchez's death. Morejón's poetic imaginings cast Sánchez as both an agent of revolutionary destruction and a harbinger of peace—she distributes bullets and roses simultaneously. Repeating the phrase "we saw her yesterday" serves both to identify the reader-viewer as a direct witness to Sánchez's life—*we saw her*—and to compress the temporal distance since her death (yesterday) in ways meant to reanimate the past. Though not as steeped in the kind of quasi-Marian imagery that characterizes most of her poetry about Sánchez, the stairway poem nonetheless retains the general flavor of Morejón's representations of Sánchez as a woman operating simultaneously on two planes—an otherworldly spiritual realm (her rising star) and the world of human needs (distributing bullets, collecting melancholy).

Just as official commemorative speeches and newspaper editorials abounded after Sánchez's death, so too did more personal reflections on Sánchez's role in the Cuban revolution. While Sánchez's intimate connection to the Cuban people may have provided the inspiration for government propaganda, there were those who reflected on their personal memories of Sánchez in other ways, and did so with, perhaps, other motivations. Among these more individualized expressions of memory, Morejón's poetry quickly rose to prominence. While her poetry was public in the sense that it appeared in Cuban newspapers and magazines—as did the various other poems cited throughout this book—it represented a uniquely personal expression of memory.

Images of Sánchez as a tender mother figure, as a friend of the people, and as the embodiment of strength and devotion are prevalent in all of Morejón's poems, just as in the commemorative speeches and public editorials that emerged in the days following Sánchez's death. Morejón was clearly familiar with the general tenor of official discourse on Sánchez's role in Cuban society, and the imagery she employed often contained subtle, and at times not so subtle, references to larger social and political issues. The language, symbolism, and message of Morejón's poetry reveal, however, a level of intimacy with the subject that sets it apart from official sites of memory.

Perhaps the most famous of Morejón's poems dedicated to the memory of Sánchez is "Elegía coral a Celia Sánchez" (Choral Elegy to Celia Sánchez), which appeared in the January 1984 issue of *Revista Revolución y Cultura*.[77] Utilizing vibrant language and a distinctly Cuban symbolism, Morejón espouses Sánchez's memory as a national treasure.

> Celia es ágil y fuerte y atraviesa una ruta de orquídeas,
>   cada día.
> Celia es cubana y nuestra como los montes de la Sierra.
> Celia, buena y sencilla, entre los pescadores de Niquero
>   y el esplendor de la bahía.
> Fusiles, hachas, flechas, piedras del río condujo hacia
>   el pico más puro.

Llega Fidel de la montaña y Ella deshierba helechos
    y los pone a sus pies
para avivar el corazón del pueblo.
Como el viento sutil en Media Luna,
Celia es así, callada, buena.
Su boca amanecida siempre pronunciará
    la palabra que amamos
la que necesitamos en la vida.
Celia es así, como era Celia, sonrisa y tempestad,
y con ella se marcha, entre mantos y orquídeas,
hacia las puertas de la eternidad.

(Celia is agile and strong and she traverses a route
    of orchids every day.
Celia is Cuban and ours like the mountains
    of the Sierra.
Celia, good and simple, among the fisherman
    of Niquero and the splendor of the bay.
Rifles, hatchets, arrows, river rocks she carried
    toward the purest peak.

Fidel arrives from the mountain and She plucks ferns
    and places them at his feet
To enliven the hearts of the people.
Like the soft wind in Media Luna,
Celia is like that, quiet, good.
Her dawning mouth will forever pronounce
    the word that we love
The one we need in this life.
Celia is this, as Celia was, smile and tempest
And she departs between robes and orchids
Toward the gates of eternity.)

For Morejón, Sánchez is a woman of mythic proportions. She is strong, sincere, and, above all, devoted to the Cuban people and to Castro. It is this devotion to others that earns Sánchez the semidivine status signaled by the capitalized pronoun "Ella." Only in the thirteenth line—where Sánchez defers to Castro—is she granted semidivine status. In all the other lines of the poem, "ella" begins with a lowercase "e." The biblical imagery present in Morejón's poem similarly serves to elevate Sánchez to divine status. Sánchez plucking ferns and placing them at Castro's feet resonates with Christian images of Mary placing palm fronds before Jesus as he enters Jerusalem. The irony, then, of Sánchez's power is that she must be willing to surrender it in order for it to be worthy of praise.

While Morejón's poetry was undoubtedly one of the most widely circulated forms of personal reflection on Sánchez's role within the Cuban revolution, at least one other significant memory text appeared in the years following Sánchez's death. In November 1985 Julio M. Llanes published a small book titled *Celia nuestra y de las flores* (Our Celia of the Flowers).[78] Illustrated throughout with brightly colored collages of flowers and butterflies interspersed with photos of Sánchez and fanciful sketches of idyllic landscapes, the slim volume actually resembles a personal scrapbook more than a scholarly biographical study. The story presented in the book centers around a young Cuban boy from Manzanillo, the boy's grandfather, and an impromptu road trip to Havana. The adventure begins with just five words from the grandfather: "I have to see her." The reader soon learns that the "her" referred to is Sánchez, and that the purpose of the trip is to lay flowers on Sánchez's coffin, where it is on display in Havana's Plaza of the Revolution.

The story of the journey is told through the grandson's own thoughts, and the focus of his reflections is primarily on his grandfather's character, habits, and talent for storytelling. In the earliest pages of the book, the grandson recalls: "There are two stories that Grandfather told, time and again, and that I have never forgotten. He told them a thousand times; however, whenever you heard them it seemed like the first time. I remember that he would light his cigar, sit back in his chair, and ask me: 'Have I told you the stories of Norma [Sánchez's nom de guerre] and the *Granma*?' . . . 'No . . . I don't remember,' I would answer him, so that he would tell them again. Then Grandfather would blow the smoke from his cigar through his nostrils and begin very slowly, with the same hoarse voice."

The long car ride to the capital becomes a pilgrimage for the bereaved grandfather and a history lesson for the grandson. As they travel through the Cuban countryside, the grandfather recounts all of his personal stories of Sánchez during the earliest years of the revolution. Using a mixture of past and present tenses, he shares intimate memories of the first time he met Sánchez in the Sierra Maestra, of the multiple beautification projects she organized around the rebel base, and of the flowers she always wore in her hair. In an especially emotional segment, the grandfather reflects on Sánchez's caretaking role, recalling that "If someone put on a pair of new boots that were sent from the *llano*, he/she thought of Celia. We knew that she was the one that had sent them. If a package arrived with uniforms or knapsacks . . . we would go crazy with happiness and think: 'Celia sent this!' . . . Such was the level of her help that we loved her like a sister, or like a mother. Because mothers are like that: always worried about the needs of others. And if someone doesn't have something, they leave no stone unturned looking for it, and they deliver it with a smile."

In reference to Sánchez's character, the grandfather states that "'she is quiet. She does a lot and says little. She doesn't like to make noise for anything. She does it all quietly, but she does it.'" Unfortunately, the grandfather's reactions to seeing the body of his beloved compatriot are not included in the story, and the book ends with a final poignant conversation between the grandfather and his grandson as they begin the journey back to Manzanillo. As the taxi passes through Havana's city limits, the boy suddenly comprehends the finality of Sánchez's death and asks innocently: "'Grandfather, now we won't see Celia anymore?' I asked him. He paused for a moment before answering me; then he said: 'Perhaps now we will see her more in photos. Now, everyone who knows something about her will say it'—he stopped talking, as if thinking. . . . 'You know something?'—he asked as he glanced at me out of the corner of his eye—'People die when they are forgotten; but when they are remembered with love, they are alive.'" In the final scene of the book, the young boy and his grandfather are clasped in a tearful embrace.

This poignant story of one man's personal memories of Sánchez illustrates how individual and collective, as well as official and unofficial, histories can intersect. In order to grasp the significance of this book as a memory text, we must first set aside the question of truth. Whether or not the characters in the book represent real people who actually experienced the events described is irrelevant. Elizabeth Van Houts has similarly stated that "if we are interested in the process of remembering and the formation of memories, the criterion of historical reliability is of little or no importance in judging the significance of the memory."[79] What is important here is the book's emotive content—the virtual reality being created in order to tell a much larger story.

While the book presents the memories of one individual's personal relationship with Sánchez, the language and symbols used to relate those memories resonate with other official and popular memory texts. Descriptions of Sánchez as a self-abnegating mother figure who was both hardworking and feminine had been in circulation for over five years at the time of the book's publication. It is at least reasonable to assume that the book's content was produced through the commingling of the personal recollections of the author, Llanes, and the existing public discourses surrounding Sánchez's memory.

Presented as an intergenerational dialogue, *Celia nuestra y de las flores* becomes the story of storytelling itself—of the dynamic social process in which memory is both transmitted and transformed. From the grandfather, to the grandson, to the reader of the book, these memories of Sánchez are passed from the imagination of the author to the imagination of the public, only to then be incorporated into new dialogues between different people at other moments in history. It is this cyclical movement of memory, from the public realm to the private realm and then back to the public realm, that permits Sánchez's memory—with all its attendant lessons, myths, and symbols—to be passed on to the next generation of Cubans.

In Morejón's poetry, Llanes's book, and the oral testimonies of individual Cubans, Sánchez becomes the embodiment of nurturing, devotion, self-abnegation, and hard work. The enumeration of these personal qualities demonstrates the persistence of a relatively standardized language and symbolism to describe Sánchez from the time of Hart Dávalos's eulogy in 1980. These popular memory texts simply ground the mythology surrounding Sánchez in the world of personal experience. At times these real or imagined experiences converge with official memory, and at other times they diverge from it, thus opening up new spaces for memory to exist.

Morejón's poetry and Llanes' book are also some of the few memory texts relating to Sánchez produced by Afro-Cuban authors. While the official state mythology of the Cuban Revolution is still grounded in and filtered through the experience of its most iconic (and primarily white) leaders, these two texts open at least some space to other voices. The fact that the Llanes text and Morejón's poems found their way onto newspaper stands and bookshelves means, however, that they were likely subject to the kind of rigorous peer review and editing processes required by large publishing houses. They are popular sources in that they were not crafted by state officials, but their content may well have been shaped by the expectations of the institutions for which they work or to which they owe the publication. Both Llanes and Morejón are closely associated with the National Union of Cuban Writers and Artists and the Casa de las Américas, two eminent literary institutions tied closely to the national government. These sources thus hang suspended—like so many things in Cuba—between the worlds of private experience and public duty.

Myths and Memorials

In his signal work *Imagined Communities: Reflections on the Origin and Spread of Nationalism*, Benedict Anderson states that "the deaths that structure the nation's biography are of a special kind."[80] The death of the Cuban revolutionary and secretary of the Council of State, Celia Sánchez Manduley, on 11 January 1980, was one such special historical event that has earned its place in the biography of Cuba. For a nation coming to terms with a turbulent and often violent history, Sánchez has become the symbol of a revolutionary ideal. The various sites of memory that were produced subsequent to Sánchez's death, by national leaders, government institutions, and individual men and women, present particular memories of her contributions to Cuban society. In turn, these memories have shaped a much larger, multifaceted national discourse concerning the relationship of the individual to the body politic, the definition of an ideal revolutionary *cubanidad*, and the proper role for women in Cuban society.

The often ambiguous, but always highly interactive, relationship between official memories of Sánchez and the memories that are transmitted by individuals highlights an important characteristic of national memory. Each story, each experience, and each conversation (whether it exists in written or oral form) that makes reference to memories of Sánchez is just one thread in the much larger memory quilt of the Cuban people. Over the years, these threads of memory have been woven together by various individuals to serve a range of purposes, from rallying the nation to collective action in the face of an economic crisis to simply recalling the lived experience of the early years of the revolution. These memories of Sánchez, in all their multiple forms, prove that "memory is not a passive depository of fact, but an active process of creation of meanings."[81] The meanings ascribed to Sánchez's memory have had ramifications far beyond the memorializing of one woman; they have played a crucial role in the creation of Cuban national identity itself. Guerra reminds us that the "Cuban Revolution [is] a verbal and visual struggle over shared, and, at times, competing texts that together generated key events as well as a simple, if conflicting, 'truth.'"[82]

The act of memorializing Sánchez's death was causally linked to her subsequent mythification, and this process has had a tremendous impact on both official and popular imaginings of the ideal socialist revolutionary. By tracing the contours of the public and private acts of memory that followed her death, we can begin to establish the links between gender, revolution, and memory. Specifically, we gain new insights into the ways in which the mythologized biography of an individual can become the embodiment of a geographical place, a collection of ideal human characteristics, and a way of life. Whether or not popular imaginings of Sánchez and her life represent the reality of who she was matters much less than their ability to reflect the ideals of a larger revolutionary discourse—one that Cubans aspire to, reformulate, or reject accordingly.

Taylor argues that "myths incorporate elements of 'reality' that contribute to their underlying pattern of values: others they omit. These elements are not included because they 'actually happened' but rather because they fit the myth: they become mythic."[83] Consequently, the fact that Sánchez is remembered as both a private and a public figure, as tough but tender, as hardworking but feminine, and as dedicated but humble perhaps tells us less about Sánchez than it does about the ways in which officials, artists, and activists attempted to (re)imagine the revolution in the face of new national challenges.

CHAPTER EIGHT

Myth, Mother, *Mujer*
Afterlife of a Revolutionary

> Do not look for her in mausoleums, but rather in the heart of
> the people . . . almost nobody remembers the sound of her voice.
> That does not matter. She was the inheritor of all voices. She was,
> in reality, all of us.
>
> —MIGUEL BARNET, "Celia: Amó lo bello porque lo bello era justo"

> In Havana, the dead are alive because they are dead.
>
> —JOSÉ QUIROGA, *Cuban Palimpsests*

Return to Media Luna

I returned to Sánchez's hometown in January 2018 to attend the thirty-eighth annual commemoration of her death. My arrival in Cuba was considerably more fraught than usual. Security officials detained me for questioning at the airport in Holguín, which first happened shortly after the passage of the Helms–Burton Law (1996), and had not happened again in the subsequent twenty-two years. Rather than buzz me forward to the arrivals area, the security agent sent me into an adjoining booth, where another agent questioned me about my travel history, personal and professional connections on the island, and the subject matter of my research. Following the thirty-minute interview, the woman decided she was satisfied with my answers and buzzed me through.

I cleared the metal detectors and moved into the baggage area, where the airport's drug-sniffing cocker spaniels moved excitedly between the assembled suitcases. A smiling woman wearing a khaki uniform greeted me as I exited the building and offered to help me find my Airbnb host. We both laughed when she shouted "Pedro? Pedro?" and six men stepped forward in response. Finally, the Pedro we sought appeared with a cigarette in hand and a concerned look on his face. My delayed exit had worried him. He quickly grabbed my suitcase handle and directed me toward the parking lot. Comfortably seated in an air-conditioned taxi that he had hired for the 184-kilometer ride to Media Luna, Pedro and I lamented the re-cooling of diplomatic relations between our two countries, which had undoubtedly triggered the additional airport screening.

The long drive to Media Luna took us along a bumpy highway past a string of sugar mill towns, agricultural cooperatives, and historical markers. The inordinately heavy rains had stalled the annual three-month *zafra* (sugar harvest), leaving cane fields partially harvested and cane cutters waiting for work. We stopped at a roadside produce stand to purchase tomatoes and cabbage for the evening's meal and at a bar to purchase a case of domestically produced Cristal beer. Pedro informed me that with carnival season over, the beer supply in Media Luna was low. He was also eager to introduce me to the local rum, Pinilla, which he considered an essential experience for all visitors to the province.

We arrived in Media Luna just as workers and students were heading home for their afternoon meal, and the town was bustling with activity. The social heart of Media Luna still sits at a bustling intersection that features a handful of stores and restaurants, a beauty shop, and a small public library. A man seated at a desktop computer sells local teenagers access to the *paquete*, a downloadable bundle of movies, music, and newspapers that arrives each week from Miami. A short drive down Raúl Podio Avenue led us to the charming guesthouse where Pedro's wife greeted us as we pulled up. I had selected Pedro's house from Airbnb—one of only two properties listed for Media Luna—both for its quaint upstairs balcony and for its location. Just outside my bedroom window, a small plastic sign mounted on a metal pole invites visitors to tour the nearby Museo Casa Natal Celia Sánchez (Celia Sánchez Childhood Home Museum).

Media Luna was exactly as I remembered—a rural community proudly rooted in its identity as Sánchez's hometown and deeply invested in preserving and promoting her story. Positioned in the province (Granma) with the greatest number of historical markers on the entire island, Media Luna's significance as a site of historical memory is unquestionable, if still largely undiscovered by foreign tourists. Beyond the history of Sánchez, Media Luna is a repository of information regarding sugar mill life, early worker mobilizations, and the spread of communist thought on the island during the early twentieth century. While public memorials and commemorative ceremonies in town revolve primarily around its most famous citizen, Media Luna provides a case study in the complexities of rural Cuban life.

Media Luna's annual tribute to Sánchez begins early on 11 January with a morning procession toward Martyrs Park. A string of concurrent ceremonies stretching from Havana to Santiago de Cuba provide a moment of national synchronicity. For the revolution's faithful, the celebration acts as connective tissue binding them to an imagined past and to a set of contemporary ideals. For its critics—provided they are not state employees, for whom attendance at the ceremony is likely compulsory—the day passes like any other.

Following breakfast on the day of the ceremony, I hailed a bicycle taxi and joined the small crowd gathering at the park. One of the local directors of the Communist Party approached to inform me that the ceremony was a political act, and was not open to the public. Fortunately, one of Pedro's family members, who was awaiting my arrival, made my formal introduction. The man excused himself and darted across the street to the local party headquarters. He returned ten minutes later and informed me that I was welcome to observe the ceremony and, with a quick parting handshake, he moved toward the front of the group.

I milled through the crowd for a few minutes, admiring the large floral arrangement standing in front of the Sánchez fountain. Three concentric rings of bright purple and pink orchids swathed with glittery ribbons bore the message, "To Celia Sánchez Manduley from the People of Media Luna." There were around eighty people of various ages in attendance, as well as a reporter and photographer from the provincial newspaper. When the first notes of the national anthem began to play over the sound system, we pressed closer to the gazebo.

The program began with a quick welcome from the director of the party, who had greeted me upon my arrival. An a cappella women's troupe dressed in peach-colored gowns performed an emotional song dedicated to Sánchez that compared her to the national mariposa flower. The chorus repeated: "May her perfume expand across the dawn / And dress the mountains in color / She gives her heart and her soul / And life is better because of her dream." The current director of the Celia Sánchez Childhood Home Museum, Marbelis Terry Pérez, then took the podium to deliver the keynote address.

As with most speeches dedicated to Cuba's revolutionary heroes, including Guevara and now Fidel Castro, Terry's speech referred only to Sánchez's "*desaparición física*" (physical disappearance) thirty-eight years ago and not to her death. At the start of his tribute to Sánchez, penned on the fifth anniversary of her death, Álvarez Tabío similarly noted that "It hardly seems possible that five years have passed since her physical disappearance. It seems that she has never stopped being present."[1] Sánchez gains a powerful afterlife through this formulation of death. No longer present in body, she lives through her example. Terry Pérez noted that Sánchez's reputation as

Castro's "most faithful interpreter" provides Cubans with an "example of unsurpassed political and ideological loyalty."

Terry Pérez applauded Sánchez's simplicity, austerity, and commitment, and was quick to claim Sánchez for Media Luna, stating, "Media Luna has the exceptional privilege of being Celia's hometown and guardian of her house, now converted into a museum, and which now forms part of our legacy." She enumerated Sánchez's contributions to the revolution, including her status as one of the principal organizers of the *Granma* landing in 1956. Terry Pérez professed that she considers Sánchez to have come from "the same lineage as Mariana Grajales and of the great women of Cuban history." "[She was a] woman of all times, [and a] genuine representation of women who can occupy any trench and maintain their gentleness, sensitivity, and tenderness," she noted. She recognized Sánchez for helping to "resolve innumerable problems from the most diverse spheres of our social and economic life: Beauty, culture, education, history, solidarity with other countries, factories, gardens, [and] flowers received as never before her emerald attention."

Terry Pérez ended her speech with a kind of secular altar call summoning the audience to reaffirm patriotic values. In her concluding remarks, she stated, "Her memory lives and will forever live in the most sacred altar of historic values; she will live eternally in every Cuban; her presence inspires, motivates, [and] drives us, [and] her works are enduring in spite of the inevitable passage of time." Terry Pérez encouraged participants too young to have made the specific sacrifices of Sánchez and her generation to answer more contemporary calls to "sacrifice" in service to something larger than self.[2] She noted, "Her legacy will remain everywhere, in difficult moments and in simple details, with every man and woman of this land, with those who work and fight to construct the future, with those who teach, with those who study and with those who heal, with those who share the dream that a better world is possible for us all. We will always remember Celia as the purest, most tender, and most native flower of the Cuban Revolution. Celia's example will live forever. Long live Fidel. Long live the Cuban Revolution." The crowd offered their warm applause and then dispersed in various directions across the park.

Icons, Symbols, and the Construction of Power

In his analysis of Guevara's legacy, Michael J. Casey notes that "mainstream political analysis ignores a vital aesthetic element to the construction of power . . . the appeal of icons and symbols."[3] He also notes that "to function . . . as an all-encompassing symbol—the identity, ideas, and life history of the author or the organization must be distilled and simplified [to] dispense with the complexity and nuance of their underlying reality."[4] By positioning Sánchez's biography at the intersection of representation, politics, and gender, we can both reconstruct the details of her life and trace a genealogy of the meanings ascribed to her story. The task is not merely to prove or disprove the details of her life as they have been preserved, communicated, and recast over the years. Instead, the task is to understand how and why interpretations of her story have developed and changed over time. As an abstracted symbol of the New Woman, Sánchez has helped shape imaginings of the Cuban Revolution as a historical experience and as an idea. By accepting that her life story is tied to a broader national performance of the ideal revolutionary state, we can move beyond the confines of traditional biography and into the terrain of gender and representation as they relate to Cuba's revolutionary process.[5]

Since her death in 1980, the number and variety of sites of memory relating to Sánchez has grown and changed. Castro biographer Tad Szulc notes that "since her death, [Sánchez] has been virtually canonized by the revolution."[6] In terms of actual physical sites, her name appears on a number of day care centers and elementary schools (including one in Zimbabwe, in Africa), a social workers' college, a hospital, two museums, and a large textile factory in Santiago de Cuba. Her image appears on two Cuban postage stamps, a commemorative one-peso coin, and in the watermark of the twenty-peso note. In 2015, the National Institute of Agricultural Science in San José de las Lajas, Mayabeque, Cuba, announced a new orchid hybrid that they named Memoria Celia Sánchez Manduley (Memory Celia Sánchez Manduley).[7]

Sánchez's story also continues to circulate through the arts. Sánchez has inspired two well-known Cuban songs, "Manzanillera combatiente" and "Y aquí en el corazón del pueblo" (And Here in the Heart of the People).[8] Both songs play regularly during television and radio broadcasts transmitted on the anniversaries of her birth and death. Shortly after Sánchez's death in 1980, Castro commissioned a group of artists to reflect on Sánchez's significance for Cuban history. The result of their collaboration was a breathtaking portfolio of large-format, limited-edition prints titled simply *Celia*.[9] The various artists called upon their unique aesthetic and interpretive skills to depict Sánchez as a woman hovering at the threshold of spiritual monumentality and earthly intimacy. They depicted her surrounded by technicolor Cuban foliage, staring wistfully into the distance with wind-blown hair, or taking the form of a mariposa bloom. Embodying the symbols of an authentic postrevolutionary *cubanidad*, Sánchez does not merely adorn her hair with a mariposa in these works, she *becomes* the mariposa.

Some artwork depicting Sánchez—like the *La Paloma* (The Dove) screen print by California-based artist and cultural worker Melanie Cervantes that is featured on the cover of this book—were produced outside of Cuba. Cervantes is the founder of the collaborative graphic arts project, Dignidad Rebelde, which draws on principles of Xicanisma (Chicana feminism) and Zapatismo (agrarian socialism) to translate stories of struggle and resistance into artwork that can be put back into the hands of the communities that inspire it. Rendered in the bold, graphic protest poster art that characterizes Cervantes's work, the *La Paloma* image claims Sánchez as an icon for Latina/Xicana activism writ large. That Sánchez's name does not appear on the poster operates as a subtle reproach to those not already familiar with her story; her historical significance obligates us to know her. If Frida Kahlo, Rigoberta Menchú, and Angela Davis need no identification in Cervantes's work, neither should Sánchez, the omission suggests.

Sánchez also appears in contemporary fiction, theater, documentaries, and radio broadcasts. In 2012, author Rosa Jordan crafted a fictional account of a Havana pediatrician, Celia Cantú, who embarks upon a life-altering exploration of Cuba's social and economic issues when her body becomes possessed by Celia Sánchez. Playwright Acie Cargill offered his take on the enduring rumors that Sánchez and Castro were romantically involved in his 2017 play *Celia Sánchez: Heroine of Cuba*. The act that takes place in the Sierra Maestra includes a racy love scene between the two guerrilla fighters.[10] Sánchez also appears briefly in Steven Soderbergh's award-winning *Che* biopic (2008).[11] Spanish actress Elvira Mínguez, who portrays Sánchez in the film, bears a striking physical resemblance to the Cuban leader. Mínguez acknowledged in an interview that while Sánchez was a woman of "tremendous historical importance," she plays only a "secondary role" in the film.[12]

Works produced within Cuba echo her official state biography and give little, if any, space to alternative readings of her life story. In 2005 Rodríguez Menéndez produced a twenty-three-chapter radio drama titled *Una muchacha llamada Celia* (A Girl Named Celia) based on his book by the same title.[13] The program weaves fact and fiction to tell a romanticized story of Sánchez, her family, and the revolution. Produced with a mass audience in mind, the goal of the program was both to educate and to entertain. A handful of film documentaries produced since Sánchez's death also follow her official biography closely. They tell a story of a heroic and loyal woman of pure revolutionary integrity who—like Castro—was born to lead Cuba into a bold new future.[14]

Commemorative sites such as Sánchez's childhood home museum in Media Luna, her monument in Lenin Park, or her crypt in Havana's Colón Cemetery are also creative spaces where visitors exchange memories about Sánchez, recount stories of their participation in the revolution, and ascribe their own meanings to their national heroine. José Quiroga encourages us to see these spaces as palimpsests that do not "reproduce the original, but [rather] dismantle it, write on top of it, [and] allow it to be seen. It is a queer form of reproduction, one where two texts, two sites, two lives, blend into one continuous present."[15] We might consider her very biography in the same manner—a palimpsest that blends memory, mythology, and experience into an evolving story of one significant woman's life. Through the interjection of new voices and experiences, the mythology surrounding Sánchez is continuously redefined and reinvented. As Nora states, "Sites of memory only exist because of their capacity for metamorphosis, an endless recycling of their meaning and an unpredictable proliferation of their ramifications."[16]

Sánchez left relatively few written reflections on her experience as a female revolutionary leader. Unlike other famous Latin American women who engaged autobiography—Eva Perón and Frida Kahlo come immediately to mind—we know little of the private choices and experiences that shaped Sánchez's public life. Fully aware that she was bearing witness to historic events, Sánchez began a personal diary during her time in the Sierra Maestra. She only ever scribbled out seventeen pages. Her personal correspondence is housed in Havana's Office of Historical Affairs, but is closely guarded by the Cuban government, which reveres the letters as national treasures. Enforced at both the individual and institutional levels, the layers of security that surround Sánchez's memory speak to the power of her position within the broader Cuban revolutionary mythos. They also shape who is able to access her story and how.

If revolution is a process, then the process of constructing collective memory is as much a part of a revolution as are the battles won and lost.[17] Through the expression of various types of collective and individual memories, Sánchez's life has assumed mythic proportions that far exceed the possibilities of any one woman. Guerra notes that in the making of the Cuban Revolution, "true military warfare [has been] replaced by symbolic forms of warfare."[18] The grand unifying historical event of the Cuban people, their revolution, and the idealized female revolutionary icon, Celia Sánchez Manduley, become common reference points against which all citizens (but perhaps women especially) are encouraged to measure their revolutionary conviction. Cubans living on the island and throughout the world either aspire to, reject, or reformulate this discourse accordingly. The process of making and remaking her story is, therefore, perpetual, because "memory is not static but alive."[19]

Final Reflections

On my most recent visit to the Museum of the Revolution in Havana I overheard a conversation between two young tourists—who I assumed were college students on holiday—standing in front of the glass case that holds a set of Sánchez's fatigues. One of the young women asked her friend, "Who is Celia Sánchez? I have never even heard of her."

Time will reveal how Cuba's changing political and economic landscape will impact the politics of remembrance with regard to the revolution in general and Sánchez in particular. Will future generations of Cubans connect to her story? Will the inevitable death of her generation of revolutionary leaders erode or fortify the powerful mythology that still hangs around her image? What will happen to her biography when a global audience gains new access to her life story after decades of relative obscurity? Sánchez's childhood home museum in Media Luna is now accessible via virtual tour to visitors across the globe, and international bike enthusiasts can participate in a fourteen-day "Celia Sánchez Tribute Ride." Every year on the anniversary of her death towns and cities across the island hold commemorative services in Sánchez's honor and the Cuban press posts to the internet articles about the celebrations. In an era when online auction venues allow for the distribution of stamps, coins, and artwork across geographic borders, Sánchez's image may circulate to new audiences who will ascribe their own (new) meanings to the national hero. How will the dissemination of her image through channels not wholly—or even primarily—controlled by the revolutionary state shape her biography? In a broader sense, what impact will these changes have on the stories we tell about the Cuban Revolution and its leaders more generally?

Sánchez's postmortem celebration within Cuba as self-abnegating, deferential, and maternal ultimately reveals the tensions inherent in Cuba's project for the New Woman and raises questions about the liberation the revolution offered. Sánchez worked within these limitations, carving her unique trajectory through the landscape of a revolutionary history still dominated by the image of bearded men in fatigues. Even for Sánchez's

naysayers and enemies—of whom there have been many over the years—
her influence and the scope of her accomplishments are too vast to ignore.
They may not agree with her politics, but most critics acknowledge her
influence. For her supporters, she remains a symbol of loyalty, persever-
ance, and courage. Her legacy for them hangs suspended in the ether of
the revolution's "golden age" before the collapse of the Soviet Union in
1989 precipitated a severe economic crisis whose effects are felt still today.
One interviewee—who asked to remain anonymous—remarked that "if
Celia were still alive, none of this would be happening."

While interpretations of Sánchez's life and legacy vary widely, she became
over the course of her life the Cuban Revolution's most influential female
leader and a link to the power of its supreme commander. Her biography has
been shaped by the vagaries of revolutionary politics, media scrutiny, diplomatic tensions, romantic speculation, and her own aspirations and desires.
It is bound to a broader revolutionary history that is continually imagined
and reimagined, made and remade. Whatever the next chapter of Sánchez's
life story looks like, it will reveal something worth knowing about where the
Cuban Revolution stands and where it is headed.

Notes

Abbreviations Used in the Notes

OAHCE/FCS   Oficina de Asuntos Históricos del Consejo de Estado, Fondo Celia Sánchez

UF/CMC   University of Florida, Cuban Miscellaneous Collection

UF/ECC   University of Florida, Ernesto Chávez Collection

Chapter One

1. The Mariana Grajales Brigade, named after the heroic mother of Cuban independence, was officially inaugurated in September 1958, with Isabela Rielo as the commanding officer. Though consisting of only fourteen women, the Marianas participated in a number of military encounters with Batista's army. Smith and Padula, *Sex and Revolution*, 30–31.

2. *Diario de la Marina* (10 May 1959): 3.

3. David Martínez Rodríguez, interview with author, 10 May 2016, Santa Clara, Cuba.

4. Luciak, *Gender and Democracy in Cuba*, 4.

5. Castro evoked this phrase in his 9 December 1966 address at the closing of the Fifth National Plenary of the FMC. See Castro, "The Revolution within the Revolution," in Stone, *Women and the Cuban Revolution*, 48–54.

6. Moreno Fonseca, interview with author.

7. Moreno Fonseca, interview with author.

8. Gónzalez López, "Para Celia."

9. For studies of Martí's social and political thought and its legacy, see López, *José Martí*, and Guerra, *The Myth of José Martí*.

10. Conte, phone interview with author.

11. Randall, phone interview with author.

12. Backscheider, *Reflections on Biography*, 146, 139.

13. Randall, phone interview with author.

14. See Álvarez Tabío, *Celia*; Stout, *One Day in December*; Haney, *Celia Sánchez*.

15. I am grateful to the anonymous manuscript reviewer who pointed me in this fruitful direction.

16. Crane, "Writing the Individual Back," 138.

17. On 9 February 1995, Senator Jesse Helms introduced the "Cuban Liberty and Democratic Solidarity (LIBERTAD) Act," which would tighten the U.S. embargo against Cuba. The full text of the Helms–Burton law is available in "Legislation and Regulations—United States." For an analysis of the events leading up to the legislation, see Ferrao, *Helms–Burton Law*.

18. Guerra, "Memory and Representations," 197. Geary discusses the notion of memory "filters" in *Phantoms of Remembrance*, 7, 177.

19. James, *Doña María's Story*, 128.

20. Here I am using the term memory as defined by Confino: "the ways in which people construct a sense of the past" (Confino, "Collective Memory and Cultural History," 1386). Noakes points out that "this sense of the past is created in two ways: through public representations and through private memory" (Noakes, *War and the British*, 12). I am also referring to the original definition of the term "sites of memory" coined by Pierre Nora. While his definition of *lieux de mémoire* ("where memory crystallizes and secretes itself") may leave room for interpretation, his three-part definition of their purpose (material, symbolic, and functional) is instructive (see Nora, "Between Memory and History," 7–24).

21. Hart Dávalos, "El ejemplo de Celia," 59.

22. Quiroga, *Cuban Palimpsests*, xi.

23. Testimony of Griselda Sánchez Manduley, in Rodríguez Menéndez, *Una muchacha llamada Celia*, 47.

24. Mangini, *Memories of Resistance*, 53.

25. Quiroga, *Cuban Palimpsests*, 2.

26. Taylor, *Eva Perón*, 9.

27. Randall, *Haydée Santamaría*; Bishop-Sánchez, *Creating Carmen Miranda*.

28. See Bayard de Volo, *Women and the Cuban Insurrection*; Chase, *Revolution within the Revolution*; Guerra, *Visions of Power*; and Serra, *The New Man in Cuba*.

29. Efraim Conte, phone interview with author, 27 June 2016.

30. Stout, *One Day in December*, 2013.

31. For a history of Julio Lobo, see Rathbone, *The Sugar King of Havana*.

32. Yolanda Díaz, email correspondence with author, 16 November 2018.

33. MGB, "Monumento a Celia," 41–42.

34. Ricardo Luís, "Celia entre nosotros."

35. "Cuso," interview with author.

36. Kish Sklar, "Coming to Terms with Florence Kelley," 31, 32.

37. Nora, "Between Memory and History," 19.

38. Quiroga, *Cuban Palimpsests*.

39. Hart Dávalos, "El ejemplo de Celia," 59.

40. Rudnick, "The Male-Identified Woman, 119.

Chapter Two

1. "Manzanillera combatiente," *Enciclopedia Digital*.

2. For a history of Media Luna, including a discussion of the Beattie enterprise, see Alarcón Mariño, *Historia de Media Luna*.

3. "Cuba," *Louisiana Planter*, 94.

4. Bécquer Céspedes, interview with author.

5. Prados-Torreira, *Mambisas*.

6. Barnet, Miguel. "Celia."

7. OAHCE/FCS, "Sobre colocación de busto de Carlos Manuel de Céspedes en parque infantil de Media Luna [11 June 1930]."

8. "Casa Natal de Celia Sánchez Manduley."

9. OAHCE/FCS, "Dr. Manuel Sánchez Silveira: Ejemplo de médico y ciudadano en el primer aniversario de su muerte [26 June 1959]."

10. Testimony of Acacia Sánchez Manduley in Chirino, "El Padre de Celia," 86.

11. Sección de Investigaciones Históricos, *Celia: Los años de Media Luna*, 9.

12. OAHCE/FCS, "Cuaderno de Manuel Sánchez Silveira sobre temas históricos."

13. Conte, phone interview with author.

14. Hart Dávalos, *Aldabonazo*, 176.

15. Reyes Rodríguez, "Cuban Heroine Celia Sánchez."

16. Reyes Rodríguez, "Cuban Heroine Celia Sánchez."

17. Reyes Rodríguez, "Cuban Heroine Celia Sánchez."

18. "Casa Natal de Celia Sánchez Manduley."

19. Casa Natal Celia Sánchez, "Casa Natal de Sánchez."

20. Los Conejitos de Celia, *Una muchacha llamada Celia*; Rodríguez Menéndez, "Celia Sánchez"; Rodriguez Menéndez, *Una muchacha llamada Celia*.

21. "Casa Natal de Celia Sánchez Manduley."

22. Rodríguez Menéndez, "Celia Sánchez."

23. Miles, *The House on Diamond Hill*, 25–26.

24. Miles, *The House on Diamond Hill*, 26.

25. Miles, *The House on Diamond Hill*, 17.

26. Sección de Investigaciones Históricos, *Celia: Los años de Media Luna*, 9.

27. Sección de Investigaciones Históricos, *Celia: Los años de Media Luna*, 9.

28. The Cuban peso and U.S. dollar exchanged at a 1:1 rate in 1947. OAHCE/FCS, "Cuenta de banco de Manuel Sánchez Silveira [29 August 1941]."

29. OAHCE/FCS, "Viaje de vacaciones de Manuel Sánchez Silveira [15 September 1949]"; OAHCE/FCS, "Viaje de vacaciones de Manuel Sánchez Silveira [7 September 1949]."

30. Palomares Ferrales, *Celia: Mi mejor regalo*, 24.

31. Rodríguez Menéndez, *Una muchacha llamada Celia*, 20–21, 28, 46.

32. Palomares Ferrales, *Celia: Mi mejor regalo*, 25.

33. For an excellent discussion of the revolutionary government's limited success in securing racial equality, see Spence Benson, *Antiracism in Cuba*, 2016, and de la Fuente, *A Nation for All*.

34. Miles, *The House on Diamond Hill*, 18.

35. Brundage, *The Southern Past*, 184.

36. Álvarez Tabío, "Celia: Cabal imágen del pueblo," 4.

37. Epstein, *Recognizing Biography*, 140.

38. Backscheider, *Reflections on Biography*, 94.

39. Bécquer Céspedes, *Celia: La más autóctona flor*, 2.

40. A copy of her birth certificate, which she must have obtained when she traveled to the United States in 1948, is housed in the Office of Historical Affairs. OAHCE/FCS, "Certificado literal de nacimiento [30 June 1948]."

41. Testimony of Dr. Adolfina Cossío in González Cabrera, "Vamos a hablar de Celia," *Mujeres* 20, no. 8 (August 1980): 10.

42. Sarabia, *Dr. Manuel Sánchez Silveira, médico rural*, 112.

43. Sección de Investigaciones Históricos, *Celia: Los años de Media Luna*, 12.

44. OAHCE/FCS, "Sobre el estado sanitario del pueblo de Media Luna [16 October 1923]."

45. Sección de Investigaciones Históricos, *Celia: Los años de Media Luna*, 12.

46. Álvarez Tabío, *Celia*, 45.

47. Álvarez Tabío, *Celia*, 46–47; Sección de Investigaciones Históricos, *Celia: Los años de Media Luna*, 11.

48. Stout, *One Day in December*, 30.

49. Testimony of Manuel Enrique Sánchez Manduley in Rodríguez Menéndez, *Una muchacha llamada Celia*, 33.

50. Testimony of Dr. Adolfina Cossío in González Cabrera, "Vamos a hablar de Celia," 10.

51. Testimony of Manuel Enrique Sánchez Manduley in Rodríguez Menéndez, *Una muchacha llamada Celia*, 32. The same testimony appears in Palomares Ferrales, *Celia: Mi mejor regalo*, 28.

52. Álvarez Tabío, *Celia*, 47; Sección de Investigaciones Históricos, *Celia: Los años de Media Luna*, 11.

53. Testimony of Silvia Sánchez Manduley in Chirino, "El Padre de Celia," 84.

54. Testimony of Griselda Sánchez Manduley in Rodríguez Menéndez, *Una muchacha llamada Celia*, 32. The same testimony appears in Palomares Ferrales, *Celia: Mi mejor regalo*, 29.

55. Rodríguez Menéndez, *Una muchacha llamada Celia*, 30.

56. Testimony of Dr. Adolfina Cossío in González Cabrera, "Vamos a hablar de Celia," 10.

57. Testimony of Griselda Sánchez Manduley in Rodríguez Menéndez, *Una muchacha llamada Celia*, 32.

58. Testimony of Silvia Sánchez Manduley in Rodríguez Menéndez, *Una muchacha llamada Celia*, 30. The same testimony also appears in Palomares Ferrales, *Celia: Mi mejor regalo*, 28.

59. Testimony of Flavia Sánchez Manduley in Chirino, "El Padre de Celia," 85.

60. Acuña Núñez, "Vida y personalidad del Dr. Manuel Sánchez Silveira," 11; Chirino, "El Padre de Celia," 86; Sarabia, *Dr. Manuel Sánchez Silveira, médico rural*, 25; testimony of Flavia Sánchez Manduley in Chirino, "El Padre de Celia," 85.

61. Testimony of Griselda Sánchez Manduley in Chirino, "El Padre de Celia," 86.

62. Testimony of Flavia Sánchez Manduley in Chirino, "El Padre de Celia," 85.

63. Álvarez Tabío, *Celia*, 93.

64. Acuña Núñez, "Vida y personalidad del Dr. Manuel Sánchez Silveira,"2; Sección de Investigaciones Históricos, *Celia: Los años de Media Luna*, 9.

65. See also Sección de Investigaciones Históricos, *Celia: Los años de Media Luna*, 12.

66. Acuña Núñez, "Vida y personalidad del Dr. Manuel Sánchez Silveira," 4–5; Rodríguez Menéndez, *Una muchacha llamada Celia*, 34.

67. Rodríguez Menéndez, *Una muchacha llamada Celia*, 39.

68. OAHCE/FCS, "Datos biográficos de la familia Sánchez Manduley [May 1922]."

69. Nydia Sarabia reproduces Dr. Sánchez's complete works in Sarabia, *Dr. Manuel Sánchez Silveira, médico rural*.

70. OAHCE/FCS, "Texto escrito por Manuel Sánchez Silveira relativo al lugar donde murió Carlos Manuel de Céspedes al parecer el documento está incompleto [n.d.]."

71. Rodríguez Menéndez, *Una muchacha llamada Celia*, 35; Acuña Núñez, "Vida y personalidad del Dr. Manuel Sánchez Silveira," 7; Sarabia, *Dr. Manuel Sánchez Silveira, médico rural*, 36. See also a four-page article he wrote about Maceo, which may have served as the kernel for the book project. OAHCE/FCS, "Homenaje Antonio Maceo [n.d.]."

72. Testimony of Silvia Sánchez Manduley in Chirino, "El Padre de Celia," 86. See also Acuña Núñez, "Vida y personalidad del Dr. Manuel Sánchez Silveira," 5.

73. Testimony of Manuel Enrique Sánchez Manduley in Palomares Ferrales, *Celia: Mi mejor regalo*, 39.

74. OAHCE/FCS, "Acreditación de Manuel Sánchez Silveira como corresponsal de la Sociedad Epeliológia de Cuba [26 December 1952]." Sección de Investigaciones Históricos, *Celia: Los años de Media Luna*, 12; Acuña Núñez, "Vida y personalidad del Dr. Manuel Sánchez Silveira," 5.

75. Certificate of membership published in Sarabia, *Dr. Manuel Sánchez Silveira, médico rural*, 18.

76. Sarabia, *Dr. Manuel Sánchez Silveira, médico rural*, 20.

77. Letters to Dr. Manuel Sánchez Silveira from general secretary, Geographical Society of Cuba, Juan Manuel Planas, dated 25 May 1934 and 9 July 1934, in Sarabia, *Dr. Manuel Sánchez Silveira, médico rural*, 16–17. See also Acuña Núñez, "Vida y personalidad del Dr. Manuel Sánchez Silveira," 9, and OAHCE/FCS, "Observaciones sobre el pueblo indio de la provincia de Macaca" [3 April 1925]."

78. Testimony of Flavia Sánchez Manduley in Chirino, "El Padre de Celia," 85.

79. Acuña Núñez, "Vida y personalidad del Dr. Manuel Sánchez Silveira," 10.

80. Sarabia transcribed the entire essay in *Dr. Manuel Sánchez Silveira, médico rural*, 45–60. The quote above can be found on page 48.

81. OAHCE/FCS, "Comunicación de Manuel Sánchez Silveira con Eugenio Fernández con una reflexión sobre el futuro de Cuba [17 September 1951]." He used the same phrase in a letter to his granddaughters Alicia Gloria and Elena Otazo Sánchez (Flavia Sánchez's daughters) the next year, OAHCE/FCS, "Comunicación de Manuel Sánchez Silveira con sus nietas [3 June 1952]."

82. Sarabia, *Dr. Manuel Sánchez Silveira, médico rural*, 25.

83. Rodríguez Menéndez, *Una muchacha llamada Celia*, 33.

84. OAHCE/FCS, "Comunicación de Manuel Sánchez Silveira con Fernando Ortiz [9 July 1934]." For biographical studies of Chibás see Ehrlich, *Eduardo Chibás*; Alvarez Martín, *Eduardo Chibás*; and Argote-Freyre, "The Political Afterlife of Eduardo Chibás."

85. OAHCE/FCS, "Sobre la filiación de Manuel Sánchez Silveira al grupo ortodoxo auténtico [19 May 1947]."

86. Testimony of Manuel Enrique Sánchez Manduley in Chirino, "El Padre de Celia," 87; Bécquer Céspedes, *Celia*, 7. For a history of the "Auténtico Years," see Ameringer, *The Cuban Democratic Experience*.

87. Correspondence cited in Chirino, "El Padre de Celia," 86.

88. I am grateful to Efraim Conte for bringing this family connection to my attention.

89. Pérez-Cisneros, *En torno al "98" cubano*, 134. For a general discussion of the Platt Amendment and the 1901 Constitutional Convention, see Pérez, *Cuba under the Platt Amendment*, 1991.

90. For a discussion of Manduley del Río's concern, as governor of Oriente, with Haitian immigration to the province, see Howard, *Black Labor, White Sugar*, 31.

91. Fernández, *Rafael Manduley del Río*, 1995.

92. Conte, email correspondence.

93. Estado Militar de la Isla de Cuba, *Guía de forasteros*, 93.

94. OAHCE/FCS, "Inscripción literal de nacimiento de Manuel Sánchez Silveira [22 September 1886]."

95. Stout, *One Day in December*, 128. Sánchez del Barro owned extensive real estate and was a supplier to the Spanish army. He also owned a general store in Manzanillo called La Spirituana, the San Miguel del Chino farm (now the Hermanos Sánchez Cooperative), and provided the financing behind the Plaza del Mercado in Manzanillo. Conte, email correspondence.

96. Conte, email correspondence.

97. For an account of the four battles fought at Manzanillo and the debacle surrounding the call for a truce, see Handfield Titherington, *A History of the Spanish-American War*. Isabel Silveira Román was the great-grandmother of Mario Girona, who was the architect for Sánchez's famed Coppelia ice cream park project (1966) in Havana's Vedado neighborhood.

98. OAHCE/FCS, "Dr. Manuel Sánchez Silveira: Ejemplo de médico y ciudadano en el primer aniversario de su muerte [26 June 1959]."

99. Chirino, "La niña que fue Celia," 6.

100. Chirino, "La niña que fue Celia," 6.

101. Álvarez Tabío, *Celia*, 55.

102. Chirino, "La niña que fue Celia," 6.

103. Palomares Ferrales, *Celia: Mi mejor regalo*, 32; Chirino, "La niña que fue Celia," 6.

104. OAHCE/FCS, "Sombra chinesca [n.d.]"; OAHCE/FCS, "Diseño de mesa [n.d.]."

105. Rodríguez Menéndez, *Una muchacha llamada Celia*, 45.

106. Testimony of Berta Llópiz in Garcia, "La joven Celia," 4; Álvarez Tabío, *Celia*, 76.

107. Chirino, "La niña que fue Celia," 7.

108. Testimony of Berta Llópiz in Garcia, "La joven Celia," 4.

109. Testimony of Berta Llópiz in Garcia, "La joven Celia," 4.

110. Bécquer Céspedes, *Celia: La más autóctona flor de la Revolución*, 16.

111. Testimony of Dr. Adolfina Cossío in González Cabrera, "Vamos a hablar de Celia," 10.

112. Testimony of Dr. Adolfina Cossío in González Cabrera, "Vamos a hablar de Celia," 11.

113. Testimony of Dr. Adolfina Cossío in González Cabrera, "Vamos a hablar de Celia," 11.

114. Sección de Investigaciones Históricos, *Celia: Los años de Media Luna*, 17.

115. Testimony of Orlando Sánchez Manduley in Rodríguez Menéndez, *Una muchacha llamada Celia*, 45–46.

116. Álvarez Tabío, *Celia*, 110.

117. Testimony of Orlando Sánchez Manduley in Rodríguez Menéndez, *Una muchacha llamada Celia*, 46.

118. Álvarez Tabío, *Celia*, 64–65; Sección de Investigaciones Históricos, *Celia: Los años de Media Luna*, 17.

119. Testimony of Dr. Adolfina Cossío in González Cabrera, "Vamos a hablar de Celia," 13.

120. Garcia, "La joven Celia," 4.

121. Sección de Investigaciones Históricos, *Celia: Los años de Media Luna*, 18.

122. Testimony of Griselda Sánchez Manduley in Garcia, "La joven Celia," 4.

123. Sección de Investigaciones Históricos, *Celia: Los años de Media Luna*, 18.

124. James, *Doña María's Story*, 172.

125. See Guerra's observations on the religious connotations of *fidelismo*. Guerra, *Visions of Power*, 17

126. Testimony of Silvia Sánchez Manduley in Rodríguez Menéndez, *Una muchacha llamada Celia*, 53.

127. Palomares Ferrales, *Celia: Mi mejor regalo*, 45.

128. Testimony of Orlando Sánchez Manduley, in Rodríguez Menéndez, *Una muchacha llamada Celia*, 70.

129. Testimony of Ana Alicia Sánchez Castellanos in Rodríguez Menéndez, *Una muchacha llamada Celia*, 52.

130. Testimony of Griselda Sánchez Manduley in Rodríguez Menéndez, *Una muchacha llamada Celia*, 53.

131. Álvarez Tabío, *Celia*, 78.

132. Stout, *One Day in December*, 37. Testimony of Griselda Sánchez Manduley in Rodríguez Menéndez, *Una muchacha llamada Celia*, 53. This same testimony appears in Palomares Ferrales, *Celia: Mi mejor regalo*, 43.

133. Conte, interview with author.

134. Palomares Ferrales, *Celia: Mi mejor regalo*, 41.

135. Acuña Núñez, "Vida y personalidad del Dr. Manuel Sánchez Silveira," 11–12.

136. Testimony of Manuel Enrique Sánchez Manduley in Palomares Ferrales, *Celia: mi mejor regalo*, 32. See also Sarabia, *Dr. Manuel Sánchez Silveira, médico rural*, 25–26.

137. OAHCE/FCS, "Dr. Manuel Sánchez Silveira: Ejemplo de médico y ciudadano en el primer aniversario de su muerte" [24 June 1959]."

138. Acuña Núñez, "Vida y personalidad del Dr. Manuel Sánchez Silveira," 12; Sarabia, *Dr. Manuel Sánchez Silveira, médico rural*, 25.

139. OAHCE/FCS, "Oposición a Fulgencio Batista [n.d.]."

140. Gott, *Cuba: A New History*, 141–43.

141. Álvarez Tabío, *Celia*, 76.

142. Stout, *One Day in December*, 34.

143. Testimony of Olga Sánchez Castellanos, in Rodríguez Menéndez, *Una muchacha llamada Celia*, 58.

144. Rodríguez Menéndez, *Una muchacha llamada Celia*, 57; Palomares Ferrales reproduces the same song fragment in *Celia: Mi mejor regalo*, 43.

145. Álvarez Tabío, *Celia*, 81.

146. Testimony of Orlando Sánchez Manduley, in Rodríguez Menéndez, *Una muchacha llamada Celia*, 61.

147. Testimony of Olga Sánchez Castellanos, in Rodríguez Menéndez, *Una muchacha llamada Celia*, 58.

148. Testimony of Flavia Sánchez Manduley in Stout, *One Day in December*, 37.

149. Stout, *One Day in December*, 34–37.

150. Randall, phone interview with author.

151. Bécquer Céspedes, interview with author.

152. Testimony of Flavia Sánchez Manduley in Palomares Ferrales, *Celia: Mi mejor regalo*, 45.

153. Testimony of Griselda Sánchez Manduley in Rodríguez Menéndez, *Una muchacha llamada Celia*, 42.

154. Núñez Mesa was elected to the House of Representatives in November 1926 and again in 1932.

155. Alarcón Mariño, *Historia de Media Luna*, 75–79.

156. Sarabia, *Dr. Manuel Sánchez Silveira, médico rural*, 15.

157. Testimony of Manuel Enrique Sánchez Manduley, Palomares Ferrales, *Celia: Mi mejor regalo*, 39.

158. Acuña Núñez, "Vida y personalidad del Dr. Manuel Sánchez Silveira," 14.

159. Bécquer Céspedes, *Celia*, 8; Sarabia, *Dr. Manuel Sánchez Silveira, médico rural*, 15.

160. Testimony of Manuel Enrique Sánchez Manduley in Chirino, "El Padre de Celia," 86.

161. Álvarez Tabío, *Celia*, 93.

162. OAHCE/FCS, "Vergüenza contra dinero [n.d.]."

163. Letter from Dr. Sánchez Silveira to Eduardo Chibás, dated 19 May 1947, reprinted in Sarabia, *Dr. Manuel Sánchez Silveira, médico rural*, 29.

164. Álvarez Tabío, *Celia*, 87.

165. Álvarez Tabío, *Celia*, 85.

166. Testimony of Ana Alicia Sánchez Castellanos in Rodríguez Menéndez, *Una muchacha llamada Celia*, 50. The same testimony appears in Palomares Ferrales, *Celia: Mi mejor regalo*, 44.

167. Álvarez Tabío, *Celia*, 87.

168. Testimony of Olga Sánchez Castellanos in Rodríguez Menéndez, *Una muchacha llamada Celia*, 45–48.

169. Stout, *One Day in December*, 39–40.

170. Álvarez Tabío, *Celia*, 89.

171. Bécquer Céspedes, interview with author.

172. Elliott, conversation with author.

Chapter Three

1. Benitez, "En recuerdo de Celia." 61–62.

2. Bécquer Céspedes, *Celia*, 17.

3. Bécquer Céspedes, *Celia*, 20

4. Chirino, "Celia: Aquella muchacha excepcional," 6.

5. Bécquer Céspedes, *Celia*, 17

6. Chirino, "Celia: Aquella muchacha excepcional," 6.

7. "Castro en la inauguración del Hospital Celia Sánchez Manduley," 52.

8. Bécquer Céspedes, *Celia*, 17–18.

9. Chirino, "Celia: Aquella muchacha excepcional," 6.

10. Chirino, "Celia: Aquella muchacha excepcional," 6.

11. Testimony of Berta Llópiz in Garcia, "La joven Celia," 4.

12. Testimony of Berta Llópiz in Garcia, "La joven Celia," 4.

13. Álvarez Tabío, *Celia*, 160.

14. Bécquer Céspedes, *Celia*, 17.

15. Bécquer Céspedes, *Celia*, 21.

16. OAHCE/FCS, "Sobre el proyecto de parque en el central Pilón [n.d.]."

17. OAHCE/FCS, "Colocación del busto de José Martí en el Pico Turquino [21 May 1953]"; Marchante Castellanos, *De cara al sol*. For testimony from a participant (he created the pedestal for the bust), see Naranjo Gauthier, "Paso a paso."

18. OAHCE/FCS, "Sobre el papel de las mujeres que participaron en el emplazamiento del busto de Martí en el Turquino [14 June 1953]."

19. The diplomatic core in attendance reported being "aghast" at the extravagant event. See Eder, "On a Peak in the Sierra Maestra."

20. Hart, "A Butterfly against Stalin."

21. Naborí, "Pido permiso a la muerte."

22. Sarabia, "Martí en Celia Sánchez," 3.

23. Testimony of Dr. Adolfina Cossío in González Cabrera, "Vamos a hablar de Celia," 11.

24. Acuña Núñez, "Vida y personalidad del Dr. Manuel Sánchez Silveira," 8.

25. OAHCE/ FCS, "Solicitud de armamentos a Elsa Castro [18 December 1957]."

26. Sarabia, *Dr. Manuel Sánchez Silveira, médico rural*, 183–85; quote on 183.

27. OAHCE/FCS, "Sobre la filiación de Manuel Sánchez Silveira al grupo ortodoxo auténtico [19 May 1947]."

28. Letter from Dr. Sánchez to Eduardo R. Chibás dated 19 May 1947 in Sarabia, *Dr. Manuel Sánchez Silveira, médico rural*, 228–29.

29. OAHCE/FCS, "Vergüenza contra dinero [n.d.]."

30. Sarabia, *Dr. Manuel Sánchez Silveira, médico rural*, 185.

31. OAHCE/FCS, "Viaje a las cataratas del Niagara [29 October 1948]"; "Tarjeta postal enviada a Acacia Sánchez Manduley [20 November 1948]."

32. OAHCE/FCS, "Viaje a las cataratas del Niagara [29 October 1948]."

33. OAHCE/FCS, "Poesía dedicada a Celia Sánchez Manduley."

34. Conte, phone interview with author.

35. Pérez, *To Die in Cuba*, 320.

36. Chirino, "Celia: Aquella muchacha excepcional," 6.

37. García Oliveras, *José Antonio Echeverría*.

38. Alvarez, *Frank País*, 22–30.

39. Guerra, *Heroes, Martyrs, and Political Messiahs*, 184.

40. Bayard de Volo, *Women and the Cuban Insurrection*, 36–38; Castro Porta, *La lección del maestro*, 31.

41. de la Cova, *The Moncada Attack*.

42. Franqui, *The Twelve*, 86.

43. Hernández, "Sesenta y dos horas," 4.

44. Smith and Padula, *Sex and Revolution*, 24.

45. Guevara, *Guerrilla Warfare*, 86.

46. Mencia, *La prisión fecunda*, 1.

47. Lechuga and Márques, "Correr la misma suerte"; Dávila, "Compañeras."

48. Quoted in Quinn, "To Die Is Much Easier," B4.

49. Mencia, *La prisión fecunda*, 128.

50. Mencia, *La prisión fecunda*, 128. For a discussion of Castro's relationship with Natalia Revuelta Clews prior to, as well as after, his imprisonment in Isla de Pinos, see Gimbel, *Havana Dreams*.

51. Mencia, *La prisión fecunda*, 125–28. For the full text of Castro's speech, see Castro Ruz, *History Will Absolve Me*.

52. Mencia, *La prisión fecunda*, 130–31.

53. Mencia, *La prisión fecunda*, 188.

54. Mencia, *La prisión fecunda*, 187.

55. Mencia, *La prisión fecunda*, 176.

56. Castro Ruz, "De Castro a Carmen," 62.

57. Bayard de Volo, *Women and the Cuban Insurrection*, 35.

58. Aída Pelayo testimony in Maloof, *Voices of Resistance*, 60.

59. Szulc, *Fidel*, 328.

60. Álvarez Tabío, *Celia*, 152. Georgina Cuervo Cerulia cites the same story in her 1983 compilation *Granma rumbo a la libertad*.

61. Franqui, *The Twelve*, 66.

62. OAHCE/FCS, "Vivencias de Sánchez [n.d.]."

63. OAHCE/FCS, "Autobiografía de Acacia Sánchez Manduley [24 November 76]."

64. Interview with Haydée Santamaría cited in Desnoes, *Los dispositivos*, 210.

65. OAHCE/FCS, "Vivencias de Sánchez [n.d.]."

66. Interview with Celia Sánchez cited in, Desnoes, *Los dispositivos*, 208.

67. OAHCE/FCS, "Vivencias de Sánchez [n.d.]."

68. OAHCE/FCS, "Acerca de la fundación del Movimiento 26 Julio [n.d.]."

69. Hart Dávalos, *Aldabonazo*, 174.

70. OAHCE/FCS, "Vivencias de Sánchez [n.d.]."

71. OAHCE/FCS, "Vales por compras realizadas por Acacia Sánchez Manduley [14 June 1956– 20 June 1957].

72. OAHCE/FCS, "Vivencias de Sánchez [n.d.]."

73. OAHCE/FCS, "Acerca de la fundación del Movimiento 26 Julio [n.d.]."

74. OAHCE/FCS, "Acerca de la fundación del Movimiento 26 Julio [n.d.]."

75. Stryker, *Cuba*, 245.

76. OAHCE/FCS, "Vivencias de Sánchez [n.d.]."

77. OAHCE/FCS, "Acerca de la fundación del Movimiento 26 Julio [n.d.]."

78. OAHCE/FCS, "Vivencias de Sánchez [n.d.]."

79. Hart Dávalos, *Aldabonazo*, 149–50.

80. OAHCE/FCS, "Vivencias de Sánchez [n.d.]."

81. OAHCE/FCS, "Vivencias de Sánchez [n.d.]."

82. OAHCE/FCS, "Acerca de la fundación del Movimiento 26 Julio [n.d.]."

83. Franqui, *The Twelve*, 68.

84. Hart Dávalos, *Aldabonazo*, 152.

85. Anderson, *Che Guevara*, 238.

86. Chase, *Revolution within the Revolution*, 71; Sweig, *Inside the Cuban Revolution*, 153.

87. Chase, *Revolution within the Revolution*, 73.

88. Chase, *Revolution within the Revolution*, 71.

89. Chase, *Revolution within the Revolution*, 50.

90. "Women of the Rebellion," 7.

91. "Women of the Rebellion," 7.

92. "Women of the Rebellion," 7.

93. See Quirk, *Fidel Castro*, and Thomas, *Cuba*.

94. Szulc, *Fidel*, 417; Quirk, *Fidel Castro*, 137.

95. See Shetterly, *The Americano*, for a discussion of American William Morgan's leadership in the El Escambray movement.

96. Castillo Bernal, "Conoció a Fidel."

97. Castro Ruz, "Por eso ese nombre es tan querido."

98. Franqui, *The Twelve*, 76.

Chapter Four

1. OAHCE/FCS, "Cuenta de gastos [n.d.]." A notation within the document registers the inclusive dates "6/12/1956–15/4/1957."

2. OAHCE/FCS, "Control de gastos [6 December 56]–[15 April 1957]."

3. Hart Dávalos, *Aldabonazo*, 175.

4. Conte, phone interview with author.

5. Torres Elers, *Frank País en la memoria*, 220–21.

6. Matthews, *Fidel Castro*, 109.

7. Franqui, *The Twelve*, 78-79.

8. Hart Dávalos, *Aldabonazo*, 176-177.

9. OAHCE/FCS, "Autobiografía de Acacia Sánchez Manduley [24 November 1976]."

10. OAHCE/FCS, "Autobiografía de Acacia Sánchez Manduley [24 November 1976]."

11. Guevara, *Reminiscences*, 77.

12. OAHCE/FCS, "Liberación de prisioneros de guerra [30 May 1957]."

13. Szulc, *Fidel*, 422.

14. Aguirre Gamboa, *Celia*, 14.

15. OAHCE/FCS, "Acerca de la fundación del Movimiento 26 Julio [n.d.]."

16. Quirk, *Fidel Castro*, 145.

17. País, interview conducted by Julio Estorino.

18. OAHCE/FCS, "Acerca de la muerte de Frank País [31 July 1957]."

19. Quirk, *Fidel Castro*, 148.

20. Szulc, *Fidel*, 422.

21. OAHCE/FCS, "Acerca de las convicciones revolucionarias de los combatientes rebeldes [29 November 1957]."

22. Alfonso, "Sánchez, leyenda Hermosa," 15.

23. UFC/ECC, MSS 91, Box 1, Folder 2, *Sierra Maestra: Órgano Oficial del Movimiento 26 de Julio en Exilio* 1, no. 4 (June 1958): 10.

24. UFC/ECC, MSS 91, Box 1, Folder 9, Acción Cívica Cubana (New York), bonds ($5, $10, $15, $25), 1958.

25. OAHCE/FCS, "Sobre el dinero recaudado por las ventas de bonos [7 July 1957]–[1 August 57]." See also "Precio de bonos del 26 de julio"; "Cuenta por la venta de bonos del 26 de julio [22 August 1957]"; and "Recaudación de fondos."

26. OAHCE/FCS, "Acerca de la muerte de Frank País [31 July 1957]."

27. Interview with Adelaida Bécquer Céspedes, Office of Historical Affairs, 4 April 2018.

28. OAHCE/FCS, "Comunicación con su padre [11 October 1957]."

29. OAHCE/FCS, "Comunicación con su hermano Manuel Enrique Sánchez Manduley relativa a la esctructura y organización del Ejército Rebelde y a la quema de caña [4 November 1957]."

30. OAHCE/FCS, "Acerca de las convicciones revolucionarias de los combatientes rebeldes [29 November 1957]."

31. de la Rosa, "Recuerdos de manzanilleros," 3.

32. See OAHCE/FCS, "Acta matrimonial de Luis Jesús Pérez Martínez y Juana Bautista de la Concepción Ramírez Figueredo expedida por Castro y con Celia Sánchez Manduley como testigo" [20 September 1958]," and "Solicitud de Nena Alarcón para ser madrina de su hija [n.d.]."

33. OAHCE/FCS, "Comunicación con Anselmo de los Santos sobre las nuevas construcciones en territorio rebelde [21 April 1958]."

34. OAHCE/FCS, "Recuento a Manuel Sánchez Silveira [15 May 1958]."

35. OAHCE/FCS, "Comunicación con su hermana Acacia Sánchez Manduley [16 January 1958]."

36. OAHCE/FCS, "Solicitud de materiales para los hospitales de la Sierra Maestra [18 May 1958]."

37. OAHCE/FCS, "Comunicación con Fidel Castro sobre el envio de suministros [28 April 1958]."

38. See OAHCE/FCS, "Comunicación con Blás González [10 May 1958]" and "Comunicación con su hermano Manuel Enrique Sánchez Manduley [22 April 1957]."

39. See OAHCE/FCS, "Recuentro a Manuel Sánchez Silveira [15 May 1958]" and "Acerca de la distribución de alimentos [23 March 1958]."

40. OAHCE/FCS, "Comunicación con su hermana Acacia Sánchez Manduley [16 January 1958]."

41. See OAHCE/FCS, "Comunicación con Fidel Castro sobre el envío de mercancias a la Sierra"; "Sobre envio de arroz para la Sierra [14 February 1958]"; "Autorización a Juan Machado para utilizar animales de carga en la subida de mercancía [30 September 1958]"; "Comunicación con Raimundo Roselló sobre traslado de mercancias [12 October 1958]"; "Comunicación con Mario Maguera [9 August 1958]."

42. OAHCE/FCS, "Comunicación con Adalberto Pesant González sobre la preparación de condiciones para la siembra de alimentos para el sustento del Ejército Rebelde [29 April 1958]."

43. See OAHCE/FCS, "Comunicación con su hermano Manuel Enrique Sánchez Manduley [22 April 1957]"; "Recuentro a Manuel Sánchez Silveira [15 May 1958]"; "Entrega de semillas a campesinos [23 January 1958]"; OAHCE/FCS, "Comunicación con Haydée Santamaría acerca de sucesos de la Sierra [n.d.]."

44. OAHCE/FCS, "Recuentro a Manuel Sánchez Silveira [15 May 1958]."

45. OAHCE/FCS, "Comunicación con Haydée Santamaría acerca de sucesos de la Sierra [n.d.]."

46. See OAHCE/FCS, "Solicitud de azucar para el hospital rebelde [26 September 1958]" and "Respuesta a solicitud de zapatos" [19 June 1958]."

47. See OAHCE/FCS, "Acerca de la existencia y distribución del armamento [18 May 1958]" and "Comunicación con Fidel Castro sobre el envio de mercancias [29 April 1958]."

48. See OAHCE/FCS, "Recuentro a Manuel Sánchez Silveira [15 May 1958]" and "Comunicación con su hermana Acacia Sánchez Manduley [12 March 1958]."

49. OAHCE/FCS, "Resfuerzo de hombres y armamentos desde Costa Rica y la incorporación de médicos a la guerrilla [2 April 1958]."

50. OAHCE/FCS, "Incorporación de Olga Lara Riera a taller de costura en la Sierra [23 January 1958]."

51. See OAHCE/FCS, "Recuentro a Manuel Sánchez Silveira [15 May 1958]" and "Sobre la confección de calzado [28 May 1958]."

52. OAHCE/FCS, "Comunicación con su hermana Acacia Sánchez Manduley [16 January 1958]."

53. OAHCE/FCS, "Comunicación con Fidel Castro sobre el envio de suministros [28 April 1958]."

54. OAHCE/FCS, "Comunicación con Fidel Castro sobre el envio de suministros [28 April 1958]"; "Comunicación con Acacia Sánchez Manduley sobre gestiones varias [10 September 1958]"; "Comunicación con Ernesto Guevara sobre envío de avituallamiento a la Sierra Maestra [19 July 1958]"; "Comunicación con su hermana Acacia Sánchez Manduley [12 March 1958]"; and "Suministros para la Sierra Maestra [20 January 1958]."

55. See OAHCE/FCS, "Comunicación con Fidel Castro sobre informaciones varias [10 May 1958]"; "Petición de medicamento [20 May 1958]"; and "Acerca de atención médica para un niño [28 September 1958]."

56. OAHCE/FCS, "Solicitud de atención médica tropa rebelde [26 June 1958]."

57. OAHCE/FCS, "Solicitud de materiales para los hospitales de la Sierra Maestra [18 May 1958]."

58. See OAHCE/FCS, "Sobre entrega de fondos para gastos de hospital del Ejército Rebelde [3 January 1958]"; "Nota de Celia Sánchez Manduley suministros para hospital de la Sierra [27 March 1958]"; and "Proyecto de hospital [18 March 1958]."

59. OAHCE/FCS, "Recuentro a Manuel Sánchez Silveira [15 May 1958]."

60. OAHCE/FCS, "Recuentro a Manuel Sánchez Silveira [15 May 1958]."

61. OAHCE/FCS, "Recuentro a Manuel Sánchez Silveira [15 May 1958]" and "Comunicación con su hermana Acacia Sánchez Manduley [12 March 1958]."

62. See, for example, OAHCE/FCS, "Comunicación con Adalberto Pesant González sobre la preparación de condiciones para la siembra de alimentos para el sustento del Ejército Rebelde [29 April 1958]"; "Control de avituallamiento [13 May 1958–3 June 1958]"; and "Constancia de pago [15 May 1958]."

63. OAHCE/FCS, "Solicitud a Acacia Sánchez Manduley de suministros para la Sierra Maestra [18 June 1958]."

64. Interview with Haydée Santamaría cited in Desnoes, *Los dispositivos en la flor*, 210.

65. OAHCE/FCS, "Comunicación con Fidel Castro sobre el envio de mercancias a la Sierra [29 April 1958]."

66. OAHCE/FCS, "Fondo de ayuda para la Sierra Maestra [3 March 1959]."

67. See OAHCE/FCS, "Nota de Celia Sánchez Manduley suministros para hospital de la Sierra [27 March 1958]"; "Viaje a la Sierra Maestra de periodistas y mercancias"; and "Acerca del traslado de periodistas [28 March 1958]."

68. OAHCE/FCS, "Recuentro a Manuel Sánchez Silveira [15 May 1958]."

69. OAHCE/FCS, "Comunicación con su hermana Acacia Sánchez Manduley [12 March 1958]."

70. OAHCE/FCS, "Diario de Celia."

71. OAHCE/FCS, "Acerca de la muerte de Manuel Sánchez Silveira; Carta de Celia Sánchez Manduley a Acacia y Griselda Sánchez Manduley relativa al impacto que le produjó la muerte del padre y pormenores de la guerra en la Sierra Maestra [17 August 58]."

72. OAHCE/FCS, "Comunicación con su hermana, Acacia Sánchez Manduley [16 January 1958]."

73. OAHCE/FCS, "Sobre la necesidad de construir un cementerio en el Zarzal [8 November 1958]."

74. OAHCE/FCS, "Recuentro a Manuel Sánchez Silveira [15 March 1958]."

75. OAHCE/FCS, "Comunicación con su hermana Acacia Sánchez Manduley [12 March 1958.]"

76. OAHCE/FCS, "Recuentro a Manuel Sánchez Silveira [15 May 1958]."

77. OAHCE/FCS, "Recuentro a Manuel Sánchez Silveira [15 May 1958]."

78. OAHCE/FCS, "Acerca del estado de salúd de Manuel Sánchez Silveira [26 February 1957]."

79. OAHCE/FCS, "Felicitaciones a los médicos por su obra; Carta de Celia Sánchez Manduley relativa a felicitación a los médicos de la guerrilla por la construcción del hospital; solicita instrumental médico para el mismo y explica sobre la enfermedad de su padre [19 May 1958]."

80. OAHCE/FCS, "Certificación de defunción de Manuel Sánchez Silveira [9 July 1958]."

81. A facsimile of the original letter is on display at the museum within the base of the Che Guevara monument in Santa Clara, Cuba.

82. OAHCE/FCS, "Acerca de la muerte de Manuel Sánchez Silveira; Carta de Celia Sánchez Manduley a Acacia y Griselda Sánchez Manduley relativa al impacto

que le produjó la muerte del padre y pormenores de la guerra en la Sierra Maestra [17 August 58]."

83. See, for example, OAHCE/FCS, "Condolencia por la muerte de su padre, Manuel Sánchez Silveira [27 June 58]" and "Condolencias por la muerte de su padre [June 1958]."

84. OAHCE/FCS, "Condolencia por la muerte de su padre, Manuel Sánchez Silveira [28 June 1958]."

85. Interview with Bécquer Céspedes.

86. Interview with Bécquer Céspedes.

87. OAHCE/FCS, "Acerca de la muerte de Manuel Sánchez Silveira; Carta de Celia Sánchez Manduley a Acacia y Griselda Sánchez Manduley relativa al impacto que le produjó la muerte del padre y pormenores de la guerra en la Sierra Maestra [17 August 58]."

88. OAHCE/FCS, "Incorporaciones de Acacia y Griselda Sánchez Manduley a la Sierra Maestra [20 December 1958]."

89. OAHCE/FCS, "Acerca de la muerte de Manuel Sánchez Silveira; Carta de Celia Sánchez Manduley a Acacia y Griselda Sánchez Manduley relativa al impacto que le produjó la muerte del padre y pormenores de la guerra en la Sierra Maestra [17 August 58]."

90. OAHCE/FCS, "Comunicación con Fidel Castro sobre el traslado de prisioneros heridos [28 July 1958]" and "[14 June 1958]."

91. OAHCE/FCS, "Solicitando al Quinteto Rebelde [14 July 1958]."

92. OAHCE/FCS, "Comunicación con Delsa Puebla Vitrales [15 July 1958]."

93. See, OAHCE/FCS, "Solicitud de combustible [2 June 1958]"; "Sobre el envio de abastacimiento [27 July 1958]"; "Solicitud de avituallamiento [28 July 1958]"; "Solicitud de medicamentos para la Sierra Maestra" [9 July 1958]"; "Sobre envio de material escolar y suminstros a la Sierra Maestra [9 October 1958]"; and "Solicitud de avituallamiento para el Cuerpo de Ingenieros del Ejército Rebelde [3 December 1958]."

94. OAHCE/FCS, "Solicitud de dinero [18 June 1958]."

95. OAHCE/FCS, "Sobre los combates de Santo Domingo y Meriño [11 July 1958]."

96. OAHCE/FCS, "Regulaciones para visitantes a la Sierra Maestra [19 September 1958]."

97. OAHCE/FCS, "Solicitud de avituallamiento a Mercedes de Varona Betancourt [8 July 1958]."

98. OAHCE/FCS, "Comunicación con Julio Martínez Dáez sobre la ocupación de armas al enemigo [21 July 1958]" and "Sobre los combates de Santo Domingo y Meriño [11 July 1958]."

99. OAHCE/FCS, "Respuesta a prisioneros enemigos [3 July 1958]."

100. See, for example, OAHCE/FCS, "Acerca de petición de libertad para Raúl Corrales Figueredo [29 August 1958]."

101. OAHCE/FCS, "Comunicación con Acacia Sánchez Manduley sobre gestiones varias [10 September 1958]."

102. OAHCE/FCS, "Sobre la construcción de escuelas, hospitales y la aplicación de la Ley Agraria en la Sierra Maestra [18 October 1958]."

103. Puebla and Waters, *Marianas en combate*.

104. *Diario de la Marina* (19 May 1959): 5.

105. OAHCE/FCS, "Felicitaciones a Juan Almeida Bosque por los triunfos alcanzados [8 October 1958]."

106. OAHCE/FCS, "Sobre la orden del Comandante en Jefe de conservar posibles objetos museables [3 June 1958]."

107. For examples of Sánchez's many requests for former combatants to contribute photos, letters, or other documentation to the OAHCE, see OAHCE/FCS, "Trabajos en prestación de servicios [4 April 1979]."

108. OAHCE/FCS, "Acerca del nombramiento de Aristedes Guerra Paza como jefe de suministro [20 October 1958]."

109. OAHCE/FCS, "Sobre envio de dinero para presos políticos [26 November 58]."

110. OAHCE/FCS, "Comunicación con Aldo Santamaría Cuadrado sobre acciones combativos [9 December 1958]."

111. OAHCE/FCS, "Comunicación con Aldo Santamaría Cuadrado sobre acciones combativos [9 December 1958]."

112. Fidel Castro promoted his brother to the rank of commander on 27 February 1958 when he commissioned him to open the Sierra Cristal front. Camilo Cienfuegos and Juan Almeida also received promotions to the rank of commander at that time. OAHCE/FCS, "Diario de Celia."

113. See OAHCE/FCS, "Autobiografía de Acacia Sánchez Manduley [24 November 1976]"; "Incorporaciones de Acacia y Griselda Sánchez Manduley a la Sierra Maestra [20 December 1958]"; and "Viaje de las hermanas hacia Las Minas de Charco Redondo [20 December 1958]."

114. "Castro-Bearded Babes in the Woods," 16–17.

115. The article noted that the costume manufacturer, Jack Noahson, was insured for $100,000 against allergy suits. The beards were apparently made with treated dog fur.

116. "Castro-Bearded Babes in the Woods," 16.

117. "Castro-Bearded Babes in the Woods," 17.

118. Accessed 1 March 2016, www.youtube.com.

119. Matthews, *Fidel Castro*, 112.

120. Thomas, *Cuba*, 1432. However, more than half of the deputies elected to the National Assembly (currently totaling 605) in 2018 were women.

Chapter Five

1. Conte, phone interview with author.

2. St. George, "The Woman behind Castro," 4.

3. Marina, "Hace 15 años ocurrió el canje," 11.

4. Several scholars have attempted to explain the prevalence of the assumption that powerful female figures achieve power through their sexual relationship with a male leader. See Elshtain, *Public Man/Private Woman*; Sawyer and Simms, *A Woman's Place*.

5. Garlick, Dixon, and Allen, *Stereotypes of Women*, 212.

6. Matthews, *Fidel Castro*, 32–33.

7. Matthews, *Fidel Castro*, 33.

8. Mallin, "Havana Adopts 'Lib,'" 40.

9. St. George, "The Woman behind Castro," 4–7.

10. Quinn, "Castro: 'El Caballero Proletariat.'"

11. Matthews, *Fidel Castro*, 37.

12. Committee on the Judiciary, "Communist Threat to the United States" (24 July 1959, 31 March 1965), 947–48.

13. Eder, "Castro Proposes Deal," 1.

14. Quiroga, *Cuban Palimpsests*, 22.

15. Efraim Conte, phone interview with author.

16. Anderson, *Che Guevara*, 235, 344; Llovio-Ménendez, *Insider*, 99.

17. Huber Matos, interview conducted by Julio Estorino.

18. Fernández, *Castro's Daughter*, 43, 47, 100–101.

19. Fuentes, *Dulces guerreros cubanos*, 139.

20. Fuentes, *Dulces guerreros cubanos*, 139.

21. Quirk, *Fidel Castro*, 174.

22. Quirk, *Fidel Castro*, 130; Matthews, *Fidel Castro*, 130; Lockwood, *Castro's Cuba*, 80.

23. Quirk, *Fidel Castro*, 174.

24. OAHCE/FCS, "Anotaciones sobre zapatos para escolares [n.d.]."

25. Hart, "A Butterfly against Stalin."

26. Matthews, *Fidel Castro*, 116.

27. Palomares Ferrales, *Celia: Mi mejor regalo*, 300–301.

28. Palomares Ferrales, *Celia: Mi mejor regalo*, 300–301.

29. Palomares Ferrales, *Celia: Mi mejor regalo*, 300.

30. Guerra, *Visions of Power*, 225.

31. Fernández Tabío, conversation with author.

32. Bécquer Céspedes, interview with author.

33. Bécquer Céspedes, *Celia: La más autóctona flor*, 1.

34. OAHCE/FCS, "Documentos para la historia" [16 March 1959])."

35. See, for example, OAHCE/FCS, "Monumento al combate de Uvero [n.d.]"; "Monumento al desembarco del Granma [26 February 1979]"; and "Proyecto de sitios históricos [27 June 1979]."

36. OAHCE/FCS, "Proyectos de sitios históricos [14 February 1978]."

37. Castillo Bernal, "Fiel guardiana," 3.

38. OAHCE/FCS, "Reconocimiento por servicios prestados [29 October 1979]."

39. Randall, phone interview with author.

40. Oliva, "Celia: Comunista, constructora, soñadora," 9.

41. Oliva, "Celia: Comunista, constructora, soñadora," 9.

42. Oliva, "Celia: Comunista, constructora, soñadora," 10.

43. Hart Dávalos, "El ejemplo de Celia," 61.

44. Oliva, "Celia: Comunista, constructora, soñadora," 10–11.

45. Sarabia, "Celia: Palma y clavellina."

46. For the complete text of his speech to the Manzanillo Lions Club, as well as a published call to convert the plantation into a national monument, see Sarabia, *Dr. Manuel Sánchez Silveira*, 61–77; 78–83. See also OAHCE/FCS, "La Demajagua y Carlos Manuel de Céspedes."

47. Hernández, "Figuras y espacios," 56–57.

48. Mallea, *Havana Living Today*, 59.

49. Molyneux, "State, Gender, and Institutional Change."

50. Castro, "The Revolution within the Revolution," in Stone, *Women and the Cuban Revolution*, 48–54.

51. The original concept of Cuba's "New Man" was the focus of many of Ernesto "Che" Guevara's writings, namely his classic essay "Man and Socialism" (1961). The full text of Guevara's essay can be found in Lothstein, ed., *"All We Are Saying,"* 365–81.

52. Geyer, "Cuban Women Freer of Male Dominance"; see Bibliography.

53. Simons, "Cuba Liberates Role of Women," 32.

54. "Las mujeres en Cuba," 2.

55. Quinn, "Castro: 'El Caballero Proletariat.'"

56. Randall, *Gathering Rage*.

57. *Mujeres ejemplares*, 10

58. Conte, phone interview with author.

59. Palomares Ferrales, *Celia*, 98.

60. Palomares Ferrales, *Celia*, 99.

61. Palomares Ferrales, *Celia*, 102; Stryker, *Cuba*, 242–43.

62. Stryker, *Cuba*, 242–43.

63. See, for example, OAHCE/FCS, "Atención médica [9 July 1968]"; "Solicitud de finca [30 June 1964]"; "Solicitud de cambio de finca para Inocencio Guerrero Ávila [15 June 1979]"; "Construcción de vivienda [11 February 1966]"; and "Recuperación por daños del ciclón [25 October 1963]."

64. See, for example, OAHCE/FCS, "Solicitud de Paulino Fonseca Ramírez [18 May 1977]."

65. OAHCE/FCS, "Atención al Dr. Márquez [3 August 1966]."

66. OAHCE/FCS, "Asistencia social [29 August 1969]."

67. OAHCE/FCS, "Asistencia social [29 August 1969]."

68. OAHCE/FCS, "Entrevista solicitada por Nestor Proenza Aguilar [n.d.]."

69. OAHCE/FCS, "Solicitud de regreso a Cuba [3 April 1977]."

70. OAHCE/FCS, "Cuaderno de Manuel Sánchez Silveira sobre temas históricos."

71. OAHCE/FCS, "Apuntes varios [n.d.]."

72. OAHCE/FCS, "Apuntes varios [n.d.]" and "Relación de gastos [n.d.]."

73. Hart Dávalos, *Aldabonazo*, 175.

74. Llovio-Menéndez, *Insider*, 103.

75. OAHCE/FCS, "Poesía dedicada a Celia Sánchez Manduley [n.d]."

76. Smith and Padula, *Sex and Revolution*, 32.

77. Sang, interview with author.

78. Porot, interview with author.

79. Conte, phone interview with author.

80. Chaney, *Supermadre*, 5.

81. Chaney, *Supermadre*, 20.

82. Garlick et al., *Stereotypes of Women in Power*, 65.

83. Chase, *Revolution within the Revolution*, 80–81.

84. Castro, "The Revolution within the Revolution," in Stone, *Women and the Cuban Revolution*, 48–54.

85. Wexler, "Emma Goldman," 39.

86. Conte, phone interview with author.

Chapter Six

1. The news of Sánchez's appointment as "Secretary to the President and the Council of Ministers" appeared in several U.S. newspapers. See "Cabinet Shuffled in Cuba."

2. St. George, "The Woman behind Castro."

3. St. George, "The Woman behind Castro," 4.

4. "Hotel Gouging Him," 1; "Raging Castro Shifts Hotels," 2, 28; "Women Remain Vital to Cuban Revolution," 52; "Women Have Many Important Posts," 20; "Women Play Major Roles," 52; "The Beardless Ones," 34.

5. Quoted in St. George, "The Woman behind Castro," 5.

6. "Castro Calls Off Strike," 1, 6.

7. Hart Phillips, "Havana Welcomes Castro," 1.

8. Battelle, "The Woman in Fidel's Life," 6; Battelle, "The Woman with Castro," 26.

9. Mallin, "Havana Adopts 'Lib,'" 40.

10. Hofmann, "Cuba Is in Fidel's Shirt Pocket," SM7.

11. Battelle, "The Woman in Fidel's Life," 6.

12. Quinn, "Castro: 'El Caballero Proletariat.'"

13. Tully, "Cuba's Prime Minister," 12.

14. "Women of the Rebellion," 7.

15. Berrellez, "Sensitivity of Castro," 15; "Cuba Receives Soviet Envoy," 6.

16. Fiorini, "An American Soldier of Fortune," 158–60; see Bibliography.

17. "Top Castro Aide," 4.

18. Hofmann, "Cuba Is in Fidel's Shirt Pocket," SM7.

19. Hofmann, "Cuba Is in Fidel's Shirt Pocket," SM7.

20. Eder, "Cuba Lives by Castro's Moods," SM12.

21. The Associated Press later linked that report to an anonymous call from a Cuban living in Miami. See "Havana Denies Reports of Castro Assassination," 6; "New Castro Death Rumor," 7.

22. Berrellez, "Castro Avoids Scandal with Secluded Life," 65.

23. Quinn, "Castro: 'El Caballero Proletariat.'"

24. Berrellez, "Women Perform Vital Tasks in Castro's Government," 76; Berrellez, "Castro Avoids Scandal," 65. See also "Castro Remains Key to Revolution," 1, 10.

25. Berrellez, "Women Perform Vital Tasks," 76.

26. Hofmann, "Cuba Is in Fidel's Shirt Pocket," SM7.

27. Quinn, "Castro: 'El Caballero Proletariat.'"

28. Berrellez, "Women Perform Vital Tasks," 76.

29. Newspapers across the United States highlighted this excerpt from the program: "Castro Opens Up in Walters Interview," 9

30. Committee on the Judiciary, "Communist Threat to the United States through the Caribbean" (24 July 1959, 31 March 1965), 950.

31. St. George, "The Woman behind Castro," 6.

32. St. George, "The Woman behind Castro," 7.

33. Mallin, "Havana Adopts 'Lib,'" 40.

34. St. George, "The Woman behind Castro," 5.

35. Battelle, "The Woman in Fidel's Life," 6.

36. OAHCE/FCS, "Juguetes para niños en la Sierra Maestra [10 January 59]."

37. Normyle, "Castro Bombs the Poor with Toys and Food," 4; "Castro ordena que den juguetes a todos," 19.

38. The information for this chapter is based on a survey of fifty-nine U.S. newspapers spanning from Seattle to Miami. In many cases, the same story appeared in several newspapers, albeit under a slightly different title. It was important for me to track printings of these articles in order to understand how widely news about Sánchez circulated within the U.S.; thus, I provide within the Bibliography the titles for all similar articles that I located.

39. Welch, *Response to Revolution*.

40. Rojas, *Fighting Over Fidel*.

41. Ross, "We Were Wrong about Castro"; see Bibliography.

42. Ross, "We Were Wrong about Castro."

43. Hart Phillips, "Havana Welcomes Castro at End of Triumphal Trip," 9.

44. Guerra, *Visions of Power in Cuba*, 152.

45. Ross, "We Were Wrong about Castro."

46. Ross, "We Were Wrong about Castro."

47. "Cuba Liberates Roles of Women," 32.

48. Mornig, "Three Women Aides to Castro," 26.

49. Berrellez, "Women Perform Vital Tasks," 76.

50. OAHCE/FCS, "Solicitud de cámara fotográfica y otros suministros a la Sierra Maestra [27 April 1957]"; Flynn, "Castro y yo," 50.

51. Tully, "Cuba's Prime Minister," 12.

52. St. George, "The Woman behind Castro," 4–7.

53. Ross, "We Were Wrong about Castro."

54. "Women Remain Vital to Cuban Revolution."

55. Battelle, "The Woman in Fidel's Life," 6.

56. "Sánchez Is No Charmer."

57. "Fue asesinada Celia Sánchez?" 1, 9.

58. This oft-repeated anecdote first appeared in "Woman Sometimes Cues Tough Chief of Cuba Rebels," 18.

59. St. George, "The Woman behind Castro," 6.

60. St. George, "The Woman behind Castro," 4.

61. St. George, "The Woman behind Castro," 4–7; Anderson, "Meet June Cobb," 162–63. See also Berrellez, "Women Perform Vital Tasks," 76. Casuso gives her own version of these events in her memoir, *Cuba and Castro*.

62. Committee on the Judiciary, "Communist Threat to the United States" (24 July 1959), 948.

63. "Women and Politics," 4.

64. "Cuba's Castro Is Surrounded by Communists," 25.

65. Ross, "We Were Wrong about Castro."

66. St. George, "The Woman behind Castro," 6.

67. For more information on the hearings, see Johnson, *Congress and the Cold War*.

68. Committee on the Judiciary, United States Senate. "Communist Threat to the United States" (22 and 23 January 1960), 501.

69. Committee on the Judiciary, United States Senate. "Testimony of Viola June Cobb," 24.

70. St. George, "The Woman behind Castro," 4-7.

71. Thomas, *Cuba*, 1048.

72. "Top Castro Aide Reported in Hub for Surgery," 4.

73. St. George, "The Woman behind Castro," 4-7.

74. St. George, "The Woman behind Castro," 5.

75. St. George, "The Woman behind Castro," 2.

76. Geyer, "Cuban Women Now Freer of Male Dominance."

77. Bécquer Céspedes, interview with author.

78. Quinn, "Castro: 'El Caballero Proletariat.'"

79. UF/CFC, MS Group 305, Box 1, *Album de la Revolución Cubana* (c. 1959).

80. "La corrupción continúa," 7.

81. "Réplica sobre reportaje de Cuba," 9.

82. "La corrupción continúa," 7.

83. Montaner, "Hablemos algo," 9.

Chapter Seven

1. Ruiz Guzmán, *Un amor de leyenda*.

2. Taylor, *Eva Perón*, 148.

3. Conte, phone interview with author.

4. The full text of the prayer, "Oración a La Milagrosa," appears in Ruiz Guzmán, *Un amor de leyenda*, 12.

5. Díaz, email correspondence with author.

6. "Será transmitida hoy," 8.

7. Conte, phone interview with author.

8. Palomares Ferrales, *Celia: Mi mejor regalo*, 25.

9. Fresnillo, "Celia vive."

10. Bécquer Céspedes, interview with author.

11. Más Martín, "Hechos e impresiones."

12. Stryker, *Cuba*, 246.

13. Anderson, *Che* 235, 344.

14. Geyer, *Guerrilla Prince*, 387.

15. Randall, phone interview with author.

16. Hart, "A Butterfly against Stalin."

17. Conte, phone interview with author.

18. Llovio-Menéndez, *Insider*, 412.

19. McLean, *Haydée Santamaría*, 88.

20. "Haydée Santamaría Cuadrado."

21. Quiroga, *Cuban Palimpsests*, 211.

22. Guerra, *Visions of Power*, 355.

23. Quiroga, *Cuban Palimpsests*, xi.

24. Pablo Rodríguez and González Bello, "Capitana del Pueblo," 53.

25. Naborí, "Pido permiso a la muerte."

26. Palomares Ferrales, *Celia: Mi mejor regalo*, 294.

27. "Castro Confidante Buried in Havana," 4; "Cuban Heroine Buried with Full Honors," 8.

28. Noakes, *War and the British*, 12–13.

29. Noakes, *War and the British*, 16. See also Cooke and Woollacott, eds., *Gendering War Talk*, 1993.

30. Wandor, *Look Back in Gender*, xiii.

31. Sang, interview with author.

32. Sang, interview with author.

33. Cartón, interview with author.

34. Guerra, *Visions of Power*, 242.

35. Stubbs, "Social and Political Motherhood of Cuba."

36. Aguirre Gamboa, *Celia*, 14.

37. OAHCE/FCS, "Acto de inauguración de la Escuela de Formación de Educadores de Círculos Infantiles de Villa Clara [20 March 1981]."

38. Casey, *Che's Afterlife*, 89.

39. Szulc, *Fidel*, 75.

40. The various continuities between Christian and revolutionary imagery have been the focus of several recent studies. Perhaps most relevant to this discussion of the semireligious imagery surrounding Celia Sánchez is J. M. Taylor's work on Eva Perón; see Taylor, *Eva Perón*, 104–10. For an interesting, albeit fairly controversial, examination of the links between Christian (specifically Catholic) imagery and male public figures, see Caudill Dealy, *The Public Man*.

41. Morejón, "Elegía coral," 58–59; Llanes, *Celia nuestra y de las flores*.

42. Kunzle, *Che Guevara*.

43. Pablo Rodríguez and González Bello, "Capitana del Pueblo," 53.

44. Quiroga, *Cuban Palimpsests*, xi.

45. Quiroga, *Cuban Palimpsests*, 2.

46. For more information on the events surrounding the Mariel boatlift, see Masud-Piloto, *With Open Arms*. For a more thorough discussion of the economic problems facing Cuba in the 1960s and 1970s, see Ruffin, *Capitalism and Socialism in Cuba*; Mesa-Lago, *The Economy of Socialist Cuba*; and Mesa-Lago, *Cuba in the 1970s*.

47. Hart Dávalos, *La más autóctona flor*, 13.

48. Nora, "Between Memory and History," 16.

49. "Fue asesinada Celia Sánchez?," 1, 9.

50. "Desmienten en Cuba," 3.

51. Conte, phone interview with author.

52. Federación de Mujeres Cubanas, "Mensaje de la Dirección Nacional de la Federación de Mujeres Cubanas," 2.

53. Guerra, *Visions of Power*, 29.

54. The concept of Cuba's "New Man" was the focus of many of Ernesto "Che" Guevara's writings, namely his classic essay "Man and Socialism" (1961). The full text of Guevara's essay can be found in Lothstein, ed., *"All We Are Saying,"* 365–81.

55. *Granma* (19 October 1967): 2–4.

56. Federación de Mujeres Cubanas, "Mensaje de la Dirección Nacional de la Federación de Mujeres Cubanas," 2.

57. Rojas, "Hemos perdido un centinela," 5.

58. Rojas, "Hemos perdido un centinela," 5.

59. Rojas, "Hemos perdido un centinela," 5.

60. "Celia," *Granma* (12 January 1980): 6.

61. "Celia," *Granma* (12 January 1980): 6.

62. Deutsch, "Gender and Sociopolitical Change," 259–306.

63. Taylor, *Eva Perón*.

64. "Celia: La más autóctona flor," *Granma* (11 January 1981): 1.

65. Bécquer Céspedes, interview with author.

66. Hart Dávalos, "El ejemplo de Celia," 61.

67. Hart Dávalos, "El ejemplo de Celia," 62.

68. Hart Dávalos, "El ejemplo de Celia," 62.

69. Aguirre Gamboa, *Celia*, 5.

70. "Inaugurará Fidel, mañana," 1. I also had the opportunity to speak with a member of the hospital's medical staff about the dedication ceremony; Gómez Satti, interview with author.

71. "Inaugurará Fidel, mañana," 1.

72. "Castro en la inauguración," 52.

73. Blanch, "Digno homenaje a Celia," 8.

74. Blanch, "Digno homenaje a Celia," 8.

75. Morejón, "Elegía coral."

76. Morejón, "Celia: Hija asombrosa."

77. Morejón, "Celia: Hija asombrosa," 59.

78. Llanes, *Celia nuestra y de las flores*.

79. Van Houts, *Memory and Gender*, 7.

80. Anderson, *Imagined Communities*, 205.

81. Portelli, *The Death of Luigi Trastulli*, 52.

82. Guerra, *Visions of Power*, 30.

83. Taylor, *Eva Perón*, 9.

Chapter Eight

1. Álvarez Tabío, "Celia: Cabal imágen del pueblo," 3.

2. Nora makes reference to a similar notion of the "impossible debt" of memory each individual feels they must pay to the nation. See Nora, "Between Memory and History," 16.

3. Casey, *Che's Afterlife*, 232.

4. Casey, *Che's Afterlife*, 63.

5. For great discussions of gendered performances of nation, see: Roach, *Cities of the Dead*; Guerra, *Visions of Power*; Quiroga, *Cuban Palimpsests*.

6. Szulc, *Fidel*, 68.

7. Suárez Guerra, "Spathoglottis," 131.

8. "Manzanillera combatiente" and "Y aquí en el corazón del pueblo."

9. Borbonet et al., *Celia*. Only 200 portfolios were ever printed. The author owns a complete collection of the prints.

10. Cargill, *Celia Sánchez*.

11. *Che*, directed by Soderbergh, 2018.

12. "La actriz vallisoletana," 2008.

13. Los Conejitos de Celia, "Una muchacha llamada Celia."; Rodríguez Menéndez, "Celia Sánchez, literatura y radio"; Rodriguez Menéndez, *Una muchacha llamada Celia*.

14. See *Celia: Leyenda y presencia*; *Celia: Fuego y canto*; and *Celia: La más hermosa flor*.

15. Quiroga, *Cuban Palimpsests*, xi.

16. Nora, "Between Memory and History," 19.

17. For a discussion of revolution as "process" (rather than end point), see Joseph and Nugent, eds., *Everyday Forms of State Formation*, xii.

18. Guerra, *Visions of Power*, 30.

19. Van Houts, *Memory and Gender in Medieval Europe*, 7.

Bibliography

Resource Collections and Historic Sites

United States

National Security Archive (Washington, D.C.)
University of Florida, Special Collections (Gainesville, Florida)
   Cuban Miscellaneous Collection
   Ernesto Chávez Collection
   Exile Newspaper Collection
University of Miami, Cuban Heritage Collection (Miami, Florida)
   Luis J. Botifoll Oral History Project
   Cuban Photograph Collection
University of Texas at Austin, Benson Latin American Library (Austin, Texas)
Yale University, Manuscripts and Archives (New Haven, Connecticut)
   Digital Images Database

Cuba

Casa de las Americas (Havana)
Celia Sánchez Childhood Home Museum (Media Luna)
Celia Sánchez Home Museum (Pilón)
Celia Sánchez Hospital (Manzanillo)
Celia Sánchez Memorial Stairway (Manzanillo)
Celia Sánchez Monument, Lenin Park (Havana)
Celia Sánchez Plaza (Manzanillo)
Federation of Cuban Women Archive (Havana)
History Institute (Havana)
José Martí National Library (Havana)
Municipal History Museum (Manzanillo)
Municipal History Museum (Media Luna)
Office of Historical Affairs (Havana)
   Fondo Celia Sánchez (OAHCE/FCS)
Revolutionary Armed Forces Mausoleum, Colón Cemetery (Havana)

Newspapers

Cuba

Bohemia	*Diario de la Marina*	*Granma*
Combate	*El Caiman Barbudo*	*Granma International*

Juventud Rebelde
Liberación
Moncada
Mujeres

Noticias de Hoy
Opina
Revista Pionero
Revolución y Cultura

Trabajadores
Verde Olivo

United States

Boston Herald
Boston Record American
Boston Sunday Advertiser
Charleston Evening Post
Cleveland Plain Dealer
Daily Record (Boston)
Dallas Morning News
El Miami Herald
El Mundo
El Mundo (Oakland,
    Calif.)
Evansville Press
Evening Star (Washing-
    ton, D.C.)
Fort Worth Star-Telegram

Greensboro Daily News
Illinois State Journal and
    Register
Jersey Journal
La Prensa (San Antonio)
Latin Times
La Verdad (Miami)
Milwaukee Journal Sentinel
Milwaukee Register
Morning Advocate
    (Baton Rouge)
New York Times
Omaha World Herald
Parade
Richmond Times Dispatch

Rockford Register-Republic
Sacramento Bee
San Diego Union
Sunday Advocate (Baton
    Rouge)
Sunday Register Star
Sunday Oregonian
    (Portland, Ore.)
Sun News (Myrtle Beach)
Times-Picayune (New
    Orleans)
Trenton Times (Trenton,
    N.J.)
Washington Post
Washington Times

Florida Exile Newspapers

13 de Marzo: Órgano
    Oficial de la Delegación
    en el Exterior (Miami)
Carta Semanal
El Heraldo de Broward
    (Fort Lauderdale)
El Matancero Libre

El Noticiero
Habla Castro: La Solución
    Revolucionaria
The Havana Times
    (Miami)
La Nación (Miami)
La Prensa de Westchester

La Verdad (Miami)
Palm Beach Latino
Panorama News
Réplica
Sierra Maestra: Órgano
    Oficial del Movimiento
    26 de Julio en Exilio

Canada

Gazette (Montreal)
The Globe and Mail

Hamilton Spectator
    (Ontario)

Toronto Star

Australia

North Shore Times (Australia)

Ireland

Belfast Telegram
The Irish Times

Scotland

The Herald (Glasgow)

England

BBC Monitoring Americas   *Sunday Times* (London)   *Times* (London)

U.S. Government Documents

Committee on the Judiciary of the United States Senate. "Communist Threat to the United States through the Caribbean. Hearings before the Subcommittee to Investigate Security Act and Other Internal Security Laws," 86th Congress, 1st Session, Part 1 (14 July 1959) Washington, D.C.: Government Printing Office, 1959.

Committee on the Judiciary of the United States Senate. "Communist Threat to the United States through the Caribbean. Hearings before the Subcommittee to Investigate Security Act and Other Internal Security Laws." 86th Congress, 2nd Session, Parts 2–7 (May 1960). Washington, D.C.: Government Printing Office, 1960.

Committee on the Judiciary of the United States Senate. "Communist Threat to the United States through the Caribbean. Hearings before the Subcommittee to Investigate Security Act and Other Internal Security Laws." 86th Congress, 2nd Session, Parts 8, 22, 23 (January 1960). Washington, D.C.: Government Printing Office, 1960.

Committee on the Judiciary of the United States Senate. "Communist Threat to the United States through the Caribbean. Hearings before the Subcommittee to Investigate the Administration of the Internal Security Laws." 89th Congress, 1st Session, Part 14 (24 July 1959; 31 March 1965). Washington, D.C.: Government Printing Office, 1965.

Committee on the Judiciary of the United States Senate. "Testimony of Robert F. Williams. Hearings before the Subcommittee to Investigate the Administration of the Internal Security Act and Other Internal Security Laws." 91st Congress, 2nd Session, Part 1 (16 February 1970). Washington, D.C.: Government Printing Office, 1970.

Committee on the Judiciary of the United States Senate. "Testimony of Viola Cobb. Hearing before the Subcommittee to Investigate the Administration of the Internal Security Act and Other Internal Security Laws." 89th Congress, 2nd Session (30 March 1962). Washington, D.C.: Government Printing, 1962.

"Legislation and Regulations—United States: Cuban Liberty and Democratic Solidarity (LIBERTAD) Act of 1996 (Helms–Burton Act)," *International Legal Materials* 35, no. 2 (1996): 359–79.

Digital, Media, and Art Sources

Álvarez, Santiago. *Celia*. Filmed interview, 3 November 1976. Havana: Instituto Cubano del Arte y la Industria Cinematográficos, 953 II-A, R2.

Borbonet, Tomás, et al. *Celia*. Havana: Taller Experimental de Seriagrafía del Fondo Cubano de Bienes Culturales, 1985.

Casa Natal Celia Sánchez. "Casa Natal de Celia: Una visita obligada en su incursión por la provincial Granma." Museum brochure, n.d.

"Casa Natal de Celia Sánchez Manduley." *EcuRed*, www.ecured.cu/Casa_Natal_de _Celia_Sánchez_Manduley (accessed 6 September 2017).

Celia: Fuego y canto. Pedro Álvarez Tabío, producer, and Haydée Tabraue Gari, director. Havana: Television Cubana, 2000.

Celia: La más hermosa flor. Documentary produced by Mundo Latino, 2015.

Celia: Leyenda y presencia. Documentary directed by Pedro Álvarez Tabío, Tele-Rebelde, 11 January 1985. http://www.cubainformacion.tv.

Che. Directed by Steven Soderbergh. New York: IFC Films, 2008.

Enciclopedia Digital: Celia Sánchez. Havana: Oficina de Asuntos Históricos del Consejo de Estado, 2016.

Los Conejitos de Celia de la UNEAC. *Una muchacha llamada Celia*. Telenovela directed by Héctor Pérez Ramírez, with script by Roberto Rodríguez Menéndez. *Enciclopedia Digital: Celia Sánchez*. Havana: Oficina de Asuntos Históricos del Consejo de Estado, 2016.

"Manzanillera combatiente." Song performed by Omara Portuondo. *Enciclopedia Digital: Celia Sánchez*. Havana: Oficina de Asuntos Históricos del Consejo de Estado, 2016.

Orozco González, Delio Gabriel. *Enciclopedia Digital: Celia Sánchez*. Havana: Oficina de Asuntos Históricos del Consejo de Estado, 2016.

Reyes Rodríguez, Dilbert. "Cuban Heroine Celia Sánchez Lives in the People's Memories," Radio Ángulo, www.radioangulo.cu/en/specials/17101 (accessed 6 September 2017).

Rodríguez Menéndez, Roberto, "Celia Sánchez, literatura y radio." In Delio Orozco, *Celia Sánchez Manduley: Enciclopedia Digital*, 2016.

"Y aquí en el corazón del pueblo." Song performed by Rafael Espín. *Enciclopedia Digital: Celia Sánchez*. Havana: Oficina de Asuntos Históricos del Consejo de Estado, 2016.

Interviews, Conversations, and Correspondence

Acuña Nuñez, Maritza. Interview with author. Museo Natal Celia Sánchez. Media Luna, Cuba, 11 January 2018.

Andino, Raquel. Conversation with author. Plaza Celia Sánchez, Manzanillo, Cuba, 12 January 2018.

Bécquer Céspedes, Adelaida. Interview with author. Office of Historical Affairs, Havana, Cuba, 4 April 2018.

Cañadilla, Bárbara. Conversation with author. Museo Histórico de Manzanillo, Manzanillo, Cuba, 12 January 2018.

Cartón, Nirma. Interview with author. Havana, Cuba, 6 July 1996.

Conte, Efraim. Interview with author. Miami, Florida, 2 January 2018.

"Cuso." Interview with author. Lenin Park, Havana, Cuba, 7 April 2018.

Díaz, Yolanda. Email correspondence with author, 16 November 2018.

Elliott. Elizabeth. Conversation with author. Museo Municipal Media Luna, Manuel Sánchez Silveira, Media Luna, Cuba, 8 January 2018.

Fambrono, Bonnie. Conversation with author. Plaza Celia Sánchez, Manzanillo, Cuba, 12 January 2018.

Fernández, Alina. Conversation with author. Auburn, Alabama, 17 September 2015.

Gómez Satti, Arnaldo. Interview with author. Hospital Celia Sánchez, Manzanillo, Cuba, 27 July 1996.

Hernández, Mirtha. Interview with author. Manzanillo, Cuba, 12 January 2018.

Llana, Nexsy. Conversation with author. Museo Histórico de Manzanillo, Manzanillo, Cuba, 12 January 2018.

Martínez, David. Conversation with author. Santa Clara, Cuba, 14 May 2016.

Matos, Huber. Interview with Julio Estorino. Luis J. Botifoll Oral History Project, Cuban Heritage Collection, University of Miami, 23 April 2008; 1 May 2008; 7 May 2008.

Moreno Fonseca, Aida Luisa. Interview with author. Office of Historical Affairs of the Council of State, Havana, Cuba, 5 July 1996.

Orozco González, Delio. Conversation with author. Museo Histórico de Manzanillo, Manzanillo, Cuba, 12 January 2018.

País, Agustín. Interview with Julio Estorino. Luis J. Botifoll Oral History Project, Cuban Heritage Collection, University of Miami, 17 October 2011.

Porot, Nilda. Conversation with author. Biblioteca Nacional José Martí, Havana, Cuba, 26 June 1998.

Randall, Margaret. Phone interview with author, 2 November 2015.

Rego Pita, Sergio. Conversation with author. Dirección Provincial de Relaciones Internacionales, Havana, Cuba, 10 July 1996.

Sang, Lourdes. Interview with author. Havana, Cuba, 8 July 1996.

Sarabia, Nydia. Interview with author. Havana, Cuba, 10 July 1996.

Published Primary Sources (Cuba)

"25 Aniversario de las FAR: 25 años de luchas y victorias. Celia." *Revista Verde Olivo*, 1981.

"A Celia: Y aquí, en el corazón del pueblo." *Tribuna*, (10 January 1993.

Aguilar, Carolina. "Con renovadas energías y confianza en el porvenir." *Mujeres* 20, no. 8 (August 1980): 4–6.

Aguilar, Onelia. "Celia Sánchez, genuina representación de la mujer revolucionaria." *Mujeres* 2, no. 14 (15 July 1962): 70.

Aguirre Gamboa, Fidel. *Celia: Heroína de la Revolución Cubana*. Havana: Editora Política, 1985.

Alfonso, Carmen. "Celia, leyenda hermosa y reciente. Ejemplo de lealtad infinita a Fidel." *Trabajadores* (11 January 1990).

Alfonso, Mireya. "Se movilizan mujeres cubanas." *Liberación* 2, no. 503 (18 October 1960): 3.

Álvarez Tabío, Pedro. "Celia: Cabal imagen del pueblo." *Bohemia* 77, no. 2 (11 January 1985): 3–15.

———. *Celia, ensayo para una biografía.* Havana: Oficina de Publicaciones del Consejo del Estado, 2003.

———. "En espera del desembarco." *Bohemia* 78, no. 47 (21 November 1986): 59–63.

———. "Todo importa después," *Bohemia* 76 (4 May 1984): 54–59.

"Anécdotas de la revolución." *Diario de la Marina* (16 January 1959): 6A.

Barnet, Enrique Pineda. "Celia." *La Gaceta de Cuba* 187 (11 July 1980): 11.

Barnet, Miguel. "Celia: Amó lo bello porque lo bello era justo." *Revolución y Cultura* 122 (October 1982): 29.

Bécquer Céspedes, Adelaida. *Celia: La más autóctona flor de la Revolución.* Havana: Editorial de Ciencias Sociales, 1999.

Benitez, Augusto E. "En recuerdo de Celia: Museo histórico de Pilón." *Bohemia* 80, no. 2 (9 January 1987): 61–62.

Benitez, José. "Celia Sánchez Manduley." *Granma* 16, no. 11 (13 January 1980): 5.

———. "Celia Sánchez Manduley." *Granma International* 15, no. 3 (20 January 1980): 9–13.

Bernal Mora, Ricardo. "La mujer estará en igual condición que el hombre para combatir." *Liberación* 3, no. 684 (26 May 1961): 1, 5.

Blanch, Gilberto. "Digno homenaje a Celia." *Mujeres* 21, no. 6 (June 1981): 6–9.

Buut, Ilse. "En la Sierra Maestra: Un encuentro con la patria y la naturaleza." *Bohemia* 77, no. 3 (18 January 1985): 43–44.

———. "Estreno del documental: 'Celia: Leyenda y presencia.'" *Bohemia* 77, no. 3 (18 January 1985): 42.

Caballero, Armando. "Ser hombre." *Liberación* 2, no. 518 (10 December 1960): 2.

Cargill, Acie. *Celia Sánchez: Heroine of Cuba: A Play.* CreateSpace Independent Publishing Platform, 2017.

Carreras Varona, Eloisa, and Armando Hart Dávalos. *Por esto.* Havana: Casa Editora Abril, 2013.

Casin Medina, Roberto. "Las armas empuñadas por mujeres," *Verde Olivo* 22, no. 35 (August 1981): 32–37.

Castaneda, Carlos M. "Jamás en mi vida toleraré conscientemente una inmoralidad." *Bohemia* 51, no. 2 (11 January 1959): 68–69, 128.

Castano, Gladys. "Mariana es la raíz." *Mujeres* 20, no. 6 (June 1980): 50–51.

Castillo Bernal, Andres. "Conoció a Fidel en febrero de 1957." *Trabajadores* (18 February 1987): 4.

———. "Fiel guardiana del legado histórico de la Revolución." *Juventud Rebelde* (14 January 1980): 3.

"Castro en la inauguración del Hospital Celia Sánchez Manduley," *Bohemia* 73, no. 3 (16 January 1981): 50–61.

Castro Medel, Osviel. "El hombre que fue raíz." *Juventud Rebelde* (21 September 2011).

Castro Porta, Carmen. *La lección del maestro*. Havana Editorial de Ciencias Sociales, 1990.

Castro Ruz, Fidel. "De Castro a Carmen," *Bohemia* (19 August 1988): 62.

———. "Decreto del Consejo de Estado Duelo Oficial." *Granma* 16, no. 10 (12 January 1980): 1.

———. *History Will Absolve Me: Castro's Self Defense Speech before the Court in Santiago de Cuba on October 16, 1953*. Havana: Radio Havana Cuba, [between 1953 and 1973].

———. "Por eso ese nombre es tan querido y familiar." *Bohemia* 73, no. 3 (16 January 1981): 50.

Casuso, Teresa. *Cuba and Castro*. New York: Random House, 1961.

"Celia." *Mujeres* 26, no. 1 (January 1986): 11.

"Celia entre nosotros." *Trabajadores* 13, no. 8 (11 January 1983): 1.

"Celia era y será siempre para todos sus compañeros la fibra mas íntima y querida de la Revolución cubana." *Juventud Rebelde* (13 January 1980): 5.

"'Celia, reportaje especial del noticiero Latinoamericano ICAIC." *Granma* 16, no. 17 (19 January 1980): 4.

"Celia Sánchez ha muerto." *Juventud Rebelde* (11 January 1980): 1.

Chirino, Lilian. "Celia: Aquella muchacha excepcional." *Juventud Rebelde* (10 January 1985): 6.

———. "El padre de Celia." *Bohemia* 75, no. 40 (7 October 1983): 84–89.

———. "La niña que fue Celia." *Relevo* (12 January 1985): 6.

"Concentración de mujeres el dia 16." *Liberación* 2, no. 437 (12 August 1960): 1.

"Consternación y tristeza en el pueblo por la muerte de Celia Sánchez." *Granma* 16, no. 10 (12 January 1980): 4.

"Constituida la Federación de Mujeres Cubanas." *Liberación* 2, no. 468 (17 September 1960): 8.

"Continúa nuestro pueblo manifestando su dolor por la muerte de Celia Sánchez." *Granma* 16, no. 13 (15 January 1980): 2.

"Crean ejecutivos las mujeres cubanas." *Liberación* 2, no. 490 (1 October 1960): 3.

Dávila, Iris. "Compañeras." *Mujeres* 13, no. 7 (July 1973): 4–5.

de la Rosa, Amado. "Recuerdos de manzanilleros que trabajaron con ella." *Juventud Rebelde* (14 January 1980): 3.

Depestre Catony, Leonardo, and Eladio Blanco Cabrera. *Cuando el país llama: Epistolario*. Havana: Editora Politica, 1990.

Díaz Sánchez, Francisco. "Mujer a tiempo y de este tiempo." *Mujeres* 20, no. 2 (February 1980): 21.

"Dolor de pueblo." *Granma* 16, no. 11 (13 January 1980): 6.

"Editorial." *Granma International* 15, no. 3 (20 January 1980): 1–6.

"Editorial Celia." *Granma* 16, no. 10 (12 January 1980): 1.

Eire Gonzalez, Mario Amador. *Heroes y heroínas de la revolución: Libro para colorear*. Havana: Editorial Pablo de la Torriente, 2010.

Ejemplo de lealtad a Castro y a la Revolución. Havana: Editora Política, 1990.

"El recuerdo de Celia." *Granma* 19, no. 8 (11 January 1983): 2.

"En Cuba." *Bohemia* 51, no. 2 (11 January 1959): 99–105.

"En Media Luna." *Granma* 19, no. 9 (12 January 1983): 5.

"En su primer aniversario: Una mujer hecha al trabajo y a la Revolución." *Liberación* 3, no. 612 (25 February 1961): 7.

"Entrevistanse esta tarde Kubitschek y Castro en Brasilia." *Diario de la Marina* (30 April 1959): 1.

Espín Guillois, Vilma. "Hoy con más ahinco y tenacidad que nunca las mujeres se proponen brindar la mayor contribución." *Granma* 19, no. 9 (21 February 1983): 2.

———. "Vilma habla de Haydée y Celia." *Bohemia* 73, no. 10 (8 March 1981): 36–39.

Estado Militar de la Isla de Cuba, *Guía de forasteros de la siempre fiel Isla de Cuba.* Havana: Imprenta del Gobierno y Capitanía General, 1873.

"Eternamente Celia seguirá viva, eternamente será maestra de todos." *Granma* 26, no. 112 (11 May 1990): 2.

"Falleció Celia Sánchez." *Granma* 16, no. 10 (12 January 1980): 1.

Federación de Mujeres Cubanas. "Mensaje de la Dirección de la Federación de Mujeres Cubanas." *Granma* 16, no. 10 (12 January 1980): 4.

Federación de Mujeres Cubanas de Cienfuegos. "Hace declaraciones: La Federación de Mujeres Cubanas." *Liberación* 2, no. 467 (16 September 1960): 8.

"Fidel en la inauguración del Hospital 'Celia Sánchez Manduley.'" *Bohemia* 73, no. 3 (16 January 1981): 50–61.

Flynn, Errol. "Castro y yo." *Bohemia* 51, no. 7 (15 February 1929): 46–50, 96–98.

Franqui, Carlos. *The Twelve.* New York: L. Stuart, 1968.

Fresnillo, Estrella. "Celia vive." *Juventud Rebelde* (11 January 1981): 8.

"Fue asesinada Celia Sánchez?" *La Verdad* (Miami) (15 January 1980): 1, 9.

Garcia, Pedro Antonio. "La joven Celia." *Granma* 26, no. 9 (11 January 1990): 4.

García Valez, Manuel. "A Celia Sánchez Manduley." *Mujeres* 20, no. 7 (July 1980): 46.

Garzón Céspedes, Francisco. "Poesías." *Muchacha* 6, no. 11 (January 1986): 35.

González Cabrera, Heidy. "Vamos a hablar de Celia." *Mujeres* 20, no. 8 (August 1980): 10–13.

González López, Waldo. "Para Celia." *Muchacha* 4, no. 11 (January 1984): 42–43.

Grau Esteban, Enrique. "En Marcha La Reforma Agraria." *Diario de la Marina* (28 February 1959): 8.

Guevara, Ernesto. *Guerrilla Warfare.* New York: Vintage, 1967.

———. "Las mujeres heroícas de la Revolución." *Noticias de hoy* 21, no. 111 (17 May 1959): 4.

Hart Dávalos, Armando. *Aldabonazo: Inside the Cuban Revolutionary Underground, 1952-1958.* New York: Pathfinder, 2004.

———. *El ejemplo de Celia: Aliento y enseñanza.* Havana: Editora Política, 1980.

———. "El ejemplo de Celia: Aliento y enseñanza para continuar el camino y marchar con decisión hacia adelante." *Bohemia* 72, no. 3 (18 January 1980): 58–62.

———. "El más alto homenaje a la inmortal guerrillera." *Granma* 16, no. 11 (13 January 1980): 4.

———. "The Greatest Honor We Can Pay to the Inmortal Guerrilla Is to Unite with Greater Force and Efficiency our Communist Vanguard." *Granma International* 15, no. 3 (20 January 1980): 14–16.

———. *La más autóctona flor de la revolución.* Havana: De la Cultura, 1990.

Hart, Sánchez. "A Butterfly against Stalin." *Marxist Internet Archive*
(14 January 2005).
———. *Haydée habla del Moncada*. Melbourne: Ocean Press, 2005.
"Heartfelt Demonstration of Grief at Funeral of Exemplary Revolutionary." *Granma International* 15, no. 3 (20 January 1980): 2–3.
Hechevarría, Frank País. "En la inauguración del nuevo hospital." *Bohemia* 73, no. 4 (17 January 1981): 57–61.
Hernández, Erena. "Figuras y espacios." *Mujeres* 20, no. 11 (November 1980): 56–57.
Hernández García, Edenia. "A la flor de la Revolución." *Mujeres* 20, no. 7 (July 1980): 46.
Hernández, Melba. "Sesenta y dos horas de mi vida desaparecieron." *Granma* (9 July 1988): 4.
Hernández Pardo, Hector. "Gracias, hermanos nicaragüenses." *Granma* 16, no. 11 (13 January 1980): 5.
"Inaugurará Fidel, mañana, el hospital clínico-quirúrgico y docente de Manzanillo." *Granma* 17:7 (10 January 1981): 1.
"Integra tres ejecutivos más la Federación de Mujeres Cubanas." *Liberación* 2, no. 480 (29 September 1960): 3.
"Integrarán las mujeres un solo organización revolucionario." *Liberación* 2, no. 441 (17 August 1960): 8.
"Intervención de Vilma Espín: Van a necesitarse los brazos de las mujeres." *Combate* (29 August 1961): 11.
Juárez, Adela E. "Como eterna flor del lomería." *Trabajadores* 13, no. 7 (10 January 1983): 4.
"La Federación de Mujeres Cubanas invita." *Liberación* 3, no. 620 (8 March 1961): 3.
"La fibra más intima y querida de la Revolución Cubana." *Bohemia* 72, no. 3 (19 January 1980): 40–49.
"La hermana entrañable." *Opina* 7 (January 1980): 5.
"Las brigadas femeninas." *Liberación* 2, no. 428 (2 August 1960): 1, 8.
Lechuga, L., and B. Márques, "Correr la misma suerte que nuestros compañeros." *Bohemia* (26 July 1974).
Lee, Susana. "Convirtamos este dolor de hoy en una fuerza más para impulsar la revolución hacia el futuro." *Juventud Rebelde* (13 January 1980): 1.
Llanes, Julio M. *Celia nuestra y de las flores*. Havana: Editorial Gente Nueva, 1985.
Martí, Julio A. "Celia por Julio A. Martí," *Moncada* (9 January 1985).
Martínez, Juan Carlos. "Celia: Monumentalizada en el corazón de los Cubanos." *Juventud Rebelde* (13 January 1980): 6.
Más Martín, Luís. "Hechos e impresiones de la Sierra Maestra: Celia Sánchez." *Noticias de Hoy* 22, no. 44 (26 February 1959): 2.
Méndez, Graziella. "Mujeres de la Revolución," *Mujeres* 4, no. 7 (July 1964): 48.
MGB. "Monumento a Celia: Un lugar como ella." *Bohemia* 77, no. 3 (18 January 1985): 541–42.
"Miles de mujeres asistirán hoy a la Asamblea Femenina Revolucionaria." *Liberación* 2, no. 440 (16 August 1960): 8.
Molina Méndez, Teresita. "Ser comunista es una actitud ante la vida. Celia." n.p.

Morejón, Nancy. "Celia: Hija asombrosa de la orquidea." *Mujeres* (January 1986): 10–11.

———. "Elegía coral a Celia Sánchez." *Revolución y Cultura* (1 January 1984): 58–59.

"Muchas gracias Celia." *Revista Pionero* 953 (1983): 8.

Mujeres ejemplares. Havana: Editorial ORBE, 1977.

"Mujeres suplen a hombres en el trabajo." *Liberación* 3, no. 616 (3 March 1961): 7.

Naborí, El Indio. "Pido permiso a la muerte." *Granma* 16, no. 10 (12 January 1980): 4.

Naranjo Gauthier, Wilfredo. "Paso a paso con el constructor del pedestal del busto de Martí en el Pico Turquino." *Viernes* 6, no. 15 (January 1986): 1–8.

"No se les escapará ni un solo de los contrarevolucionarios." *Liberación* 3, no. 587 (26 January 1961): 5.

Oliva, Milgros. "Celia: Comunista, constructora, soñadora." *Mujeres* 24, no. 1 (January 1984): 8–11.

Oramas, Joaquín. "Más flores para Celia." *Granma* 16, no. 12 (14 January 1980): 3.

Ortega, Anthony. "Los barbudos." *Bohemia* 51, no. 2 (11 January 1959): 72–73.

"Our People Pay Tribute to Celia." *Granma International* 15, no. 3 (20 January 1980): 1.

Pablo Rodríguez, Pedro, and Manuel González Bello. "Capitana del pueblo." *Bohemia* 72 (18 January 1980): 52.

"Para siempre en el corazón del pueblo." *Bohemia* 72, no. 4 (19 January 1980): 49–62.

Pardo Llada, José. "De un diario de guerra: Como se enteró Castro de la caída de Batista." *Bohemia* 51, no. 2 (11 January 1959): 42–44.

Peña, Jacinto E. *Celia en la clandestinidad*. Bayamo: José Joaquín Palma, 1990.

Petinaud, Jorge. "Celia en la hora cero." *Granma* 16, no. 51 (20 December 1981): 5.

"Recorrido del Doctor Castro por las provincias de Camaguey y Oriente." *Diario de la Marina* (1 July 1959): 1.

Remigio Montero, Maria del Carmen, and Nancy Babiel Gutierrez. *Celia: alas y raices*. Havana: Oficina de Publicaciones del Consejo de Estado, 2011.

"Réplica: La Habana." *La Verdad* (Miami) (23 January 1980): 5.

Ricardo Luis, Roger. "Celia entre nosotros." *Bohemia* 78, no. 2 (10 January 1986): 38.

"Rindió nuestro pueblo postrer homenaje a Celia." *Granma* 16, no. 11 (13 January 1980): 1, 5.

Rivero Suárez, Aleida. "Celia de todos los días." *Granma* 16, no. 12 (14 January 1980): 3.

Robinson Calvet, Nancy. "Y aquí en el corazón del pueblo." *Granma* 16, no. 11 (13 January 1980): 5.

Rodríguez, José Alejandro. "En clave, la decisión de luchar." *Trabajadores* (8 March 1986): 4.

Rojas, Marta. "Celia en función del diseño y su obra ambiental: Contemporaneidad, belleza, utilidad y cubanía." *Granma* 26, no. 9 (11 January 1990): 4.

———. "En la base del monumento a José Martí: Millares de personas rinden homenaje a Celia Sánchez." *Granma* 16, no. 10 (12 January 1980): 4.

———. "Hemos perdido un centinela a toda prueba." *Granma* 16, no. 10 (12 January 1980): 2.

————. "We've Lost a Battle-Tested Fighter." *Granma International* 15, no. 3 (20 January 1980): 7–8.

Ruiz Guzmán, María Antonia. *Un amor de leyenda*. Havana: n.p., 1996.

St. George, Andrew. "The Woman behind Castro." *Parade* (11 April 1965).

Sánchez Ochoa, Magaly. "Mujer tu eres una Mariana Grajales." *Mujeres* 19, no. 10 (October 1979): 6–9.

Sánchez Parra, Ramon. "Celia en el recuerdo." *Granma* 26, no. 9 (11 January 1990): 1.

Sarabia, Nydia. "Celia: Palma y clavellina." *Revolución y Cultura* (July 1982): 7–13.

————. *Dr. Manuel Sánchez Silveira, médico rural*. Havana: Instituto Cubano del Libro, 1971.

————. "Martí en Celia." *Juventud Rebelde* (14 January 1980): 3.

Sección de Investigaciones Históricos, Comité Provincial. *Celia: Los años de Media Luna*. Bayamo: José Joaquín Palma, La Plata, 1990

"Será trasmitido hoy por radio y televisión la despedida de duelo de Celia Sánchez." *Granma* 16, no. 10 (12 January 1980): 4.

"Un aspecto general de la asamblea de la Federación de Mujeres Cubanas." *Liberación* 2, no. 472 (21 September 1960): 8.

Union Femenina de Las Villas. "Aumenta el entusiasmo por la concentración." *Liberación* 2, no. 438 (13 August 1960): 1.

Vázquez, Adelina. "Celia: Sentimiento y raiz de pueblo." *Mujeres* 20, no. 2 (February 1980): 4–7.

Vázquez, Omar. "Inauguran la exposición 'Flores para Celia' en el museo histórico de Plaza de la Revolución." *Granma* 19, no. 9 (12 January 1983): 5.

"Visita de sorpresa hizo el Dr. Castro a Baracoa, Oriente." *Diario de la Marina* (29 June 1959): 1–2.

"Visita el doctor Castro la Marina de Guerra." *Diario de la Marina* (22 February 1959): 8.

"Visita realizada a la finca 'Kuquine.'" *Diario de la Marina* (18 January 1959): 9.

Published Primary Sources (U.S. and Global)

"1950s: March 8, 1959; An Intimate Lunch with Fidel." *New York Times* (14 April 1996): 104.

Adamski, Kat. "The Revolutionary's Lover." *North Shore Times* (10 September 2010): 12.

Anderson, Jack. "Meet June Cobb: She's a Soldier of Fortune." *San Diego Union* (12 August 1962): 162–63.

"An Honest Woman to Greet Raisa." *Washington Times* (29 March 1989): 4.

"Anniversary Celebration Gave Outsiders Two Sides of Castro." *Sun News* (Myrtle Beach) (1 August 1983): 18.

"Anticomunismo no influyó en veredicto, dice jurado." *El Miami Herald* (21 November 1980): 1–2.

Aubery, Richard, and Geoff Bottoms. "Shield of the Needy." *Morning Star* (5 June 2002): 10.

Balmaseda, Liz. "La cuna de la Revolución: La comandancia de Castro en la Sierra está fija en el tiempo." *El Miami Herald* (11 December 1983): 24–25.

Batelle, Phyllis. "The Woman with Fidel." *Omaha World Herald* (14 January 1959): 26.

———. "The Woman in Fidel's Life." *Fort Worth Star-Telegram*" (14 January 1959): 6.

Bauza, Vanessa. "Cuba's Revolution Bypasses Women." *Gazette* (Montreal, Canada) (18 January 2003): E1.

"The Beardless Ones: Powerful Women in Castro's Cuba." *Illinois State Journal and Register* (27 November 1960): 34.

Benson, Todd "Cuba Mourns Leading Lady of Revolution" *Irish Times* (20 June 2007): 12.

Berrellez, Robert. "Castro Avoids Scandal with Secluded Life." *Fort Worth Star-Telegram* (27 November 1960): 65.

———. "Sensitivity of Castro to Criticism Growing." *Times-Picayune* (New Orleans) (18 July 1959): 15.

———. "Women Perform Vital Tasks in Castro's Government." *Morning Advocate* (Baton Rouge) (27 November 1960): 76.

Betancourt, Ernesto. "¿Dónde estara Fidel, en Venezuela?" *El Nuevo Herald* (6 December 2003): 22A.

Blakeslee, Sandra. "Pedaling with a Revolutionary Spirit." *New York Times* (18 February 2001).

Bohning, Don. "Castro asume el control directo." *El Miami Herald* (12 January 1980): 1, 10.

———. "Informan se suicidó Haydée Santamaría." *El Miami Herald* (30 July 1980): 1, 3.

"Bryant: Vuelvo aunque me espere la silla eléctrica." *El Nuevo Herald* (18 January 1981): 1, 10–11.

"Cabinet Shuffled in Cuba." *Sunday Advocate* (Baton Rouge) (25 March 1962): 29.

Capen, Richard G., Jr. "Dentro de Cuba: Un panorama sombrio." *El Miami Herald* (19 June 1983): 1–4.

"Castro-Bearded Babes in the Woods." *Life* 46, no. 15 (13 April 1959): 16–17.

"Castro Calls Off Strike, Sure of Hold on Cuba." *Miami Herald* (5 January 1959): 1–2.

"Castro Can't See Formal U.S.-Cuban Diplomatic Ties." *Trenton Times* (9 June 1977): 10.

"Castro Confidante Buried in Havana." *Sunday Register Star* (13 January 1980): 4.

"Castro Flies to Las Villas." *Omaha World Herald* (13 August 1959): 11.

"Castro Flies to Las Villas." *Times-Picayune* (New Orleans) (13 August 1959): 11.

"Castro ha preparado la gran trampa." *El Miami Herald* (31 March 1977): 6.

"Castro Off to Area of Reported Battle." *San Diego Union* (13 August 1959): 9.

"Castro Opens Up in Walters Interview." *Charleston Evening Post* (9 June 1977): 9.

"Castro ordena que den juguetes a todos los niños de Sierra Maestra." *La Prensa* (San Antonio) (12 February 1959): 19.

"Castro perdió su conexión con Satan." *El Miami Herald* (7 February 1980): 6.

"Castro Remains Key to Revolution." *Greensboro Daily News* (14 August 1964): 1, 10

"Castro Says 'Maybe 2–3000' Still Prisoners." *Sun-News* (Myrtle Beach) (9 June 1977): 25.

"Cede Cuba un barco." *El Miami Herald* (16 February 1980): 7.

"Communist Gets Post in Cuban Cabinet Shift." *Sunday Start* (25 March 1962): 14.

Crossettes, Barbara. "Reporter's Notebook: Two Galas for Two Cubas." *New York Times* (1 August 1983): A3.

"Cuba." *Louisiana Planter and Sugar Manufacturer* (New Orleans), 51, no. 52 (2 August 1913): 94.

"Cuba Denies Report of a Castro Fight." *San Francisco Chronicle* (25 January 1980): 16.

"Cuba: Highlights of Cuban Rebelde Radio News." *BBC Monitoring Americas* (19 July 2004).

"Cuba Letter Tells Hate toward U.S." *San Diego Union* (6 June 1980): 15.

"Cuba Liberates Roles of Women." *Milwaukee Journal Sentinel* (7 December 1971): 32.

"Cuba Officials Switch Jobs." *Omaha World Herald* (25 March 1962): 15.

"Cuba Political Prisoners." *Dallas Morning News* (9 June 1977): 3.

"Cuba Receives Soviet Envoy." *Richmond Times Dispatch* (18 January 1971): 6.

"Cuba Releases Figures." *Fort Worth Star-Telegram* (9 June 1977): 59.

"Cuba Shifts Top Echelon." *Sunday Oregonian* (25 March 1962): 5.

"Cuban Heroine Buried with Full Honors." *Omaha World Herald* (13 January 1980): 8.

"Cuban Red Steps Up in Cabinet Reshuffle." *Plain Dealer* (Cleveland) (25 March 1962): 11.

"Cubans Pay Tribute to Revolutionary Hero Celia Sánchez." *Info-Prod Research* (Middle East) (10 May 2012).

"Cuba's Castro Is Surrounded by Communists, Far Leftists." *Richmond Times Dispatch* (19 April 1959): 25.

Cuza Male, Belkis. "Los hijos de Fidel." *El Nuevo Herald* (29 June 2001): 19A.

"Desmienten en Cuba versión de muerte de Celia Sánchez y Raúl Castro." *El Miami Herald* (24 January 1980): 3.

Diebel, Linda. "Even Pilots Lose Track of Time on the Flight That 'Doesn't Exist.'" *Toronto Start* (7 May 1990): A12.

Dorschner, John. "Castro: The Man and His Revolution Age Together." *Times-Picayune* (New Orleans) (11 December 1983): 10.

Eder, Richard. "Castro Proposes Deal to Halt Aid to Latin Rebels." *New York Times* (6 July 1964): 1, 12.

———. "Cuba Lives by Castro's Moods." *New York Times* (26 July 1964): SM12, 47–48.

———. "On a Peak in the Sierra Maestra, Premier Castro and 1,000 Followers Reaffirm Cuban Revolution's Goals." *New York Times* (18 November 1965): 25.

"Elsewhere." *Dallas Morning News* (12 January 1980): 44.

"Entierran hoy a Celia Sánchez en La Habana." *El Miami Herald* (12 January 1980): 1, 10.

Esrati, Stephen. "We're Taking a Licking on Barred Issues." *Plain Dealer* (Cleveland) (2 June 1985): 183.

"Eventos de esta semana en Cuba." *El Miami Herald* (13 January 1980): 6.

"Exclusive: Inside Cuba's Revolution. In a Savage Civil War, Castro and 1,000 Rebels Fight Cuba's 'Rifle Rule.'" *Look* (4 February 1958): 22, 30.

"Figuras de la revolución." *El Miami Herald* (11 December 1983): 5C.

Fiorini, Frank País. "An American Soldier of Fortune in Cuba Says: 'We Will Finish the Job.'" *San Diego Union* (14 May 1961): 158–60.

———. "An American Soldier of Fortune in Cuba Says: 'We Will Finish the Job.'" *Sacramento Bee* (14 May 1961): 136–38.

———. "An American Soldier of Fortune in Cuba Says: 'We Will Finish the Job.'" *Sunday Advocate* (14 May 1961): 91–93.

Frank Paísel, Max. "Castro Arrives in Subdued Mood." *New York Times* (19 September 1960): 1, 18.

Geyer, Georgie Anne. "Cuban Women Now Freer of Male Dominance." *Richmond Times Dispatch* (18 September 1966): 25.

———. "In Castro's Cuba, a Woman's Place Is on the Job." *Milwaukee Journal* (12 September 1966): 11.

———. "Revolution Brings New Life to Cuban Woman." *Fort Worth Star-Telegram* (11 September 1966): 77.

Guevara, Ernesto. *Reminiscences of the Cuban Revolutionary War*. Melbourne: Ocean Press, 2016.

Gugliotta, Guy, and Liz Balmaseda. "Cuba Transformed since Castro's Takeover." *Sunday Oregonian* (11 December 1983): A2–A3.

Hanley, Charles. "Castro Stepping through World's Minefields with Care." *Sunday Advocate* (Baton Rouge) (22 January 1984): 16.

Hart Phillips, R. "Castro Directing Fighting in Cuba." *New York Times* (13 August 1959): 1, 5.

———. "Havana Welcomes Castro at End of Triumphal Trip." *New York Times* (9 January 1959): 1, 9.

"Havana Denies Reports of Castro Assassination." *New York Times* (28 January 1964): 6.

"Haydée Santamaría Cuadrado, Early Castroite, Commits Suicide." *Boston Herald* (30 July 1980): 3.

Hofmann, Paul. "Cuba Is in Fidel's Shirt Pocket." *New York Times* (13 June 1965): SM7, 88–90.

"Hotel Gouging Him, Castro Charges, Moves to Harlem." *San Diego Union* (20 September 1960): 1.

Kakutani, Michiko. "When Life in Cuba Was Elegant and Sweet." *New York Times* (13 August 2010): C22.

Kaufman Purcell, Susan. "Was Communism an Afterthought?" *New York Times* (19 October 1986): 415.

Keeley, Graham. "Castro's One True Love Returns to Cuba after Absence of 40 Years." *Belfast Telegraph* (24 August 2006).

"La corrupción continúa en la Cuba de Castro." *El Miami Herald* (27 February 1979): 7.

"Las mujeres en Cuba: Igualdad está cerca." *El Mundo* (Oakland, Calif.) (5 July 1973): 2.

"Latin Troubles Seen: Changes Made in Cuba." *Richmond Times Dispatch* (25 March 1962): 12.

"Leader of Guerrillas in Bolivia Is Believed to Be 'Che' Guevara." *Evansville Press* (20 July 1967): 32.

"Los cuatro García Márquez." *El Miami Herald* (5 July 1981): 9.

"Los fracasos de Castro lo hacen perder impulso." *El Miami Herald* (30 July 1980): 10.

Mallin, Jay. "Havana Adopts 'Lib.'" *Boston Herald* (27 April 1973): 40.

Marina, Gloria. "Hace 15 años ocurrió el canje de los brigadistas." *El Miami Herald* (17 April 1977): 11.

"Más técnicos Cubanos." *El Miami Herald* (15 March 1980): 5.

Matthews, Herbert. "Castro Revisited." *War and Peace Report* (December 1967): 3–5.

———. "Now Castro Faces the Harder Fight." *New York Times* (8 March 1959): 288, 333–35.

———. "One Morning at Moncada." *New York Times* (26 July 1973): 37.

Meluza, Lourdes. "Fin de 20 años en sintonía con Cuba." *El Miami Herald* (26 June 1982): 7.

Midgley, Carol. "Our Man in Havana." *Times* (London) (22 May 2006): 2.

Montaner, Carlos Alberto. "Hablemos algo de los que se fueron a la porra." *El Miami Herald* (6 December 1979): 9.

Mornig, Roberta. "Three Women Aides to Castro Tell of Struggle to Power." *Evening Star* (Washington, D.C.) (16 April 1959): 26.

"New Castro Death Rumor." *Boston Record American* (28 January 1964): 7.

Normyle, William. "Castro Bombs the Poor with Toys and Food." *Milwaukee Journal* (5 February 1959): 4.

"Ola de resusitaciones." *El Miami Herald* (15 June 1983): 6.

"Pastors for Peace Pay Homage to Heroine Celia Sánchez." *Info-Prod Research* (Middle East) (2 August 2012).

Prieres, Manuel. "El dictador y su juguete favorito." *El Miami Herald* (28 October 1980): 4.

Pukas, Anna. "Castro's Life of Luxury." *The Express* (12 May 2015): 24.

Quinn, Sally. "Aura of Castro Felt throughout Cuba." *Omaha World Herald* (30 March 1977): 5.

———. "Castro: An Enigma; He Can Change to Fit Events." *Plain Dealer* (Cleveland) (7 April 1977): 44.

———. "Castro: 'El Caballero Proletariat.'" *Washington Post* (27 March 1977): K1.

———. "Castro: Lo que le dijo a un periodista." *El Miami Herald* (3 April 1977): 10–11.

———. "Spaghetti, Hemingway, Women, Movies Turn Castro On." *Times-Picayune* (New Orleans) (3 April 1977): 66

———. "To Die Is Much Easier." *Washington Post* (21 March 1977): B4.

"Raging Castro Shifts Hotels." *Daily Record* (Boston) (20 September 1960): 2, 28.

"Raúl Castro Tours Eastern Zones under Recovery after Sandy." *Info-Prod Research* (Middle East) (4 February 2013).

"Rebels Cheered the New Year In with a New Cuba." *Fort Worth Star-Telegram* (1 January 1984): 1, 7AA.

"Refiagse en E.U. 'Hijo de la Revolución' Cubana." *El Miami Herald* (28 May 1980): 1.

"Refugee Doctors Say Castro Near Breakdown." *Evansville Press* (8 July 1980): 2.

Regalado, Tomás. "Balance de otro año para Castro." *El Miami Herald* (29 December 1982): 5.

———. "El discurso de Castro." *El Miami Herald* (8 December 1982): 5.

"Regreso de naufragio y volvió al combate." *El Nuevo Herald* (17 January 1982): 1, 6–8.

"Réplica sobre reportaje de Cuba." *El Miami Herald* (15 March 1977): 9.

Rohter, Larry. "The World: Castro Is Anxious about His Military." *New York Times* (25 June 1989): 2.

Ross, Stanley. "We Were Wrong about Castro!" *Times-Picayune* (New Orleans) (12 June 1960): 197.

———. "We Were Wrong about Castro!" *Cleveland Plain Dealer* (12 June 1960): 293.

———. "We Were Wrong about Castro!" *Sunday Oregonian* (12 June 1960): 165.

———. "We Were Wrong about Castro!" *Boston Sunday Advertiser* (12 June 1960): 54–55.

"Rumores 'explican' muerte de Celia Sánchez." *El Nuevo Herald* (23 January 1980): 3.

Sales, Miguel. "Los dispositivos de la sumisión." *El Miami Herald* (1 June 1982): 5.

"Sánchez Is No Charmer." *Milwaukee Journal* (27 November 1960): 52.

Simons, Marlise. "Cuba Liberates Role of Women." *Milwaukee Journal Sentinel* (7 December 1971): 32.

Suárez Guerra, L. "Spathoglottis 'Memoria Celia Sánchez Manduley,' nuevo híbrido de orquídea terrestre." *Cultivos Tropicales* 36, no. 1 (2015): 131.

Szulc, Tad. "Speech by Castro Indicates Curbs on Red Militants." *New York Times* (4 April 1962): 1, 3.

Tedd, Carlos. "The Women of the Revolution." *Times of Havana* (27–29 1962): 4.

Thomas, Jo. "Cuban Who Fought beside Castro Commits Suicide." *New York Times* (30 July 1980): A8.

Todd, Dave. "Even Cuban Elite Prefer Refugee Life in Canada." *Hamilton Spectator* (Ontario, Canada) (20 November 1993): A13

Toomey, Christine. "The Life and Loves of inFidelity Castro." *Sunday Times* (London) (28 December 2009): 12–15, 17.

"Top Castro Aide Reported in Hub for Surgery." *Boston Record American* (28 July 1971): 4.

Towers, Roy. "The Reckless Revolutionary." *The Herald* (Glasgow) (13 August 1996): 11.

Treadway, Joan. "Cuban Visit Confining." *Times-Picayune* (New Orleans) (16 June 1980): 1, 6.

Tully, Andrew. "Cuban Prime Minister Acts like Kid Who Hates to Leave Party for Bed." *Evansville Press* (16 April 1959): 12.

"Un soldado americano en busca de fortuna en Cuba afirma termineremos nuestra obra." *Latin Times* (Chicago) (19 May 1961): 1–2.

"U.S., Cuba Still Far Apart: Castro." *Rockford Register-Republic* (9 June 1977): 3.

Verdecia, Carlos. "El padre Gúzman, un testigo excepcional." *El Miami Herald* (24 January 1982): 13–14.

"The Woman behind Castro." *Sunday Oregonian* (11 April 1965): 156–59.

"The Woman behind Castro." *Sacramento Bee* (11 April 1965): 106–9.

"The Woman behind Castro." *San Diego Union* (11 April 1965): 169–72.

"Woman Sometimes Cues Tough Chief of Cuban Rebels." *Omaha World Herald* (1 April 1958): 18.

"Women and Politics." *Morning Advocate* (Baton Rouge) (9 September 1967): 4.

"Women Are Playing Hob with Politics All over the World." *Jersey Journal* (9 September 1967): 22.

"Women behind Castro." *Jersey Journal* (10 April 1965): 2.

"Women Have Many Important Posts in Castro Government." *Sunday Oregonian* (27 November 1960): 20.

"Women of the Rebellion." *Dallas Morning News* (18 January 1959): 7.

"Women Play Major Roles in Castro Revolt and Rule." *Times-Picayune* (New Orleans) (26 February 1961): 52.

"Women Remain Vital to Cuban Revolution." *Milwaukee Journal Sentinel* (27 November 1960): 52.

Secondary Sources

Acuña Núñez, Maritza. "Vida y personalidad del Dr. Manuel Sánchez Silveira." Master's thesis, Museo Municipal de Manzanillo, n.d.

Alarcón Mariño, Roberto. *Historia de Media Luna*. Havana: Editorial de Ciencias Sociales, 2005.

Alvarez, José. *Frank País: Architect of Cuba's Betrayed Revolution*. Boca Raton, Fla.: Universal, 2009.

Alvarez Martín, Elena. *Eduardo Chibás: Clarinada Fecunda*. Havana: Editorial de Ciencias Sociales, 2009.

Álvarez Tabío, Pedro. *Celia: Ensayo para una biografía*. Havana: Cámara Cubana del Libro, 2004.

Ameringer, Charles. *The Cuban Democratic Experience: The Auténtico Years, 1944–1952*. Gainesville: University Press of Florida, 2000.

Anderson, Benedict. *Imagined Communities: Reflections on the Origin and Spread of Nationalism*. London: Verso, 1991.

Anderson, John Lee. *Che Guevara: A Revolutionary Life*. New York: Grove Press, 1997.

Argote-Freyre, Frank. "The Political Afterlife of Eduardo Chibás: Evolution of a Symbol, 1951–1991." *Cuban Studies* 32 (2001): 76–77.

Arredondo Gutiérrez, Alberto. *La historia secreta del comunismo cubano y sus purgas*. Miami: Editorial AIP, 1965.

Backscheider, Paula. *Reflections on Biography*. New York: Oxford University Press, 1999.

Bayard de Volo, Lorraine. *Women and the Cuban Insurrection: How Gender Shaped Castro's Victory*. New York: Cambridge University Press, 2018.

Bishop-Sánchez, Kathryn. *Creating Carmen Miranda: Race, Camp, and Transnational Stardom*. Nashville: Vanderbilt University Press, 2016.

Bokovoy, Melissa, and Jane Slaughter. "Memory, Gender, and War." *Choice* (February 2001): 1023–30.

Brundage, W. Fitzhugh, *The Southern Past: A Clash of Race and Memory*. Cambridge, Mass.: Belknap, 2005.

Casaventes Bradford, Anita. *The Revolution Is for the Children: The Politics of Childhood in Havana and Miami, 1959–1962*. Chapel Hill: University of North Carolina Press, 2014.

Casey, Michael J. *Che's Afterlife: The Legacy of an Image*. New York: Vintage, 2009.

Castañeda, Jorge. *Compañero: The Life and Times of Che Guevara*. New York: Knopf, 1997.

Casuso Morin, Teresa. *Cuba and Castro*. New York: Random House, 1961.

Caudill Dealy, Glen. *The Public Man: An Interpretation of Latin American and Other Catholic Countries*. Amherst: University of Massachusetts Press, 1997.

Chaney, Elsa M. *Supermadre: Women in Politics in Latin America*. Austin: University of Texas Press, 1979.

Chase, Michelle, *Revolution within the Revolution: Women and Gender Politics in Cuba, 1952-1962*. Chapel Hill: University of North Carolina Press, 2015.

Confino, Alon. "Collective Memory and Cultural History: Problems of Method." *American Historical Review* (December 1997): 1386–1403.

Cooke, Miriam, and Angela Woollacott, eds. *Gendering War Talk*. Princeton, N.J.: Princeton University Press, 1993.

Crane, Susan. "Writing the Individual Back into Collective Memory." *American Historical Review* (December 1997): 1372–85.

Cuba, Consejo de Estado. *Camilo, imagenes de la memoria*. Havana: Centro de Arte Contemporáneo Wilfredo Lam, 1999.

Cuervo Cerulia, Georgina, ed. *Granma: Rumbo a la libertad*. Havana: Editorial Gente Nueva, 1983.

de la Cova, Antonio Rafael. *The Moncada Attack: Birth of the Cuban Revolution*. Columbia: University of South Carolina Press, 2007.

de la Fuente, Alejandro. *A Nation for All: Race, Inequality, and Politics in Twentieth-Century Cuba*. Chapel Hill: University of North Carolina Press, 2001.

Desnoes, Edmundo. *Los dispositivos en la flor: Cuba: Literatura desde la revolución*. Mexico City: Ediciones del Norte, 1981.

Deutsch, Sandra McGee. "Gender and Sociopolitical Change in Twentieth-Century Latin America." *Hispanic American Historical Review* 71 (May 1991): 259–306.

Ehrlich, Ilan. *Eduardo Chibás: The Incorrigible Man of Cuban Politics*. Lanham, Md.: Rowman & Littlefield, 2015.

Elshtain, Jean B. *Public Man/Private Woman: Women in Social Political Thought*. Princeton, N.J.: Princeton University Press, 1981.

Epstein, William H., *Recognizing Biography*. Philadelphia: University of Pennsylvania Press, 1987.

Fernández, Alina. *Castro's Daughter: An Exile's Memoir of Cuba*. New York: St. Martin's, 1997.

Fernández, Fernando. *Rafael Manduley del Río: Un estrénuo mambí*. Holguín, Cuba: Ediciones Holguín, 1995.

Ferrao, Joaquín. *Helms–Burton Law: Historical Background and Analysis*. Miami: Endowment for Cuban American Studies of the Cuban American National Foundation, 1998.

Fuentes, Norberto. *Dulces guerreros cubanos*. Barcelona: Seix Barral, 1999.

García, Gladys Marel. *Insurrection and Revolution: Armed Struggle in Cuba, 1952-1959*. Boulder: Lynn Rienner, 1998.

García Oliveras, Julio A. *José Antonio Echeverría: La Lucha Estudiantil Contra Batista*. Havana: Editora Política, 2001.

Garlick, Barbara, Suzanne Dixon, and Pauline Allen. *Stereotypes of Women in Power: Historical Perspectives and Revisionist Views*. New York: Greenwood, 1992.

Geary, Patrick J. *Phantoms of Remembrance: Memory and Oblivion at the End of the First Millennium*. Princeton, N.J.: Princeton University Press, 1994.

Geyer, Georgie Anne. *Guerrilla Prince: The Untold Story of Fidel Castro*. Boston: Little, Brown, 1991.

Gillis, John R., ed. *Commemorations: The Politics of National Identity*. Princeton, N.J.: Princeton University Press, 1994.

Gimbel, Wendy. *Havana Dreams*. New York: Alfred A. Knopf, 1998.

Gott, Richard. *Cuba: A New History*. New Haven, Conn.: Yale University Press, 2005.

Gronbeck-Tedesco, John. *Cuba, the United States, and Cultures of the Transnational Left, 1930–1975*. New York: Cambridge University Press, 2015.

Guerra, Elda. "Memory and Representations of Fascism." In *Italian Fascism: History, Memory, and Representation*, edited by R. J. B. Bosworth and Patrizia Dogliani. London: Macmillan, 1999.

Guerra, Lillian. *Heroes, Martyrs, and Political Messiahs in Revolutionary Cuba, 1946–1958*. Yale University Press, 2018.

———. *The Myth of José Martí: Conflicting Nationalisms in Early Twentieth-Century Cuba*. Chapel Hill: University of North Carolina Press, 2005.

———. *Visions of Power in Cuba: Revolution, Redemption, and Resistance, 1959–1971*. Chapel Hill: University of North Carolina Press, 2012.

Guerra, Wendy. *Nunca fui primera dama*. Barcelona: Ediciones B, 2008.

Guerrero Rodriguez, Antonio. *Exposición y retratos de patriotas cubanas: Toda la patria está en la mujer del 9 de enero al 9 de febrero de 2008*. Havana: Centro de Prensa Internacional, 2008.

Hall, Stuart. "Notes on Deconstructing 'The Popular.'" In *People's History and Socialist Theory*, edited by Raphael Samuel, 227–39. London: Routledge & Kegan Paul, 1981.

Hamilton, Carrie. *Sexual Revolutions in Cuba: Passion, Politics, and Memory*. Chapel Hill: University of North Carolina Press, 2012.

Handfield Titherington, Richard. *A History of the Spanish-American War*. New York: D. Appleton, 1900.

Haney, Richard. *Celia Sánchez: The Legend of Cuba's Revolutionary Heart*. New York: Algora, 2005.

Howard, Phillip. *Black Labor, White Sugar: Caribbean Braceros and Their Struggle for Power in the Cuban Sugar Industry*. Baton Rouge: Louisiana State University Press, 2015.

Hunsaker, Steven. *Autobiography and National Identity in the Americas*. Charlottesville: University Press of Virginia. 1999.

James, Daniel. *Doña María's Story: Life History, Memory, and Political Identity*. Durham, N.C.: Duke University Press, 2001.

Johnson, Robert David. *Congress and the Cold War*. New York: Cambridge University Press, 2005.

Jordan, Rosa. *The Woman She Was*. Victoria, B.C.: Brindle & Glass, 2012.

Joseph, Gilbert M., and Daniel Nugent, eds. *Everyday Forms of State Formation: Revolution and Negotiation of Rule in Modern Mexico*. Durham, N.C.: Duke University Press, 1994.

Ker Conway, Jill. *When Memory Lives: Reflections on Autobiography*. New York: Alfred A. Knopf, 1998.

Kish Sklar, Kathryn. "Coming to Terms with Florence Kelley: The Tale of a Reluctant Biographer." In *The Challenge of Feminist Biography: Writing the Lives of Modern American Women*, edited by Sara Alpern et al. Chicago: University of Illinois Press, 1992.

Klouzal, Linda. *Women and Rebel Communities in the Cuban Insurgent Movement, 1952–1959*. Amherst, N.Y.: Cambria, 2008.

Kunzle, David. *Che Guevara: Icon, Myth, and Message*. Berkeley: University of California Museum of Art, 1997.

"La actriz vallisoletana Elvira Mínguez da vida a Celia Sánchez a las órdenes de Soderbergh." *El Mundo*, https://www.elmundo.es/elmundo/2008/08/03/castillayleon/1217753711.html (accessed 1 December 2018).

Lefebvre, Georges. *La Révolution française: La fuite du roi*. Paris: Centre de documentation universitaire, 1951.

Llovio-Ménendez, José. *Insider: My Hidden Life as a Revolutionary in Cuba*. New York: Bantam Books, 1988.

Lockwood, Lee. *Castro's Cuba, Cuba's Fidel*. New York: World, 1967.

López, Alfred J. *José Martí: A Revolutionary Life*. Austin: University of Texas Press, 2014.

Lothstein, Arthur, ed. *"All We Are Saying . . .": The Philosophy of the New Left*. New York: Capricorn, 1971.

Luciak, Ilja A. *Gender and Democracy in Cuba*. Gainesville: University Press of Florida, 2007.

Mallea, Hermes. *Havana Living Today: Cuban Home Style Now*. New York: Rizzoli, 2017.

Maloof, Judy. *Voices of Resistance: Testimonies of Cuban and Chilean Women*. Louisville: University of Kentucky Press, 1998.

Mangini, Shirley. *Memories of Resistance: Women's Voices from the Spanish Civil War*. New Haven, Conn.: Yale University Press, 1995.

Marchante Castellanos, Carlos Manuel. *De cara al sol y en lo alto del Turquino*. Havana. Oficina de Publicaciones del Consejo de Estado, 2012.

Masud-Piloto, Felix Roberto. *With Open Arms: Cuban Migration to the United States*. Totowa, N.J.: Rowman & Littlefield, 1988.

Matsuda, Matt. *The Memory of the Modern*. New York: Oxford University Press, 1996.

Matthews, Herbert L. *Fidel Castro*. New York: Simon and Schuster, 1969.

McLean, Betsy, ed. *Haydée Santamaría*. Melbourne: Ocean, 2003.

Melman, Billie. "Gender, History, and Memory: The Invention of Women's Past in the Nineteenth Century and Early Twentieth Century." *History and Memory* 5 (1993): 5–41.

Mencia, Mario. *La prisión fecunda*. Havana: Editora Política, 1980.

Mesa-Lago, Carmelo. *Cuba in the 1970s: Pragmatism and Institutionalization*. Albuquerque: University of New Mexico Press, 1978.

———. *The Economy of Socialist Cuba: A Two-Decade Appraisal*. Albuquerque: University of New Mexico Press, 1981.

Miles, Tiya. *The House on Diamond Hill: A Cherokee Plantation Story*. Chapel Hill: University of North Carolina Press, 2012.

Molyneux, Maxine. "State, Gender, and Institutional Change: The Federación de Mujeres Cubanas." In *Hidden Histories of Gender and the State in Latin America*, edited by Elizabeth Dore and Maxine Molyneux, 291–321. Durham, N.C.: Duke University Press, 2000.

Noakes, Lucy. *War and the British: Gender, Memory and National Identity, 1939–91*. London: I. B. Tauris, 1998.

Nora, Pierre. "Between Memory and History: Les Lieux de Memoire." *Representations* 26 (Spring 1989): 7–24.

Olick, Jeffrey, ed., *States of Memory: Continuities, Conflicts, and Transformations in National Retrospection*. Durham, N.C.: Duke University Press, 2003.

Palomares Ferrales, Eugenia, *Celia: Mi mejor regalo*. Havana: Casa Editorial Verde Olivo, 2015.

Passerini, Luisa. *Fascism in Popular Memory: The Cultural Experience of the Turin Working Class*. London: Cambridge University Press, 1987.

Pérez, Louis A., Jr. *Cuba under the Platt Amendment, 1902–1934*. Pittsburgh: University of Pittsburgh Press, 1991.

———. *To Die in Cuba: Suicide and Society*. Chapel Hill: University of North Carolina Press, 2005.

Pérez-Cisneros, Enrique. *En torno al "98" Cubano*. Madrid: Editorial Verbum, 1997.

Portelli, Alessandro. *The Death of Luigi Trastulli and Other Stories: Form and Meaning in Oral History*. New York: State University of New York Press, 1991.

Prados-Torreira, Teresa. *Mambisas: Rebel Women in Nineteenth-Century Cuba*. Gainesville: University Press of Florida, 2005.

Puebla, Teté, and Mary-Alice Waters. *Marianas en combate: Teté Puebla y el peloton femenino en la guerra revolucionaria cubana, 1956–58*. New York: Pathfinder, 2003.

Quirk, Robert E. *Fidel Castro*. New York: Norton, 1993.

Quiroga, José, *Cuban Palimpsests*. Minneapolis: University of Minnesota Press, 2005.

Randall, Margaret. *Gathering Rage: The Failure of Twentieth-Century Revolutions to Develop a Feminist Agenda*. New York: Monthly Review, 1992.

———. *Haydée Santamaría, Cuban Revolutionary: She Led by Transgression*. Duke University Press, 2015.

Rathbone, John Paul. *The Sugar King of Havana: The Rise and Fall of Julio Lobo, Cuba's Last Tycoon*. London: Penguin, 2010.

Roach, Joseph. *Cities of the Dead: Circum-Atlantic Performance*. New York: Columbia University Press, 1996.

Rodriguez Menéndez, Roberto. *Una muchacha llamada Celia*. Havana: Editorial Pueblo y Educación, 1996.

Rojas, Rafael. *Fighting over Fidel: The New York Intellectuals and the Cuban Revolution*. Princeton, N.J.: Princeton University Press, 2016.

Rousso, Henry. *The Vichy Syndrome: History and Memory in France since 1944*. Cambridge, Mass.: Harvard University Press, 1991.

Rudnick, Lois. "The Male-Identified Woman and Other Anxieties: The Life of Mabel Dodge Luhan." In *The Challenge of Feminist Biography: Writing the Lives of Modern*

American Women, edited by Sara Alpern et al. Chicago: University of Illinois Press, 1992.

Ruffin, Patricia. *Capitalism and Socialism in Cuba: A Study of Dependency, Development and Underdevelopment*. London: MacMillan Press, 1990.

Saldaña-Portillo, Maria Josefina. *Revolutionary Imagination in the Americas and the Age of Development*. Durham, N.C.: Duke University Press, 2003.

Sawyer, Marian, and Marian Simms. *A Woman's Place: Women and Politics in Australia*. Sydney: George Allen and Unwin, 1984.

Serra, Ana. *The New Man in Cuba: Culture and Identity in the Revolution*. Gainesville: University Press of Florida, 2007.

Sherman, Daniel. *The Construction of Memory in Interwar France*. Chicago: University of Chicago Press, 1999.

———. "Monuments, Mourning, and Masculinity in France after World War I." *Gender and History* 8, no. 1 (April 1996): 82–107.

Shetterly, Aran. *The Americano: Fighting with Castro for Cuba's Freedom*. Chapel Hill, N.C.: Algonquin, 2007.

Smith, Lois, and Alfred Padula. *Sex and Revolution: Women in Socialist Cuba*. New York: Oxford University Press, 1996.

Spence Benson, Devyn. *Antiracism in Cuba: The Unfinished Revolution*. Chapel Hill: University of North Carolina Press, 2016.

Stone, Elizabeth. *Women and the Cuban Revolution*. New York: Pathfinder, 1981.

Stoner, K. Lynn. "Militant Heroines and the Consecration of the Patriarchal State." *Cuban Studies* 34 (February 2004): 71–96.

Stout, Nancy. *One Day in December: Celia Sánchez and the Cuban Revolution*. New York: Monthly Review, 2013.

Stryker, Deena. *Cuba: A Diary of the Revolution, Inside the Cuban Revolution with Fidel, Raúl, Che, and Celia Sánchez*. Oakland, Calif.: Next Revelation, 2015.

Stubbs, Jean. "Social and Political Motherhood of Cuba: Mariana Grajales Cuello." In *Engendering History: Caribbean Women in Historical Perspective*, edited by Verene Shepherd, Bridget Brereton, Barbara Bailey. New York: St. Martin's, 1995.

Sweig, Julia. *Inside the Cuban Revolution: Castro and the Urban Underground*. Cambridge, Mass.: Harvard University Press, 2001.

Szulc, Tad. *Fidel: A Critical Portrait*. New York: Harper, 2000.

Taylor, J. M. *Eva Perón: The Myths of a Woman*. Chicago: University of Chicago Press, 1979.

Teel, Leonard Ray. *Reporting the Cuban Revolution: How Castro Manipulated American Journalism*. Baton Rouge: LSU Press, 2015.

Thomas, Hugh. *Cuba, or, The Pursuit of Freedom*. New York: Da Capo, 1998.

Torres Elers, Damian A. *Frank País en la memoria*. Havana: Editoria Historia, 2012.

Tumarkin, Nina. *Lenin Lives! The Lenin Cult in Soviet Russia*. Cambridge, Mass.: Harvard University Press, 1983.

———. *The Living and the Dead: The Rise and Fall of the Cult of World War II in Russia*. New York: Basic Books, 1994.

Van Houts, Elisabeth. *Memory and Gender in Medieval Europe, 900–1200*. Toronto: University of Toronto Press, 1999.

Verdery, Katherine. *The Political Lives of Dead Bodies: Reburial and Postsocialist Change*. New York: Columbia University Press, 2000.

Wandor, Michelene. *Look Back in Gender*. London: Methuen, 1987.

Welch, Richard E. *Response to Revolution: The United States and the Cuban Revolution, 1959–1961*. Chapel Hill: University of North Carolina Press, 1985.

Wexler, Alice. "Emma Goldman and the Anxiety of Biography." In *The Challenge of Feminist Biography: Writing the Lives of Modern American Women*, edited by Sara Alpern et al. Chicago: University of Illinois Press, 1992.

Winter, Jay, and Emmanuel Sivan. *War and Remembrance in the Twentieth Century*. Cambridge: Cambridge University Press, 1999.

Wood, Elizabeth. *The Baba and the Comrade: Gender and Politics in Revolutionary Russia*. Bloomington: Indiana University Press, 1997.

Index

Botello Ávila, Olvein Manuel, 100
Brooks, Ignacio, 27
Buena Vista Social Club, 157

Calixto García Hospital (Havana), xx, 97
Cape Cruz sugar mill (Pilón), 11, 49, 80
capitalism, 134
Cargill, Acie, 194; *Celia Sánchez, Heroine of Cuba*, 194
Carlos Enrique Carracedo sugar mill, 49
Carranza Rivero, Mario "Guatemala," 100
Carta de México (1956), 65
Cartón, Nirma, 4, 132, 167
Casa de las Américas, 106, 128, 186
Casa Natal Celia Sánchez. *See* Celia Sánchez Childhood Home Museum
Casey, Michael J., 169, 192–93
Castro, Fidel, 3, 22, 34, 54, 135, 152, 214n112; assassination plot against, 110; background of, 113, 133, 142, 143; biographies of, 2; birthplace of, 18–19; CIA assassination attempts on, 105; communism and, 152 (*see also* Cuban Communist Party); Cuban émigrés and, 144; early political career of, 58–59, 60, 61; *fidelismo* and, 39, 170, 172; *fidelista* and, 135, 152; gender roles and, 101, 126, 134, 168; grave site of, 168; Havana apartment of, 109, 110; imprisonment of, 62; as longest-serving non-royal head of state, 105; machismo and, 126; Mexican headquarters, 65–66; Miami press rumors about, 172; mistress of, 64, 111; Moncada Barracks attack and, 41, 61–62, 63, 66; Murrow TV interview of, 104; New York visits, 124, 126, 127; nom de guerre of, 88, 96; notoriety of, 104; País death and, 85, 86; personality cult, 169; preservation of papers of, 119–20; public works projects, 121; rumored death of, 71–72; socialist reform agenda,

105, 143–44; speculation on private life of, 140–41 (*see also* Castro-Sánchez relationship); survival of, 72; tombstone of, 169; ubiquity of image of, 169; U.S. press and, xx, 72–73, 74, 81, 82, 138–46, 153–56; vision for Cuba, 152 *See also* Cuban Revolution; Sierra Maestra
Castro, Fidel, Jr., 104
Castro, Lidia, 64–65
Castro, Rafael, 88
Castro, Raúl, 16, 22, 48, 54, 62, 72, 105, 133, 214n112; as Cuban president, 105; guerrilla unit, 87; imprisonment of, 62; marriage to Vilma Espín, 107, 142, 150; revolution's second front and, 103; rumored death of, 172; Sánchez funeral and, 164, 165; Sánchez's symbolic motherhood and, 168; Uvero battle and, 83–84
"Castro Cap" costumes, 104
Castro de Rodriguez, María, 64
Castro Mestre, Elsa, 55, 87, 90
Castro Porta, Carmen, 61, 63, 65–66
Castro-Sánchez relationship, 12–13, 14, 18, 24, 29, 42, 43, 46, 47, 79, 84, 87–89, 93, 98, 107–12, 191–92; counter-memories of, 111–12; Cuban Revolution and, 109–10, 113, 138, 143; dismissive ideas about, 124; dramatization of, 194; first meeting, xx, 66, 75–78; memorialization of, 174; Miami press rumors about, 172; New York visits, 124–25; photo montage of, 174; as quasi-marital, 112; questions on nature of, 109–10; Sánchez governmental roles and, 12, 13, 117–19; Sánchez museum and, 24; Sánchez's death and, 154, 162, 164, 165, 173, 178; Sánchez's faith in leadership of, 152; Sánchez's influence on, 139–40; and Sánchez's unmarried status, 129; as sexual, 112–13, 141–42; in Sierra Maestra, 112, 141, 149–51; similar back-

Envisioning Cuba

TIFFANY A. SIPPIAL, *Celia Sánchez Manduley: The Life and Legacy of a Cuban Revolutionary* (2020).

ARIEL MAE LAMBE, *No Barrier Can Contain It: Cuban Antifascism and the Spanish Civil War* (2019).

HENRY B. LOVEJOY, *Prieto: Yorùbá Kingship in Colonial Cuba during the Age of Revolutions* (2018).

A. JAVIER TREVIÑO, *C. Wright Mills and the Cuban Revolution: An Exercise in the Art of Sociological Imagination* (2017).

ANTONIA DALIA MULLER, *Cuban Émigrés and Independence in the Nineteenth-Century Gulf World* (2017).

JENNIFER L. LAMBE, *Madhouse: Psychiatry and Politics in Cuban History* (2017).

DEVYN SPENCE BENSON, *Antiracism in Cuba: The Unfinished Revolution* (2016).

MICHELLE CHASE, *Revolution within the Revolution: Women and Gender Politics in Cuba, 1952–1962* (2015).

AISHA K. FINCH, *Rethinking Slave Rebellion in Cuba: La Escalera and the Insurgencies of 1841–1844* (2015).

CHRISTINA D. ABREU, *Rhythms of Race: Cuban Musicians and the Making of Latino New York City and Miami, 1940–1960* (2015).

ANITA CASAVANTES BRADFORD, *The Revolution Is for the Children: The Politics of Childhood in Havana and Miami, 1959–1962* (2014).

TIFFANY A. SIPPIAL, *Prostitution, Modernity, and the Making of the Cuban Republic, 1840–1920* (2013).

KATHLEEN LÓPEZ, *Chinese Cubans: A Transnational History* (2013).

LILLIAN GUERRA, *Visions of Power in Cuba: Revolution, Redemption, and Resistance, 1959–1971* (2012).

CARRIE HAMILTON, *Sexual Revolutions in Cuba: Passion, Politics, and Memory* (2012).

SHERRY JOHNSON, *Climate and Catastrophe in Cuba and the Atlantic World during the Age of Revolution* (2011).

MELINA PAPPADEMOS, *Black Political Activism and the Cuban Republic* (2011).

FRANK ANDRE GURIDY, *Forging Diaspora: Afro-Cubans and African Americans in a World of Empire and Jim Crow* (2010).

ANN MARIE STOCK, *On Location in Cuba: Street Filmmaking during Times of Transition* (2009).

ALEJANDRO DE LA FUENTE, *Havana and the Atlantic in the Sixteenth Century* (2008).

REINALDO FUNES MONZOTE, *From Rainforest to Cane Field in Cuba: An Environmental History since 1492* (2008).

MATT D. CHILDS, *The 1812 Aponte Rebellion in Cuba and the Struggle against Atlantic Slavery* (2006).

EDUARDO GONZÁLEZ, *Cuba and the Tempest: Literature and Cinema in the Time of Diaspora* (2006).

JOHN LAWRENCE TONE, *War and Genocide in Cuba, 1895–1898* (2006).

SAMUEL FARBER, *The Origins of the Cuban Revolution Reconsidered* (2006).

LILLIAN GUERRA, *The Myth of José Martí: Conflicting Nationalisms in Early Twentieth-Century Cuba* (2005).

RODRIGO LAZO, *Writing to Cuba: Filibustering and Cuban Exiles in the United States* (2005).

ALEJANDRA BRONFMAN, *Measures of Equality: Social Science, Citizenship, and Race in Cuba, 1902–1940* (2004).

EDNA M. RODRÍGUEZ-MANGUAL, *Lydia Cabrera and the Construction of an Afro-Cuban Cultural Identity* (2004).

GABINO LA ROSA CORZO, *Runaway Slave Settlements in Cuba: Resistance and Repression* (2003).

PIERO GLEIJESES, *Conflicting Missions: Havana, Washington, and Africa, 1959–1976* (2002).

ROBERT WHITNEY, *State and Revolution in Cuba: Mass Mobilization and Political Change, 1920–1940* (2001).

ALEJANDRO DE LA FUENTE, *A Nation for All: Race, Inequality, and Politics in Twentieth-Century Cuba* (2001).